Medea's Chorus

Studies in Modern Poetry

Peter Baker
General Editor

Vol. 19

This book is a volume in a Peter Lang monograph series.
Every volume is peer reviewed and meets
the highest quality standards for content and production.

PETER LANG
New York · Washington, D.C./Baltimore · Bern
Frankfurt · Berlin · Brussels · Vienna · Oxford

Veronica House

Medea's Chorus

Myth and Women's Poetry Since 1950

PETER LANG
New York · Washington, D.C./Baltimore · Bern
Frankfurt · Berlin · Brussels · Vienna · Oxford

Library of Congress Cataloging-in-Publication Data

House, Veronica.
Medea's chorus: myth and women's poetry since 1950 / Veronica House.
p. cm. — (Studies in modern poetry; v. 19)
Includes bibliographical references and index.
1. English poetry—Women authors—History and criticism.
2. English literature—20th century—History and criticism.
3. American poetry—Women authors—History and criticism.
4. English literature—20th century—History and criticism.
5. Myth in literature. I. Title.
PR605.W6H68   821'.91099287—dc23   2012026554
ISBN 978-1-4331-2064-0 (hardcover)
ISBN 978-1-4539-0938-6 (e-book)
ISSN 1069-4145

Bibliographic information published by **Die Deutsche Nationalbibliothek.**
Die Deutsche Nationalbibliothek lists this publication in the "Deutsche
Nationalbibliografie"; detailed bibliographic data is available
on the Internet at http://dnb.d-nb.de/.

The paper in this book meets the guidelines for permanence and durability
of the Committee on Production Guidelines for Book Longevity
of the Council of Library Resources.

© 2014 Peter Lang Publishing, Inc., New York
29 Broadway, 18th floor, New York, NY 10006
www.peterlang.com

Printed in Germany

Table of Contents

Acknowledgments

How grateful I am that one summer twenty years ago, while home from college visiting my parents, I enrolled in Gregory Staley's Introduction to Greek Mythology course at the University of Maryland. Greg has been my teacher, mentor, and friend ever since, and for his selfless and continual guidance and encouragement, I am tremendously grateful. As a 'wise man' figure in my life, Greg helped to guide me toward my belief in the power of myth. Also from the University of Maryland, I would like to thank Phillis Levin and Michael Collier. It was in their poetry workshops that I first began to make connections between myth and contemporary women's poetry.

From the University of Texas at Austin, I wish to thank a whole host of people who supported me through my doctoral work, which culminated in a distant draft of this book. Chuck Rossman, Brian Breman, and Lesley-Dean Jones offered valuable criticism, ideas, and encouragement. Lisa Moore, whose insights and friendship in her Feminist Theory course helped me to first feel that I had found my community at UT. This project could not have happened without Liz Cullingford, my super-star director who offered such support, astute critique, and belief in my project. I thank her for her guidance every step of the way. I don't know how I would have made it through those difficult years of writing the first drafts of this book without my wonderful group of friends in Austin who supported me through it all: Stacy Macdiarmid, Miriam Schacht, Peter Caster, Paul Minifee, Lee Rumburger, Susanna Childress. A heartfelt thanks goes to my dear friend Colleen Hynes, at whose house I wrote the initial drafts of this work. She read many of those drafts and offered critique and encouragement. Along with her home-cooking, her friendship helped to sustain me. A special thanks to Dave Eddington, whose belief in me and my work never waned, whose love and generosity meant so much. I miss him deeply and thank him for his tremendous role in motivating me throughout the early stages of writing.

I am lucky to have so many wonderful colleagues at the University of Colorado Boulder, that it would be difficult to thank them all. Marty Bickman has been a friend and advocate of my work from the start. Nona Olivia read drafts of several chapters. John Ackerman has supported my career from the beginning and has offered invaluable advice over the years.

A big thank you goes to Peter Steinberg for his helpful comments on my Sylvia Plath chapter.

I wish to say a special thanks to my mother, Laraine. It was nestled under her arm as a little girl that I first heard Greek myths and fell in love with language. I thank her for the countless hours that she spent reading to me and talking with me about literature. A huge thank you is owed to my father, Art, my sister, Jessie, and my grandparents, Sally, Billie, and Stan, for their belief in me and for their support of my pursuits, in all of their colorful manifestations. I am also grateful to Harley and Marie for their support.

The most significant events to have happened to me during the writing of this book include meeting my husband, Kevin, and having our daughter, Cassidy. Kevin has read many versions of this book, and has, each time, offered thoughtful suggestions combined with love and encouragement. He has been my rock through this process. And to Cassidy, who will grow up knowing that she can do and be anything that she wants, and that I love her infinitely, I thank her for her sweetness and love.

Grateful acknowledgement is given for permission to quote from the following copyrighted works:

Veronica House, "Words We Can Grow Old and Die In': Earth Mother and Ageing Mother in Eavan Boland's Poetry" in *The Body and Desire in Contemporary Irish Poetry*. Irish Academic Press, copyright © 2006. Reprinted by permission of the publisher. All rights reserved.

By H.D. (Hilda Doolittle), from *Helen In Egypt*, copyright 1961 by Norman Holmes Pearson. Reprinted by permission of New Directions Publishing Corp.

By H.D. (Hilda Doolittle), from *Helen In Egypt*, copyright 1961 by Norman Holmes Pearson. Reprinted by permission of Carcanet Press Limited.

By H.D. (Hilda Doolittle), from *Collected Poems, 1912–1944*, copyright 1944, 1945, 1946 by Oxford University Press, renewed 1973 by Norman Holmes Pearson. Reprinted by permission of New Directions Publishing Corp.

By H.D. (Hilda Doolittle), from *H.D. Selected Poems*, copyright 1988. Reprinted by permission of Carcanet Press Limited.

By Aurelia Schober Plath, from *Letters Home by Sylvia Plath: Correspondence 1950–1963*, copyright 1975. Reprinted by Permission of HarperCollins Publishers.

By Aurelia Schober Plath, from *Letters Home by Sylvia Plath: Correspondence 1950–1963*, copyright 1975. Reprinted by permission of Faber and Faber Ltd.

Excerpts from thirteen poems [125 lines in total] from *The Collected Poems of Sylvia Plath*, Edited by Ted Hughes. Copyright © 1960, 65, 71, 81 by the Estate of Sylvia Plath. Editorial mat'l copyright © 1981 by Ted Hughes. Reprinted by permission of HarperCollins Publishers.

"The Colossus" from *The Colossus and Other Poems* by Sylvia Plath, copyright © 1957, 1958, 1959, 1960, 1961, 1962 by Sylvia Plath. Used by permission of Alfred A. Knopf, a division of Random House, Inc. Any third party use of this material, outside of this publication, is prohibited. Interested parties must apply directly to Random House, Inc. for permission.

From *The Dream of a Common Language: Poems 1974–1977* by Adrienne Rich. Copyright © 1978 by W.W. Norton & Company, Inc. Used by permission of W.W. Norton & Company, Inc.

From *On Lies, Secrets, and Silence: Selected Prose 1966–1978* by Adrienne Rich. Copyright © 1979 by W.W. Norton & Company, Inc. Used by permission of W.W. Norton & Company, Inc.

Foley, Helene P.; *The Homeric Hymn to Demeter.* © 1994 Princeton University Press Reprinted by permission of Princeton University Press.

From *Helen* by Euripides in *The Complete Tragedies: Euripides II*, translated and with an Introduction by Richard Lattimore. Copyright © 1952, 1956 by The University of Chicago. All rights reserved. Reprinted by permission of The University of Chicago Press.

From *Medea* by Euripides in *The Complete Tragedies: Euripides I*, translated by Rex Warner. Copyright © 1955 by The University of Chicago. First published 1944, reprinted 1946 by John Lane, The Bodley Head Limited, London, England. All rights reserved. Reprinted by permission of The University of Chicago Press.

Introduction

"Backward to your sources, sacred rivers!"

What does it mean to claim that myths are timeless? That figures are archetypal? Implicit in our understanding of ancient mythologies is the notion that they contain a truth that resonates through the ages and across cultures. There is also, in the modern conception of the word "myth," an understanding of falsehood. This definitional tension is inherent in what Alicia Ostriker famously calls feminist "revisionist mythmaking," challenges to and revisions of representations of female characters from mythology (213).[1] Myth is a powerful form of persuasion—it teaches people how to live and encodes and transmits cultural values. Feminist writers have capitalized on myth's potency while they expose the ways in which existing myths marginalize female characters, often portraying them as victims, virgins, murderers, or deceivers, as reflections of male fantasies and fears. If archetypal gender roles allotted to mythic figures are not timeless, however, but malleable, and if the archetype is in fact an artifact of a culture that no longer exists, then writers can set out for new terrain, enact new cultural scripts, and create characters who are not bound by their previous incarnations. Myth is neither inherently misogynistic nor paternalistic. It is an imaginative rendering of a culture's beliefs, which implies that as a culture changes, the wellsprings of the culture's imagination should change along with it to remain viable. When the women poets in this study engage in mythic revision, they are doing far more than re-writing old stories. They are embarking on the radical work of cultural transformation, work that confronts latent assumptions and drives modern culture to venture into new psychological landscapes.

This book is an exploration of the dilemma female poets writing in the last half of the twentieth century face when they take Greek mythology as their central topos. In their poetry and prose, the writers engage with modern cultural discourses about literary authority, gender, oppression, violence, and age. Yet even while the poets rework certain aspects of the Greek myths that they find troubling, they see the inherent power in the stories and use that power for personal and social revelation. By "myths," I mean particular written versions of the broader category of Greek myth, which comprises all variations of the stories, including those passed down orally from one generation to the next. Because the myths existed in multiple versions, ancient writers did not create from scratch; their artistic contribution lay in how they *changed* the stories. Revision is inherent to mythmaking. Modern female poets are engaging, therefore, in a several millennia-old tradition of mythic revision. This book delves into the fertile tradition and tracks mythic revision from the 1950s through the second-wave feminist movement, and into turn-of-the-century feminism, to highlight individual achievements and to show the collective effect of these highly varied works on post-WWII literature and feminist thought and practice.

Greek myths offer some of literature's strongest and most eloquent female characters, and yet they provide the model for misogynist representations of women in the arts. From the ancient Greeks to the poets of High Modernism, men who wrote mythological poetry fought to keep mythic production out of female hands and wielded a powerful exclusionary rhetoric that denied women a place in the creation and transmission of mythological poetry. Poets such as T.S. Eliot and Ezra Pound consistently and often openly worked to stifle women's ability to publish poetry that did not fit into their particular definition of acceptable substance and style, and in their appropriation of the classics, they hoped for a subject matter and style that they thought of as decidedly masculine.

The male high modernist agenda was often so deliberately anti-woman that it became an essential project for female poets to inscribe feminine experiences into the classical stories that this group of men sought to protect as its own.[2] Poet and scholar Alicia Ostriker has confessed, for example, "During my school years I wrote poems that appropriated the cadences of T.S. Eliot but twisted angrily away from his meaning. Writing what he would hate, in forms approximating bits of his rhythms, was a form of battle" ("My H.D." 6). Eavan Boland echoes Ostriker's sentiment in her explanation of women poets' uses of myth: "We took the language in which we were humiliated and made it tell our story" (poetry reading).

My purpose here is not to analyze the value of male high modernist texts but rather to acknowledge the influence that the movement had in shaping the collective reaction of later women writers.

The High Modernist Homeric Return

In 1908 T.E. Hulme and the Poets' Club met for the first time to discuss the state of poetry, which Hulme argued, "needed an antidote to Romanticism in the form of 'dry, hard, classical verse'" (*Speculations* 131).[3] Although Hulme died during WWI, Pound and Eliot continued to advocate his beliefs.[4] The stereotypical association of classicism with masculinity helps to explain later women writers' reactions against the powerful rhetoric that used the epithet "feminine" to indicate weakness. The competing classicisms of the first half of the century must be examined, because the topic of literary legitimacy so affected women's writing in the second half of the century.

In *The Birth of Tragedy* (1877), Friedrich Nietzsche proclaims his "faith in the imminent rebirth of classical antiquity," a prescience that proved accurate according to T.S. Eliot, who declared in a 1916 lecture at Oxford, "The beginning of the twentieth-century has witnessed a return to the ideals of classicism" (70, Schuchard 165). Modernist classicism involved not only the study of ancient literature and the use or revision of those texts, but also the study of archaeology, ancient philosophy, art, religion, and the translation of texts by "educated poets," as Eliot writes in "Euripides and Professor Murray" (1920). Classicism, according to Eliot in his 1923 review of Joyce's *Ulysses*, was "a goal toward which all good literature strives, so far as it is good" (*Selected Prose* 176).[5] Eliot's classicism mirrored Hulme's, but it contained a political as well as an artistic component.

The literature of the classical revival reflected the devastation of war-torn Europe and the spiritual wasteland of the twentieth century. Eliot defines the "ideals of classicism" as "form and restraint in art, discipline and authority in religion, centralization in government (either as socialism or monarchy)" (Schuchard, "Extension" 165). Modernist classicism advocated a return to the heroic, masculine war culture of the Trojan War. T.S. Eliot explains, "Classicism is in a sense reactionary, but it must be in a profounder sense revolutionary" ("Commentary"). He expands on this statement in his assertion that Hulme was "the forerunner of a new attitude of mind, which should be the twentieth-century mind, if the twentieth century is to have a mind of its own. Hulme is classical, reactionary, and revolutionary; he is the antipodes of the eclectic, tolerant and democratic mind of the end of the last century" (Criterion, 1924). His brand of classicism, which rejected democracy for socialism or monarchy, is not unrelated to Pound's eventual adoption of fascism and, in fact, helps to explain why many modernist figures came to espouse authoritarian political ideals. The overthrow of the present and the reclamation of the past constituted a kind of cultural purgation. The high modernists returned to classical literature in order to "alter," to "readjust" the state of the modern world (Eliot, "Tradition and the Individual Talent).

The male modernist *nostos* had consequences for women writers, because Ancient Greek heroic criteria were necessarily masculine. In their polemic against Romanticism, Hulme, Eliot and their followers reasserted the Homeric and Aeschylean classical tradition as authentic, while criticizing other strains of classical literature as antithetical to the particular type of classicism espoused by their circle of male poets. For example, Eliot writes, "H. D. and the other poets of the 'Poets' Translation Series' have so far done no more than pick up some of the more romantic crumbs of Greek literature; none of them has yet shown himself competent to attack the *Agamemnon*" ("Euripides and Professor Murray"). He is referring specifically to H.D.'s translations of Euripides's choruses, which I discuss in chapter one.

Hulme's call for "dry, hard classical verse" reflects the masculine association of classicism and poetry espoused by Eliot and Pound that emerged not only as a means of defining the political environment, but also in response to the growing number of women involved in publishing poetry, especially in small magazines between 1913–1917. *The Little Review*, edited by Margaret Anderson out of Chicago and New York, and *Poetry*, edited by Harriet Monroe and Alice Corbin Henderson out of Chicago, sought a wide readership and, in order to enlarge the community of women writers, accepted virtually all writing submitted by women. Eliot and Pound worried that when female publicists sacrificed quality merely to encourage women to write and publish, they put the state of modern poetry in jeopardy. The two men often blamed women writers for infusing poetry with sentimentalism, emotionalism, and a lack of craft. In fact, Eliot wrote in a letter to his father, "I struggle to keep the writing as much as possible in Male hands, as I distrust the Feminine in literature, and also, once a woman has had anything printed in your paper, it is very difficult to make her see why you should not print everything she sends in" (1 *Letters* 204).[6] In 1915 Pound expressed his dream of running his own magazine: "No woman shall be allowed to write for this magazine" (quoted in Watson 385). His takeover of *The Little Review* in 1917 virtually eradicated women's writing from the journal.

Because writers like Pound, Eliot, and Hulme foregrounded supposedly masculine qualities as essential to good writing, many women writers were not taken seriously.[7] Pound wrote, "Not wildly anti-feminist we are yet to be convinced that any woman ever *invented* anything in the arts" (*New Age*, 1 Aug 1918, emphasis added). Given his critique of women's lack of inventiveness, it is paradoxical that Pound urged younger male poets to imitate ancient Greek epic in an attempt to "purify the language of the tribe" (*Literary Essays* 409).[8]

High modernists were preoccupied with establishing the male as intellectually superior to the female and as the only suitable audience for the intellectual discussion of classicism. In the late 1920s, Pound wrote to the young Louis Zukofsky to urge him to form a literary group of writers, but warned, "NOT too many women, and if possible no wives at assembly. If some insist on accompanying their *mariti*, make sure they are bored and don't repeat offense." He advised Zukofsky on how to choose publishable work for a new magazine: "AND the verse used MUST be good . . . preferably by men under 30" (*Selected Letters,* original capitals and italics).[9] The extent of Pound's paranoia appears in the following violent image of rape: "originality is the phallus or spermatozoid charging, head-on, the female chaos . . . Even oneself has felt it, driving any new idea into the great passive vulva of London" (postscript to his translation of de Gourmont's *Natural Philosophy of Love* 169). In his image of attacking and penetrating "the female chaos," he enacts his own creation myth: like God, Zeus, and other male mythic deities, he establishes order over chaos. Such self-representation demonstrates both his egotism and the violent misogyny of his poetic enterprise.

When Pound and Eliot called for a return to ancient Greek ideals, they imposed a male-authored mythological literature in which women are, for the most part, either victims and mutes like Alcestis, Iphigenia, and Philomela, monsters and murderers like Medusa, Clytemnaestra, and Medea, or beautiful deceivers like Pandora and Helen. Even though Homer offers several of Greek literature's most sympathetic and honorable female characters, they were not the focus of Pound's or Eliot's interest. The new classicism meant a return to and an embrace of a patrilineal, hero-driven culture defined in Homer's epics and Aeschylus's *Oresteia*. Eliot writes in his controversial essay, "*Ulysses*, Order, and Myth," that James Joyce's use of Homer's *Odyssey*

> is simply a way of controlling, of ordering, of giving a shape and a significance
> to the immense panorama of futility and anarchy which is contemporary history.
> . . . Instead of narrative method, we may now use the mythical method. It is . . .
> a step toward making the modern world possible for art. (681)

Many Joyceans would disagree with Eliot's assessment of *Ulysses,* and his description tells us more about his own interest in the mythical method than about Joyce. Several years earlier, he indicated his philosophical perspective on modern literature in "Tradition and the Individual Talent" (1920) in his famous belief that "No poet, no artist of any art, has his complete meaning alone. His significance, his appreciation is the appreciation of his relation to the dead poets and artists." Engagement with great literature of the past is the *only way* to make a modern literature that matters. Pound agreed not only with Eliot's assessment of Joyce's work, but also with his conviction that modern poets needed the mythical method to reinvent the Golden Age of the classics.[10] He and Eliot saw themselves as saviors of Poetry.

The high modernist criteria for poetic selection and discrimination had a profound impact on the women poets in this study who were raised on modernism's literary exclusivity and misogyny and who were taught to emulate poets such as Ezra Pound and T.S. Eliot if they wanted to be taken seriously as writers. How then could women poets reconcile the power of the classical tradition, which offered literary legitimacy, with the victimization, oppression, and marginalization of women at its heart?

Women Writers' Call to Re-Action

Despite the deliberate androcentrism of much high modernist writing, an alternate modernism grew out of the archaeological and anthropological discoveries made by James Frazer, Jane Ellen Harrison, and Sir Arthur Evans. Harrison, in particular, offered an image of Greece that was quite different from the one that male modernists espoused, based on Dionysian urges and the supremacy of an earth goddess: Isis, Cybele, or Demeter.[11] Scholars who challenged traditional male-centered history inevitably began to influence women writers. A separate and distinct classic modernism emerged among many writers and artists. H.D., Louise Bogan, and Edna St. Vincent Millay, for example, wrote mythological poetry; Naomi Mitchison, Laura Riding, and Winifred Bryher wrote classical/historical fiction; Renee Vivien and Natalie Barney imagined Sapphic communities of women.[12] The diverse and international network of women writers was not simply a marginal group of a few women, but was at the center of modernism.[13] Numerous scholars have discussed this alternate classicism, which included revisions of Greek mythology by modernist women writers.[14] Nevertheless, revisions of Greek myths by women poets who wrote during the second half of the century have been under-explored, despite several breakthrough articles, written between 1985 and 1990, on "revisionist mythmaking."

During the period from 1985 through 1990, Alicia Ostriker, Rachel Blau DuPlessis, Paula Bennett, and Susan Stanford Friedman carved out a new area of feminist scholarship on H.D.'s and later women poets' uses of Greek mythology. Ostriker was the first to write on women poets who reworked female characters from mythology to challenge the status of contemporary women.[12] This book builds on landmark articles and chapters written by the women mentioned above and is indebted to the prior conversation. Poets continue to work with myth and to place themselves within the tradition of revisionist mythmakers by citing one another in their writing and interviews and by dedicating poems to one another.[16]

The chapters that follow focus on several major, canonical poets in order to emphasize the centrality of the subject of mythic revision to the larger twentieth-century poetic enterprise. While some of the poets in this book are contemporaries, I have organized my investigation chronologically in terms of dates the poems were published, in order to follow the poetic and cultural dialogue as it unfolded in these poets' lives, and sometimes to show the different ways in which the women contested at the same historical moment. In my chronological progression, I do not mean to imply advances in thought, but rather a continual addition of voices to the tradition of mythic revision. Indeed, years and sometimes decades apart, women continue to wrestle with similar questions. The texts in this study are dialogic: as the poets consider previous mythic revisions, they become aware of their role in maintaining the tradition and shaping its reception. Many of the 1970s and 1980s literary critics who wrote the first articles on mythic revision are also poets. They laid claim to classical mythology as material through which to rewrite conventional gender roles and to explore female subjectivity. Feminist theory developed in tandem with these literary endeavors as women asked: How can we (can we?) include "real" women in mythology and literature? How do we emphasize everyday domestic experiences of motherhood, love, sex, and aging that differ from and sometimes oppose cultural norms? Is there a female "essence" that is separate from male "essence," a set of female cultural values that are different from male cultural values? Is there a "truth" that women must inscribe into the canon, or is "truth" illusory? What does a continued return to past myths teach us about our own culture and ourselves?

Each chapter contains a section on biographical background to illuminate what led the poet to choose to revise the particular myth and a section on literary and theoretical background to ground the analysis of the poet's work. More than a mere account of the myths that influenced the poet, I delve into the complex history of intertextuality, influence, and the feminist questions surrounding the poems. I am interested in biography so far as it illuminates each poet's reasons for revision and her choice of myths. I consider who and what she reads and what cultural pressures she feels as a poet and woman. To help contextualize the poetry and to determine each writer's mythic framework, I examine her journals, letters, and non-fiction, when they are available. My goal has been to explore the role of myth in these women's lives and work without decontextualizing either them or it. In mapping myth's place and function for these poets, I chart the personal, cultural, and political motivations underlying their mythic revisions and locate them within the feminist social and theoretical movements of the second half of the twentieth century.

In the following chapters, I examine the use of Greek myth in works by H.D., Sylvia Plath, Adrienne Rich, Margaret Atwood, and Eavan Boland to highlight larger cultural, political, and feminist issues. Some of these writers identify as feminists, some do not; some are actively involved in political and social movements, others are not. All read other women writers and are aware of their place in a wider literary tradition. I have chosen to focus on particular moments of mythic revision in these poets' careers to offer one possible reading of the dense and complicated history of post-WWII women's writing. The book offers a variety of voices and perspectives, from women of different ages, sexual identities, and nationalities, to emphasize that revisionist mythmaking is not a monolithic or monologic tradition, but one that is as dynamic and multivocal as the Greek corpus that the women revise.

In the first chapter, I trace this dialogue through H.D.'s *Helen in Egypt* (1961), in which the archetypal figures of Helen and Achilles rewrite their lives in defiance of the identities ascribed to them. Through her engagement with the *Iliad*'s concept of imperishable glory, H.D. revises cultural ideas of masculinity and femininity, literary reputation, and a woman's ability to shape her own vision of her identity. More often than with any other modernist woman poet, H.D. and her work are cited by later generations of women as central to their understanding of possibilities for mythic revision. In "Creating a Woman's Mythology" (2000) Susan Stanford Friedman places H.D. at the forefront of the revisionist movement.[17] Later women poets often cite *Helen in Egypt* as a crucial text for understanding their own objectives for revisionist mythmaking.[18] For this reason, I begin my book with H.D, who acts as a bridge between modernist and postmodernist poets.

The second chapter tracks the gradual transformation of Sylvia Plath's poetic persona during the 1950s and early 1960s from victim, Electra, to avenger, Clytemnestra, due to Plath's growing sense of anger at gendered social injustice. H.D.'s investigations into gender identity and Plath's poetics of rage would influence the mythic revisions of second-wave feminist poets such as Adrienne Rich, who is the subject of the third chapter.

During the 1970s, Rich used the Demeter/Persephone myth and the accompanying Eleusinian Mysteries to explore what she perceived as the principal problem in patriarchal cultures—the ruptured relationship between women and their need for reunion through lesbianism. Rich's prose, *Of Woman Born* (1976), and poetry, *Dream of a Common Language* (1978), reflected and influenced radical feminist thought of the time.

The fourth chapter addresses the intersection of myth with domestic violence and psychological abuse, social problems that were becoming visible when Margaret Atwood revised the Circe/Odysseus relationship in her poetic sequence "Circe / Mud Poems" (1974). The chapter asserts that Atwood's revision of the myth is not a condemnation of *The Odyssey*, as previous scholars have argued, but rather an embrace of the epic's central message: the need to return to what makes us human.

The fifth chapter turns to the contemporary Irish poet Eavan Boland's use of Demeter and Persephone to tackle the dearth of representations of aging women in poetry. Her two collections, *In a Time of Violence* (1994) and *The Lost Land* (1998), mirror questions central to age studies in current feminist scholarship.

The conclusion studies the state of revisionist mythmaking at the turn of the millennium, using Rita Dove's *Mother Love* and Anne Carson's sequence "Rome: A Traveller's Guide" as representative of contemporary revisionist mythmaking.

Of course, Greek mythology itself teems with powerful female figures and rebellions against the tyranny of the patriarchal mythmaker. In 431 B.C.E. the classical playwright Euripides, whose plays often contain scathing social commentary on the repression of women, produced his *Medea*. Just before Jason appears on stage for the first time in all his unapologetic egotism and declares his determination to send Medea and their sons into exile so that he may remarry, a thoroughly fed-up all-female chorus sings,

> Flow backward to your sources, sacred rivers,
> And let the world's great order be reversed.
> It is the thoughts of *men* that are deceitful,
> *Their* pledges that are loose.
> Story shall now turn my condition to a fair one,
> Women are paid their due.
> No more shall evil-sounding fame be theirs.
>
> Cease now, you muses of the ancient singers,
> To tell the tale of my unfaithfulness;
> For not on us did Phoebus, lord of music,
> Bestow the lyre's divine
> Power, for otherwise I should have sung an answer
> To the other sex. (*Medea* ll. 410–429, original italics)

Twenty-five hundred years after this radical call for women to tell their own stories, female poets are claiming Phoebus's lyre to answer male-authored mythological literature.

Myth functions at the crossroads between the human subconscious and temporal reality—it is an artifact of cultural imagination, a product of a specific place and time. New places and new times allow for the expansion of the boundaries of existing mythologies. The revisionist poets in this study do not have to go the journey alone— their poems work in dialogue with other women's poetry, as they form a chorus of voices "sing[ing] an answer / To the other sex." In so doing, they allow the myths to endure in altered and newly relevant forms.

And the ambiguous allure of myth is reborn.

CHAPTER ONE

H.D.'s Revision of *Kleos* Culture in *Helen In Egypt*

H.D.'s Mythic Mirror

When Hilda Doolittle accepted Ezra Pound's name for her, "H.D. Imagiste," she could hardly have imagined the muscle his words would have in shaping her lifelong reputation. He and his contemporaries wielded the power to create and destroy literary lives, and they executed it with definitive and unforgiving strokes. In 1952, forty years after her "naming," when H.D. looked back at her career, from her poetic fragments to her long poems and novels, she found a lifetime of her mythic revisions of female characters conscribed to limited roles by their male creators. During the next four years, H.D. wrote *Helen in Egypt* to challenge prevailing ideas about her own identity, gender constructions, and literary authority. Using the earliest literature in the Greek language, Homer's *Iliad*, she critiqued both the dominant culture and the Western literary tradition. This choice was a direct response to Pound. In *Helen in Egypt*, H.D. challenges his ideas about the appropriate use of the classics and asserts her poetic legitimacy. Indeed, the issue of reputation is at the heart of *Helen in Egypt*. The ancient Greek concept of *kleos* (glory, renown, fame) as it relates to the figure of Helen in H.D.'s four major classical predecessors (Homer, Stesichorus, Euripides, and Sappho) guided her vision of her heroine in *Helen in Egypt* and her own conception of herself as a writer.

H.D. and Pound shared a love of ancient Greece and classical learning. Pound initially encouraged her writing of concise mythic fragments and named her "H.D. Imagiste" in 1912 after reading one of her poems. Pound's early requirements for Imagism were precision, concreteness, and economy of diction. He asserted in *Literary Essays*, "At least for myself, I want it so, austere, direct, free from emotional slither" (12). He wrote in a note accompanying several of H.D.'s poems that he sent to Harriet Monroe, editor of *Poetry* magazine, that H.D.'s poetry was "Objective—no slither; direct—no excessive use of adjectives, no metaphors that won't permit examination. It's straight talk, straight as the Greek!" (*Letters* 11). H.D.'s early writing followed Pound's criteria for successful poetry.

Despite Pound's initial acceptance of H.D., she did not share the male high modernist admiration for the hard-edged masculinity of Archaic epic or Aeschylean drama. While different versions of classicism circulated during the modernist period, Pound embraced a classical literary tradition that celebrated male power. Unlike many of her male contemporaries who valorized the heroic and militaristic traditions in Greek poetry, H.D. revised the older works to incorporate female protagonists who sought to define themselves against the prescribed notions of femininity.[1] She favored Euripides, and by the 1920s, she had moved away from Imagism in her poetry, two choices that Pound and those who supported his brand of modernism could not tolerate. By the 1920s, Pound began to openly disapprove of H.D.'s classical subject matter as she started her translations of the "lyrical" and "feminine" Euripides (H.D., *Notes on Euripides*). These were exactly the qualities in poetry that Pound disliked. He urged her to reconsider her direction, calling her a Circe who should "get out of her pig-sty," and telling her that it was "time to go back to an effort of 1912, to get down into meaning and leave off the school room Hellenism" (*Letters*). He believed that her work on the tragedian did not constitute serious classicism. He wanted a return to 1912, the year that he had written to Monroe that H.D.'s poetry was "straight as the Greek," the year that he "named" her and gave H.D. her poetic identity.

Others were also displeased with H.D.'s work. In 1921, T.S. Eliot wrote to Richard Aldington about H.D.'s second volume of poems, *Hymen*: "I think you overrate H.D.'s poetry. I do find it fatiguingly monotonous and lacking in the element of surprise. I mean that this last book is inferior to her earlier work; that many words should be expunged and many phrases amended; that the Hellenism lacks vitality" (*Letters* 488). Eliot's criticism of H.D.'s work is based on her lack of "form, restraint, and discipline," qualities that he used as his measure for good poetry. Other critics followed suit. In 1927 Laura Riding and Robert Graves wrote in *A Survey of Modernist Poetry*, "[H.D.'s] work was so thin, so poor, that its emptiness seemed 'perfection,' its insipidity to be concealing a 'secret,' its superficiality so 'glacial' that it created a false 'classical' atmosphere" (118–123). In his famous "H.D.'s Greece" (1937) Douglas Bush argues that:

> Her refuge is a dream-world of ideal beauty which she calls Greece; her self-conscious, even agonized, pursuit of elusive beauty is quite un-Greek . . . The fact is that the hard, bright shell of H.D.'s poetry partly conceals a soft romantic nostalgia, which however altered and feminized, is that of the Victorian Hellenists. (505–506)

While Bush is correct that H.D. dreamed up a Greek world, so did Pound and her contemporaries who conjured their own versions of the ancient civilization. She can hardly be criticized for that. Bush's objection to H.D.'s "soft," "romantic," "feminized" poetry echoes T.E. Hulme's injunction against writing that he believed threatened the serious work of classic modernist poets. H.D.'s legitimacy was repeatedly questioned, and she was so effectively consigned to the margins of the modernist movement that in 1975 feminist critic Susan Stanford Friedman had to ask, "Who Buried H.D.?"[2]

Even before the second-wave feminist revival of interest in her work, H.D. was thinking about her literary standing. Her engagement in *Helen in Egypt* with the Greek concept of *kleos* came at an important time in her career, when she was reassessing her past work, her reputation, and her relationship with Pound. As teenagers, they had been briefly engaged, until she discovered his engagement to another woman. While she married poet Richard Aldington and, after leaving him, spent the rest of her life with her partner Winifred Bryher, H.D. claimed that nothing afterwards had the power of the "electric, magnetic" kisses she shared with Pound when she was a girl (*End to Torment* 4). She saw those moments as "out of time, eternal," mythical, and they would figure in her poetry for the rest of her life, particularly in the relationship between Helen and Achilles in *Helen in Egypt* (*End to Torment* 26). From H.D.'s early days as an Imagist until her death, she perceived her life as an enactment of mythic patterns. Her poetry, letters, and prose demonstrate her fluid movement between her own life and myth. After a nervous breakdown in 1946, caused by the horrors of World War II and perhaps in part by Pound's fascist and anti-Semitic ravings in his early 1940s radio broadcasts from Rome to America and his subsequent incarceration for treason, H.D. moved to a Swiss clinic, Kusnacht. While there, she resumed psychotherapy, which she had undergone years earlier as a patient of Freud. Her new analyst, Erich Heydt, helped her realize the deep sentiments she still had for Pound. When she received Pound's *Pisan Cantos*, which he drafted from the Italian Disciplinary Training Center where he suffered a nervous breakdown, she determined to start her own cantos, *Helen in Egypt*.

H.D. began her poem in 1952, partially in response to her fresh look at her failed relationship with Pound. She called her writing "an attempt, not unsuccessful, to retain a relationship, materially 'ditched'" (*End to Torment* 58). She felt Pound's rejection not only personally, but especially in terms of her poetic legitimacy. Pound's name, "H.D. Imagiste," and categorization of her had stuck, although she had long since moved away from Imagism. In the final years of her life, as she delved into her own past to determine how she and Pound had become what they were, H.D. wrote a poem that investigates the difficulty of reconciling conflicting identities. In *Helen in Egypt*, she explores male and female characters who seek to define themselves against an externally-constructed, public identity. She did this by returning to two archetypal figures of woman and man from mythology: Helen and Achilles.

The many versions of Helen that came to H.D. from antiquity and the tradition of revision inherent in mythology complicate H.D.'s definition of her protagonist. Any time H.D. refers to one version, it is crucial to remember that she knew that the Greeks did not consider Helen's character to be definitively established.[3] Throughout her poem, H.D. presents different versions of Helen and deliberately refuses to pin down Helen's identity. *Helen in Egypt* hinges on H.D.'s careful reading of Homer and classical revisions of Homer's Helen. H.D. chose Helen because her character has more variety than any other mythic woman, and H.D. repeatedly poses a version of the question, "Is this Helen actually that Helen?" (*Helen in Egypt* 47). There are so many different Helen stories that H.D.'s Helen wants to know if there is such a thing as a real or essential identity.

Questions concerning Helen's nature do not only appear in classical literature. Even in H.D.'s lifetime, scholars debated Helen's historicity. Was there a Trojan War, and was Helen at Troy during the ten-year period? H.D. knew of the controversy surrounding Heinrich Schliemann's removal of "Helen's" jewels from Turkey to Berlin in the late 1800s, and their subsequent disappearance from the Berlin Museum during World War II.[4] Schliemann had photographs taken of his wife, Sophia, whom he called his own Helen of Troy, donning the jewels that he wrongly dated to the Trojan War period. Critics later argued that the jewels were not found at Troy at all. These advances and scandals in archaeology led to debates concerning the nature of history and myth. They also added another layer to the male-fabricated stories about Helen and help to explain the frequency of archeological references in H.D.'s poem. *Helen in Egypt* follows Helen as she, like an archaeologist, uncovers and reconstructs her identity layer by layer, piece by piece.

H.D. was fascinated with the concept of palimpsests, and her extensive career is filled with revisions of classical myths and characters whose themes and experiences relate to her own time and life. In keeping with the cultural moment of 1950s feminism in which she wrote, H.D.'s revision of Greek *kleos* is an example of her use of palimpsest: through Helen's examination of various versions of her life that only partially define her, H.D. shows the courage, strength, and determination that women of her own time demonstrated in their efforts toward self-definition. H.D.'s Helen asks radical questions about the roles that her culture constructed for her. No longer simply temptress, beauty, or possession, she interrogates the identities ascribed to her and redefines herself in her own terms. In the end, she realizes that there is no "essential" Helen, no "true" self, but rather a series of constructions among which she can choose.

Helen in Egypt prefigures the second-wave feminist investigations into culturally scripted identity. Feminist critic and poet Rachael Blau DuPlessis stresses the influence of H.D.'s endeavor on subsequent feminist thought: "Her whole work was answering questions we had just begun to formulate" ("Haibun" 118). H.D. became a model for the next generation of women poets: "We [women] had sought," DuPlessis continues, "the story of modern female cultural position, the portrait of the artist as a struggling and investigative woman. We had sought women's contributions, women's intervention in the western cultural compact. At every moment that the bucket went down into [H.D.'s] vast and capacious oeuvre, it came up full, full, full" ("Haibun" 118). Indeed, H.D.'s Helen and Achilles show what women and men must do if they have no clear history with which they can identify: they must transcribe a new history with each thought, with each vision and revision. In creating Helen and Achilles as characters who question their culture's stories about them, H.D. challenged the validity of the archetypal literary figures for Woman and Man, and helped to set the stage for later women poets to revise classical prototypes.

Helen's Multiple Personalities

In her revision of the Helen myths, H.D. drew on Homer, Stesichorus, Euripides, and Sappho, whose conceptions of *kleos* as related to Helen affected H.D.'s ethical and aesthetic choices. In Greek heroic epic, identity was not defined by an internalized sense of honor, but by the approbation or blame spoken by others. In Homer's *Iliad*, warriors fight to gain *kleos*, glory or fame that persists in praise poetry after they are dead or that is acknowledged by spoils of war. Dean Hammer explains that "an individual's identity and sense of worth . . . are defined by reference to [a] social system, which distributes punishments and rewards for the fulfillment of one's social roles" (59–60). *Tīmē* (honor) refers to the external, tangible objects given to a man by his peers for his *aretē* (excellence in battle); it is the booty, prizes, slaves, and women that a man rightfully earned through conquest. The more *tīmē* a warrior had, the more *kleos* he could expect to receive from the poets who would sing his praises.[5] This glory was the only form of immortality that a warrior could have and it was, therefore, the ultimate objective. Homer's epic opens with Achilles's wrath over Agamemnon's seizure of Briseis, Achilles's war prize. She represents the external recognition of Achilles's value, and he fears that losing the outward evidence of his excellence in battle will diminish his *kleos*. H.D's *Helen in Egypt* recognizes the desire, so prominent in Homer, for favorable remembrance in song. H.D. describes the host of terrified warriors in a storm at sea who cry, "did I miss glorious death on the Walls / . . . to be swept / by the waves to ignoble death?" (122). If their performance is not marked by *tīmē*, or if they do not die fighting at Troy, they will not be immortalized in song.

In Greek literature, men are not alone in their concern about reputation; Helen, too, worries what others say about her. Praise poetry, *kalōn epainos* (praise of the noble), is balanced by blame poetry, *aiskhron psogos* (blame of the base).[6] In *The Iliad*, Achilles is "best" in masculine form—*aristos Akhaiōn* (best of the Achaeans); Helen is "best" in feminine form—*kallistē* (most beautiful); but whereas Achilles wants to be an "icon of glory," Helen fears that she is an "icon of shame."[7] H.D. says that the Greek warriors fought, "cursing Helen through eternity" (*Helen in Egypt* 4). In her poem, she establishes a dialectic: the men will be heroic and gain *kleos*; Helen will be cursed and gain shame. H.D.'s Achilles wonders, "had she enchanted us / with a dream of daring, of peril, / as yet un-writ in the scrolls of history, / un-sung as yet by the poets?" (50). In the song yet un-sung, Helen would be vilified. The question "who will forget Helen?" recurs in H.D.'s poem (122, 123, 124, 127). The implied answer is that no one can forget, but her immortality through song, her infamy, is not the kind of *kleos* that male heroes desired.[8]

Even in *The Iliad*, Helen is already a liminal figure, both an articulate women who voices her concerns and an object of other people's fantasies and speculations. Rachael Blau DuPlessis offers a popular misconception about H.D.'s use of Helen: "H.D. here gives voice to one of the female figures left voiceless" (*Writing* 77). In fact, Helen has a voice in Homer's epics; far from having been silenced, she relates her experiences in her own words. In Book Six of *The Iliad*, Helen considers the potential damage to her reputation and worries that she will be dishonored for generations. She says to Hector, "I am indeed a shameless, evil-minded and abominable creature . . . all through my own shame . . . tormented by Heaven to figure in the songs of people yet unborn" (126). Nancy Worman explains, "Her sense of public reputation is anomalous among the female figures in Homeric epic; *kleos* is rightfully the concern of the warrior, not of the warrior's prize. Like any good warrior . . . she fears the insults of others . . . and recognizes the vulnerability of her public position" (24). Despite Helen's fears about how she will be remembered, the Homeric Helen is *not* shamed. In fact, the men she encounters in the epics are good to her: Priam is paternal and generous; Hector assures her that she is "kind"; in *The Odyssey*, Helen is safely home in Sparta after the war, and Menelaus has forgiven her transgression. In her speech to Telemachus, Helen claims that she is glad to be home with her husband. Although Menelaus is quick to remind her of how she took on the multiple voices of the wives of several Greek soldiers hidden inside the Trojan Horse in order to make them give themselves away, no one dwells on her deception. She, like the crafty Odysseus, has the *mêtis* (cunning, wily intelligence) to use the power of speech to deflect blame.

A centuries-long tradition of revisions of Homer began in the sixth century B.C.E. with the Sicilian poet Stesichorus. He claimed that Helen blinded him as punishment for writing a poem that repeated the traditional story about Helen's adultery. Stesichorus quickly revised his poem to assert that Helen was never at Troy, whereupon Helen restored his sight. His "Palinode" (counter-song; apology), which removes Helen from Troy in order that her character's moral ambiguities would disappear, simply states: "The story is not true. / You did not board the well-benched ships, / You did not reach the towers of Troy."[9] Stesichorus was perhaps the first poet to posit that Helen of Troy was a fiction. He wrote that Helen stayed with Proteus in Egypt while the gods sent her phantom to Troy.[10] Norman Austin explains the revelation associated with this revision: "this revised Helen [would no] longer [be] both wife and mistress, or both Greek and Trojan. She would be all Greek, and a wife plain and simple, with her deadly gaze and her wayward libido displaced onto her idol. Helen, divested of all false projections, would be a whole woman at last" (Austin 115). While Stesichorus's Helen is simplified, to simplify does not necessarily mean to make "whole." Stesichorus's Helen gains *kleos* as a pure, virtuous wife, never having committed adultery. The phantom-Helen becomes the depository for all negative projections. While Stesichorus saves both Helen and Greek womanhood from disgrace, H.D. rejects his simplification of the Homeric Helen's dualities. Regardless of the reductive nature of Stesichorus's revision, an amazing thing happens in the legend that develops *around* his Palinode: Helen is responsible for getting her own *kleos,* and she makes sure that she is remembered in the way she wants to be remembered. In fact, she is the only mythic character ever to force a poet to revise his myth.

While H.D. roots herself in the Homeric tradition that recognizes Helen's complexity, and she mentions Stesichorus's "Palinode" in the opening lines of *Helen in Egypt,* she turns to the revolutionary playwright Euripides as her model for a rejection of war culture.[11] Thirty-four years earlier, she wrote in "Notes on Euripides" (1918), "Euripides is a white rose, lyric, feminine, a spirit" and "the

Shakespeare of Greece." For H.D., he was "feminine" in his sharp critique of Greek culture and politics and his revelation of the effect of the male heroic code on the home and on women. Although H.D.'s understanding of Euripides's career offers only one of several interpretations, she venerated him not only as a radical writer, but also for his strong and vocal female characters. His plays often concern the domestic implications of war and "heroism." H.D. admired Euripides's subversiveness, his de-heroization of heroic figures, and his questioning of old myths. Having lived through two world wars, H.D. identified with Euripides's condemnation of the Peloponnesian War and read into his plays the argument that "'empire' like 'woman' is a fantasy, a fact that does not diminish the mad intensity with which men pursue it" (Meagher xxv).

In her own counter-song, H.D. would build on Euripides's *Helen* (412–411 B.C.E.), in which he splits his heroine into self and *eidolon* (phantom). But Euripides's portrait of Helen is, though progressive in some ways, still reductive and problematic in others. Her insistence on her purity is the most significant revision of her character: "though I wear the name of guilt in Greece, yet here / I keep my body uncontaminated by disgrace" and "I have done nothing wrong and yet my reputation / is bad (193, 202). She is innocent of any wrongdoing, is devoted to Menelaus, and promises him that she would "Die by the sword that kills [him], and be laid to rest / beside [him]. . . . [She] swear[s] to forsake the daylight when [he] die[s]" (227). While Euripides's version seems as reductive as Stesichorus's, the play's political background underscores its somber message.

Euripides's *Helen* connects gendered oppression with Athenian imperialist oppression. In 415 B.C.E. Athens launched a military campaign against Sicily. The final disastrous battles took place between 413–412 B.C.E., a year before Euripides wrote his play, which was based on the Sicilian Stesichorus's revision of the Helen myth. Colin Leach has argued that the play raises significant questions about the Athenian campaign through the lens of the Trojan War: "The Trojan War was fought over a phantom: for what, precisely, after nineteen years, was the Peloponnesian War being fought? Was Sicily's gold real, or another phantom? Did the public attitude of Athens . . . really accord with its real-world behavior?" (14). Euripides's *Helen* is a metaphor for Athens's defeated dream of extending its influence to the borders of the known world. Meagher explains, "In presenting a faithful Helen, chaste and secure in Egypt, Euripides not only left the Trojan War without its traditional excuse, but also left Athens' most recent folly without excuse as well . . . The lightness and brightness of *Helen* only served to highlight ironically the unremitting darkness of what lay behind it" (xxiv-xxv). In 1958, H.D. wrote in her marginal notes on the typescript of her 1918 essay "Notes on Euripides": "Re-reading *Helen*, some quarter century later, or more, gave me an entirely new idea of this enigmatic drama. This play, in the light of history, the ill-fated Sicilian expedition, is one of the most poignant & devout of the series" (18).[12] H.D. continuously made parallels in her writing between Euripides's historical situation and her own, and between gendered oppression and war.

Euripides's vindication of Helen in his play is a philosophical and political move, but not necessarily a feminist one. Notions of shame and glory still drive the plot, and Helen's innocence is as fabricated as her guilt. Euripides's *Helen* offers a rare example of what Helene Foley calls the atypical woman in drama, who "acts to secure her husband's survival and wins a glorious reputation in her private capacity as wife" (302). Menelaus promises that the world will hear the truth, and adds that she simply must be a loyal wife to him. Helen gains *kleos* as a faithful wife, and although she is the play's central character, she arguably has less complexity than she does in either of Homer's epics. At the end of the play, Helen is promised a cult role as a model to virgins. Ultimately, *kleos* is still essential, and for a woman, it is tied to a vindication of marriage and a wife's fidelity.

H.D. was also inspired by Sappho's lyric poetry from the early sixth century B.C.E., with its opposition to epic values and its elevation of love over war. In 1909 the Berlin Parchment, an Egyptian manuscript containing Sapphic fragments, was first translated into English by J.M. Edmonds and published in the *Classical Review*. Among Edmonds's translations of the Oxyrhynchus papyri fragments was the famous fragment 16. H.D. read these issues of the *Classical Review*, sending transcriptions of the fragments to Richard Aldington.[13]

In fragment 16 Sappho's speaker specifies that while some may praise the beauty of armies, whatever one loves is most beautiful on Earth to that individual. In so stating, she challenges the war-drive of male-authored epic. Jack Winkler argues,

> Sappho speaks as a woman opponent entering the lists with men, but her proposition is not that men value military forces whereas she values desire, but rather that all valuation is an act of desire. Men are perhaps unwilling to see their values as erotic in nature, their ambitions for victory and strength as a kind of choice, but it is clear enough to Sappho that men are in love with masculinity and that epic poets are in love with military prowess. (97)

Sappho establishes a tripartite argument in which each "desire" (men for armies, Helen for Paris, and Sappho for Anaktoria) is equally weighed:

> Some men say an army of horses and some men say an army on foot
> And some men say an army of ships is the most beautiful thing
> On the black earth. But I say it is
>   What you love.

Easy to make this understood by all.
For she who overcame everyone
in beauty (Helen)
      left her fine husband

behind and went sailing to Troy.
Not for her children nor her dear parents
had she a thought, no—
. . .
] reminded me now of Anaktoria
who is gone.

I would rather see her lovely step
And the motion of light on her face
than chariots of Lydians or ranks
      of foot soldiers in arms. (Fragment 16)[14]

Epic subordinated the things women pursued and loved. Sappho elevates them to equal status with men's desire to pursue war, but indicates her preference for love. In fact, while Menelaus began the most infamous war in Greek mythology in his relentless pursuit of Helen, Sappho allows Anaktoria's departure in recognition of the value of the pursuit of "what you love."

Sappho frames her argument with images of war that are traditionally central to epic poetry, but the heart of her poem centers on the desire of one person for another. Helen's love for Paris provides the ultimate example. Helen, the quintessential object of desire and fantasy, becomes, in Sappho's poem, the subject who pursues her own desire. She is no longer the Helen whose glory or shame rests on the most famous choice in Greek mythology: Paris's selection of the most beautiful woman in the world, in which Helen is, depending on the source, the happy or unhappy prize. Rather, Sappho makes Helen the one who chooses "the most beautiful thing," the object of her desire (Paris). In that moment, Sappho un-writes the entire literary tradition of Helen. Jack Winkler agrees that Sappho's Helen is not the Helen of epic: "Homer's Helen cursed herself for abandoning her husband and coming to Troy; Sappho's Helen, on the contrary, is held up as proof that it is right to desire one thing above all others, and to follow the beauty perceived no matter where it leads" (97). H.D. appreciated Sappho's subversion of tradition and elevation of love and desire. She used Sappho's ideas in *Helen in Egypt*. In a 1952 letter to her friend Norman Pearson, H.D. wrote of her own Helen poem, "It is the 'phantasmagoria' or unreality of war as against the reality of the eternal and of Love" (*Between History* 127). Whereas Sappho's Helen chose to pursue Paris, H.D.'s Helen chooses Achilles. In *Helen in Egypt*, against the backdrop of epic, Helen's erotic encounter with Achilles will be central.

H.D.'s Helen transcends the categories of hated lover/adulteress and virtuous wife/mother. H.D. questions the male heroic code's emphasis on externally-constructed reputation and engages with the concept of *kleos* to expose how damaging it is for men or women to ground their identities in the perceptions of others. She replaces externally-bestowed reputation with one that is self-constructed. Despite H.D.'s acknowledgement of Euripides and Stesichorus as her classical inspirations, her engagement with and revision of Homer and Sappho are equally crucial to *Helen in Egypt*.[15] H.D. participated in the classical tradition of Homeric revision and followed Sappho's model by making Helen the subject of her quest and elevating love above war. She also admired Homer's Helen for her complexity and for the verbal mastery that allowed her a role in singing her own praise, in bestowing her own *kleos*. As a stand-in for H.D.'s own struggle for self-definition, her Helen sorts through the various accounts of her life and accepts or rejects parts of each version to write a new story of herself.

"There is a voice within me": Helen's Reconciled Identity

H.D. wrote *Helen in Egypt*, in part, as a response to the damage done to her reputation by male-created criteria for poetic legitimacy. Her Helen works to establish an alternative means of identity formation that is not based on externally-constructed *kleos*, but rather on the praise and blame that she accords herself. In order to begin this process Helen confronts previous myths not only about herself but also about other women. She establishes her own tradition of goddesses and mortal women with whom she can identify and against whom she can define herself. The poem opens with Helen wandering through the Amen temple in Egypt where, she thinks, Hermes brought her to wait out the Trojan War; a phantom, she believes, took her place at Troy. As she studies the painted hieroglyphs on the temple walls, she begins to construct a story of her past. She will be able to draw strength and understanding of her own frustrations from the various characters that she sees and recalls.

One such character is her twin sister Clytemnestra, whose experience leads Helen to recognize the flaws in a culture that bases itself on a masculine heroic code. One of Helen's memories concerns Clytemnestra's attempt to avenge the sacrifice of her daughter Iphigenia. H.D.'s Helen asks,

> does it even the Balance
> if a wife repeats a husband's folly?
>
> never; the law is different;
> if a woman fights,
> she must fight by stealth,

with invisible gear;
no sword, no dagger, no spear
in a woman's hands

can make wrong, right. (97)

Helen refers to "the law" established by Athena's court in Athens that determined
Orestes's innocence of bloodguilt after he killed his mother. Whereas Clytemnestra
is found guilty of avenging her daughter's murder, Athena determines that Orestes
is justified in avenging his father's murder, and Apollo declares that a mother
has no legitimate claim to her child.[16] Several Greek tragedies, from Euripides's
Medea to Aeschylus's trilogy, *The Orestia*, demonstrate the disastrous effects of a
woman's attempts to follow the heroic code of retribution that would bring *kleos*
to a man in war. Helen's statement that the law is different for women adduces
Clytemnestra as an embodiment of the incompatibility of Homeric heroism with
Greek womanhood. Helen begins to formulate her identity through her realization
that she is a part of a history, or "family," of women whose choices and reputations
were determined for them by men and by societal definitions of femininity and
masculinity. While Euripides shows in several of his plays that under the Homeric
code women could not act heroically and remain feminine, H.D. challenges the
very notion of masculine glory, and asks how women can avenge themselves, "make
wrong, right," if not through violence.

This question transcends the concept of physical sacrifice that Helen raises in
her reference to Iphigenia, and evokes the ways that women's multidimensional-
ity was "sacrificed" in much male-authored literature and history.[17] Referring to
the male sacrifice of innocent women such as Polyxena, Chryseis, and Briseis,
Paris says to Helen later in the poem, "It was not only Iphigenia / . . . / there
was always another and another and another" (218). Helen's identification with
numerous women, both passive victims and autonomous goddesses, suggests each
individual's potential multiplicity. The myths about Helen (and other women)
represent fractured parts of a whole; H.D.'s Helen tries to piece together the frag-
ments that work and to discard those that do not. When Helen sees a glyph of Isis
with her sister Nephthys, she recalls her closeness to her own sister, Clytemnestra.
They are "inseparable / as substance and shadow, / as shadow and substance are"
(68). If Helen and her "shadow" sister are inseparable, perhaps Helen and her
"shadow," or phantom, upon the ramparts at Troy are also inseparable; Helen is
not one or the other, as previous writers have suggested, but both. She constructs
her identity piece by piece as she assembles a group of women to whom she can
relate. This network of women proves integral to Helen's ability to define herself.
Through these connections Helen begins her own process of *anagnorisis* (the
coming to self-awareness), a result of many Greek male heroes' quests.[16]

While recalling previous male sacrifices of women such as Iphigenia, Helen focuses, too, on the concept of re-birth, imagining her own movement beyond the stories others tell about her. She contemplates this as she sees glyphs of Isis and Osiris, which in turn lead her to think of the Demeter and Persephone Mysteries. H.D. believed that male violence results from a rejection of maternal love and that a return to the mother Goddess would be restorative. In fact, as Gregory explains, H.D. saw Euripides's *Helen* as "Eleusinian in that [it] concern[s] the recovery of one who has been lost . . . and clearly [H.D.] sees her work, like the Helen of her *Helen in Egypt,* in relation to these mysteries of recurrent losing and finding and losing again" (182). H.D. draws a parallel between the Eleusinian experience of Demeter losing and finding Persephone or Isis's experience of burying and resurrecting Osiris, and Helen's experience of searching for and reconstructing her own identity. As Hollenberg argues, in linking the motif of the Mysteries of loss and rebirth to Helen's own quest, "H.D. shows the painful self-division, the loss of a part of the soul, caused by woman's internalization of culture's traditional ambivalence toward her sexuality; and she dramatizes the obsessive convolutions of the slow process of recovery" (*H.D.*, 180). Hollenberg's argument can extend beyond sexuality to identity in general. Indeed, subsequent poets hailed H.D. as a model for their own ability to challenge culturally-scripted identity.

At the end of Book I of *Helen in Egypt,* Achilles's mother, Thetis, informs Helen that while her association with these women might be significant, it is not the endpoint of her quest. Thetis tells her that she should find her answers in Greece rather than in Egypt. Helen must take her new understanding of the need to strive for internal valuation back to Greece, the stand-in for Western culture in general, in order "that enchantment may find a place / where desolation ruled, / and a warrior race, / Agamemnon and Menelaus" (90). In other words, H.D. neither advocates a withdrawal from the world nor the construction of a female community that would exist separately from traditional communities; rather, she suggests that the familiar world be enriched through an incorporation of the lost appreciation for the feminine principle and through the devaluation of a war culture that praises men for their excellence in killing and destruction. Helen is called "home" from the foreign to the familiar, to Leuke, the White Island, where, in Greek mythology, she and Achilles meet.[18]

The "new phase" of *Helen in Egypt* concerns Helen's struggles on Leuke as men tell her who they think she is. H.D. felt this struggle in her own life, as well. She wrote to Pearson, "I am all right, but bored and claustrophobic, as I have a mad desire to travel, to get right away. I am taking it out in re-reading some of Euripides and working toward a new phase of the *Helen,* in which, as I see it, she will leave Egypt; then, we have the whole Greek mythology to draw on.

But I will not hurry this – it is my 'travel' at the moment" (Hollenberg, *Between History* 138). H.D. was restless with her new relationship with her therapist Dr. Erich Heydt. He was dredging up painful and difficult memories of Pound. H.D. named Heydt as her Paris, Freud as her Theseus, and told Pearson in September of 1952, "It is fascinating . . . that there are these stories that so perfectly fit *my* legend" (Hollenberg, *Between History* 129, emphasis added). "I am writing this as I am living it," H.D. exclaimed in another letter dated a year later, "a sort of poetic analysis, complete with couch and father-symbol" (Hollenberg, *Between History* 150). She felt a cathartic identification with Helen's investigation into her past to make sense of the present. Like the poem's first section, "Pallinode," the second section on Leuke plays on external versus internal definitions of identity.

Once on Leuke, Helen must discern if there is truth in the various accounts of her life that she hears from her two former lovers, Paris and Theseus.[19] Because their different "memories" of her reveal that, to them, she merely reflects what they want her to be, she must confront the men who seek to categorize her. In Book One, Helen had been consumed with forgetting everything about her life except for her encounter with Achilles on the beach in Egypt; Book Two deals with others urging her to remember parts of her repressed past and to forget Achilles.

Helen goes back in time to her escape from Sparta with Paris, acknowledging that she was, she now believes, at Troy. The narrator situates us initially in Paris's memory: "we are in King Priam's palace before the death of Paris, or rather we are with Paris who in his delirium sees Helen as he saw her for the last time" (123). Is Paris's representation of Helen truth or fantasy? The poem's narrator explains, "we see, through the eyes of Paris, an earlier Helen. It is a vibrant, violent Helen" (125). Paris says,

> you were eaten away by fire.
>
> . . .
>
> And Helen? the story the harpers tell
> reached us, even here upon Leuke;
> how she was rapt away
>
> by Hermes, at Zeus' command,
> how she returned to Sparta,
> how in Rhodes she was hanged
>
> and the cord turned to a rainbow,
> how she met Achilles . . .
> in Egypt. (125, 129)

After repeating these "canonical" accounts of Helen's fate after the war, he adds, "but the harpers / never touch their strings / to name Helena and Death" (130). Paris's version of what happened is new: "I am the first in all history / to say, she died, died, died / when the Walls fell" (131). He claims that Achilles "was never your lover / . . . / you fell on his spear, / like a bird out of the air" (139).[20] This is Paris's "reality." He asks, "what is Helen without the spears, / what is Love without arrows?" (140). In other words, as would be typical in a *kleos* culture in which Helen is what others say about her, he cannot separate Helen from the war stories in which she figures. To Paris, she is a conflation of his "delirious" memories and what the "harpers" have made her out to be.

Dissatisfied with Paris's account, Helen next meets with Theseus, her Freud figure, to seek guidance. He, too, asks her the question, "Do you remember?" (147). Each person who asks this of Helen means by the question: does she remember *his* version of her life. Theseus asks Helen to remember a part of her past, not for her benefit, but for his own gratification. He asks, "are you the Palladium, / the olive-wood statue / that directed [my] Quest?" (150). He views her as helper, as statue or icon. To him, she was not the subject of her own quest, but an object in his. Theseus continues to ask and answer questions that lead one to wonder if the multiple "Helens" from men's versions of her life are "one of these / or all . . .?" (163). Unlike Paris, Theseus persistently re-enforces the possibility of multiple perspectives and realities. This concept will influence Helen as she ultimately picks and chooses from various stories the aspects that she accepts in her own construction of her life.

From the beginning of H.D's poem, Helen searches for identity. The notion is so new and foreign, however, that when she begins to speak during her encounter with Theseus, neither she nor the narrator is sure that the voice is her own. She describes this acquisition of a voice as breath returning to the dead shrouded and entombed in marble and snow:

> It comes to me, lying here,
> it comes to me, Helena;
> do you see the cloth move,
>
> or the folds, to my breathing?
> no, I breathe quietly,
> I lie quietly as the snow,
>
> drifted outside; how did I find
> the threshold? marble and snow
> were one; is this a snow palace?

does the ember glow
in the heart of the snow?
Yes—I drifted here,

blown (you asked) by what winter-sorrow?
but it is not sorrow;
draw near, draw nearer;

do you hear me? do I whisper?
there is a voice within me,
listen—let it speak for me. (174–175)

The glowing ember, the source of light and power, is a voice. While the narrator explains, "It is an heroic voice, the voice of Helen of Sparta," Helen finishes her speech, "do I love War? / is this Helena?" (176, 177). Is she merely a vessel for the conflicting voices that blow through her or will she have the agency to claim the voice as her own? The image of the glowing, yet un-appropriated voice recalls the poem's earlier question, "Is this Helen that Helen?" Her search for a definitive identity turns into an embrace of a composite identity that includes multiple and seemingly contradictory accounts.

Helen listens as her ex-lovers describe their versions of her until she finally declares her need to "review all the past / in the new light of a new day" (226). There are "truths," she finds,

that break through the legend,
the fame of Achilles,
the beauty of Helen,

like fire
through the broken pictures
on a marble-floor. (258–259)

Helen realizes that the "truths" of her multifaceted character have the destructive potential to break apart the myth-mosaic. The legends about her and Achilles were created "because Apollo granted a lute-player / a rhythm" (229). Her newfound understanding of the legends' fictive nature frees her to shatter the previous male-created versions of her identity, to explore her own creative rhythms, and to tell her own story. Helen includes aspects of her life from various accounts: the flight from Sparta with Paris, the escape from burning Troy, and the experience in Egypt. Whereas in a *kleos* culture, what others say about Helen is what she will be remembered for, H.D.'s Helen must figure out what to remember and what to forget in her search for "everlasting memory / the glory" (3). She often frames her thoughts with the supplication "let me forget . . . let me remember" (17). Helen dares to challenge the notion of *kleos* as she continuously suggests the limitations of the stories about her that "the harpers will sing forever" (6). The cultural, collective memory preserved in myth is different from the "Troy-gates broken / in memory of the Body" (7). Helen must strive for body-memory, or individual memory, through a realization that none of the stories matters except for the one that she constructs for herself.

Helen asserts her boredom with the old stories of war and *kleos*: "I do not want to hear of Agamemnon / and the Trojan Walls, / I do not want to recall / shield, helmet, greaves" (18). As Euripides's Helen understands that her "life's a myth," H.D.'s Helen insists,

> I am not nor mean to be
> the Daemon that they made of me
> . . .
> let them sing Helena for a thousand years,
> let them name and re-name Helen (109–110)

She articulates the problem that *men* sing the songs of war and posits that Greek myths generally relegated women to certain marginal roles, often ignoring the personal, domestic elements that Helen sifts through here. She says,

> I am called back to the Walls
> to find the answer,
> [. . .]
> to return and sort over and over,
> my bracelets, sandals and scarves --
> [. . .]
> these intimate, personal things (232–233)

When Helen tries to recite what happened at Troy, she breaks off, "I can not remember . . . / I only remember the shells, / whiter than bone, / on the ledge of a desolate beach" (235). In a revision of the concept of *kleos*, Helen authors the story of her own life based on the "personal things" that do not find their way into epic. At the heart of her revision beats her moment of love with Achilles. This is what she wants to be remembered for.

"A challenge . . . to all song forever": A Different Kind of Glory

Helen in Egypt allows a female character to claim her own identity; it also challenges the ancient and contemporary social systems that make that claim so difficult for both women *and* men. In order to change society, H.D. argues, men must redefine themselves, too. With Helen's help, Achilles re-conceptualizes his life and legacy. Both he and she leave behind the war-language of epic to enter an alternate existence in which each tries to determine which of their experiences are real and which are dream or myth.

Helen moves between moments in time and space as she jumps between memories. The lack of linear chronology in the poem mirrors the psychoanalytic effect of Helen's quest: she revisits specific moments in her past or accounts that she has heard about herself as they present themselves to her conscious mind. Once these latent moments become manifest, she is able to incorporate them into the narrative of herself that she is constructing. As Helen and Achilles talk of things "that had not yet happened, / had happened long ago," she relates herself and him to the hieroglyphs she sees as she walks through the Amen Temple in Egypt (55). As the comparisons between Helen and other women help her to weave a web of stories and traits with which she can identify, the comparisons that she creates between herself and Achilles reflect the fictive and amorphous natures of "character" and "self" that she recognizes in the mythic figures "Helen" and "Achilles":

> War, Ares, Achilles, Amor;
> Karnak was her temple;
> Amen-Zeus is her father, my father,
>
> his temple is our temple,
> there, I sought Clytaemnestra;
> I called my sister Astarte
>
> or Nephthys, twin sister of Isis,
> and Isis is Cypris, Cypria;
> [. . .]
>
> could Achilles be father of Amor,
> begotten of Love and of War?
> [. . .]
>
> was Proteus his father?
> could Proteus, king of Egypt,
> of many names, of many shapes,
>
> manifest as Achilles?
> stop—O voice prompting my strophies,
> stop—how could that be?

if Thetis was Cypris, Cypria,
(you say) who could not Achilles be? (178–180)

All of these shape-shifters could be multiple ("who could not Achilles be?"). Helen's thoughts beget and unite them. These identifications help her to understand her connection with Achilles, a goal of her quest. Theseus says to Helen, "you were destined forever to know this dual companionship/ . . ./ yourself in another/ . . ./ O tiny world, O world of infinity" (188). When she asks where he and Achilles "reconcile" or "cross," Theseus answers her, "Helen in Egypt, / Helen at home, / Helen in Hellas forever" (190). In other words, all of the mythic figures whom Helen has been contemplating come together in her thoughts, in her "strophies." Once she acknowledges her power to make these connections and to recognize the interchangeability of mythic characters, she begins to see them as fictions that she can manipulate. And once she "break[s] through the legend," she can rewrite it (258).

Helen determines the centrality of the moment in which she and Achilles meet, the defining moment in "timeless time" around which all other moments revolve. According to H.D.'s poem, at Troy, at the moment Paris's arrow pierced his heel, the dying Achilles locked eyes with Helen as she watched the battle from the ramparts. In another dimension of time and space, Helen and Achilles meet on a beach in Egypt, when Achilles suddenly challenges her, "Are you Hecate? Are you a witch?" She calls on his mother, Thetis, and at the mention of her name, Achilles grabs Helen's throat. The violence turns to passion and they make love under his cloak. These two scenes of connection lock in Helen's mind as the "ever-recurring eternal moment[s]" when "l'Amour [and] La Mort merge in the final illumination" (271). In *Helen in Egypt*'s penultimate poem, H.D. inscribes the significance of the finite moment that becomes the infinite:

there is no before and no after,
there is one finite moment
that no infinite joy can disperse

or no thought of past happiness
tempt from or dissipate
[. . .]

the seasons revolve around
a pause in the infinite rhythm
of the heart and of heaven. (303–304)

Helen's experiences are all born from her moment of erotic fulfillment with Achilles. In creating this central lyric moment, H.D. engages in a challenge to the *Iliad*'s narrative, which is propelled by the heroes' war-drive for *kleos*.

So powerful is the allure of *kleos* that in Greek mythology, Achilles rejects the offer of a long and happy life, choosing instead to die during the Trojan War to gain imperishable glory. Achilles admits in H.D.'s poem, "[Helen] enchanted us / with a dream of daring, of peril, / as yet un-writ in the scrolls of history, / un-sung as yet by the poets" (50). In other words, in the warriors' quest to achieve excellence (*aretē*) and win her back, Helen represented the possibility of immortality through song.

In H.D.'s poem, however, "present is past, past is future," and in this "time-less-time" previous preconceptions about character do not matter and *kleos* as the reward for prowess in war becomes irrelevant (51, 39). In Egypt Achilles turns into "the new Mortal, / shedding his glory" and rejecting *The Iliad*'s masculine war culture that values "deathless glory" above all else (10, 41). Unlike Achilles in *The Iliad*, who prizes the external show of honor (*tīmē*), "this Achilles [is not to be recognized] by accoutrements of valour" (7). In the Hades episode of *The Odyssey*, Achilles regrets his choice for a short life with *kleos*, confessing to Odysseus, "I would rather work the soil as a serf on hire to some landless impoverished peasant than be King of all these lifeless dead" (173). Homer himself established the tradition of revision of his earlier epic that H.D. follows here. Echoing *The Odyssey*, H.D.'s Achilles says to Helen, "I was shot like an underling, / like the least servant, / following the last luggage-carts / and the burdened beasts" (60). His *kleos* disappears when he sees Helen, and he questions his former desire to "control the world" (52). Achilles realizes that his

> body honoured
> by the Grecian host
> was but an iron casement,
>
> it was God's plan
> to melt the icy fortress of the soul
> and free the man;
> . . .
> *as the new Mortal,*
> *shedding his glory,*
> *limped slowly across the sand.* (italics mine, 9–10)

This image of the "new Mortal" emerging out of the shell of the body prefigures the image of the "truths" about the two lovers "that break through the legend/ . . . / like fire / through the broken pictures / on a marble floor" (258–259). Achilles is vulnerable, as his limp suggests. Like Helen, who is depicted as a moth "with half-dried wings" just emerged from its cocoon, Achilles has metamorphosed, has shed a shell that was socially imposed, to emerge as the "new Mortal" (166, 300).

H.D. imagined that this transformation of consciousness could result from a rejection of a patriarchy based on war, supplanted by an embrace of what she envisioned as maternal love.[40] DuPlessis argues that "*Helen in Egypt* seriously intends itself as an anti-war text, which uses an examination of the roots of violence in repression of love of the mother to propose an alternative" (*Career* 114). H.D. places Helen's and Achilles's moment of love at the center of her inquiry, thereby de-emphasizing war and adventure. Helen's reference to Achilles's mother, Thetis, precipitates their moment of union. Achilles initially reacts violently to Helen's mention of his mother's name. Helen perceives his anger as "a treasure," as it leads her to reassess his legend, as well as her own. Helen thinks of the young Achilles longing for his mother, who had left him to be trained by the centaur, Chiron, and then by the king of Scyros, to "learn to rule a kingdom" (287). Thetis wanted Achilles to be instructed on Scyros "in the laws and the arts of peace" (286). She knew, the narrator explains, that "the prophecy of Achilles' fame could only be fulfilled if he died in battle" (295). Despite the cultural importance of *kleos*, Thetis chose to hide Achilles away to save him. Achilles had "forgotten his vows of allegiance" to Thetis, however, when he "followed the lure of war" and entered "The Command," "the adamant rule of the inner circle of the warrior caste" (287, 61). The narrator defines Achilles as ruler of The Command (with Agamemnon, Menelaus, and Odysseus): "This is the Achilles of legend, Lord of the Myrmidons, indisputable dictator with his select body-guard" (51). Achilles describes the power he had:

> I had broken the proud
> and re-moulded them to my whim;
> the elect, asleep in their tents,
>
> were my slaves, my servants;
> we were an iron-ring, unbreakable (51)

In his encounter with Helen, for the first time since he had joined the iron-ring, Achilles "wondered why he forgot / and why he just now remembered" his vows to pursue peace (287). He tries to strangle Helen in a rage that, she realizes, stems from his loss of his mother.

When Helen confronts the son/Achilles who is angry at his inability to fulfill his mother's wishes, it sparks her memory of her own daughter, Hermione, whom she had left in Sparta. Earlier in the poem, Helen had declared, "I am only a daughter; / no, no, I am not a mother," as she tried to deny the guilt that other mothers such as Jocasta and Hecuba may have felt about abandoning their sons. So too, when she relates herself to the Persephone myth, she claims, "I am only a daughter, / no I'm not Demeter / . . . / I am Kore, Persephone" (195). This denial changes after Helen recalls her departure from Sparta. In a lyric that is reminiscent of Sappho's description of Helen's departure, Helen remembers:

> I had . . . everything,
> my Lord's devotion, my child
> prattling of a bird-nest,
>
> playing with my work-basket;
> the reels rolled to the floor
> and she did not stoop to pick up
>
> the scattered spools but stared
> with wide eyes in a white face,
> at a stranger – and stared at her mother,
>
> a stranger – that was all,
> I placed my foot on the last step
> of the marble water-stair
>
> and never looked back (228)

As she "look[s] back" now and accepts her forgotten memory of abandoning her child, she can bring a new perspective to her relationship with Achilles, who was "abandoned" by his mother and who "abandoned" his mother's wishes. She asks why she and Achilles both forgot their "domestic" connections, his promise to his mother to work for peace and her promise as a mother to her daughter.

Sappho's fragment 5 offered H.D. a model for Helen's prayer that Achilles be cleansed of his warrior past to fulfill, instead, his mother's wish that he lead a life centered on peace:

> O Kypris and Nereids, undamaged I pray you
> Grant my brother to arrive here.
> And all that in his heart he wants to be,
>   make it be.
>
> And all the wrong he did before, loose it.
> Make him a joy to his friends,
> A pain to his enemies and let there exist for us
> Not one further sorrow.

In the same vein, in *Helen in Egypt*, Helen prays to Amen that Achilles be able to forget the war (12). She asks, "what does it matter, / who won, who lost? / must the Battle be fought and fought / in his memory?" (35). In a *kleos* culture, the answer would be yes. Replaying the moments of heroic battle would be essential in conferring glory; but memory functions differently for Helen than it does for Greek men. Achilles thinks,

> The Command was bequest from the past,
> from father to son,
>
> . . .
>
> the Command was my father, my brother,
> my lover, my God
>
> . . .
>
> [Helen] is stronger than God, they say
> She is stronger than fate. (61)

Weary of the fallout from patriarchy, Helen prays that she and Achilles be allowed to forget the negative events of the war and remember only the instant of their love. Achilles asks, "who am I? am I a ghost?" to which Helen responds, "you are living, O child of Thetis, / as you never lived before" (16). This is an alternate way of life to patrilineal war culture, one instead based on matrilineal connection. The life that Helen wants to remember is based on love, not on "the whole powerful war-faction" and "deathless glory" (18, 41).

This concept goes back to an ancient rejection of war and *kleos* based on *aretē*. In their place was honored a new type of *kleos* based on the winning of love, or excellence in love. The poetic tradition that emphasizes this new *kleos* is one that goes from Sappho to Ovid to Horace, and says that the lover and beloved will live in poetry, will receive immortality through the song of their love. For example, Sappho's fragment 147 declares that the love of which she spoke in her poetry would confer a new kind of *kleos*: "someone will remember us / I say / even in another time." H.D. establishes Helen within this tradition by providing an alternate means of attaining *kleos* that does not require killing or dying. The most crucial deviation, however, is that Helen, not other poets, can confer this glory, renown, fame upon herself. It is no longer a question of what others sing about her, but what she defines herself to be.

As Achilles seizes her throat, Helen claims the story and Paris's death-dealing arrow as her own in a curative gesture:

> mine, the great spread of wings,
> the thousand sails,
> the thousand feathered darts
>
> that sped them home,
> mine, the one dart in the Achilles-heel,
> the thousand-and-one, mine. (25)

Helen prays to Theseus to help her, "so that none of the heroes be lost, / teach me to remember, / (there is one prayer, / may he find the way)" (207). If she can take over the power of poetry, she can turn the greatest war story into one in which no one dies and Achilles is not alone. Step by step she re-writes the war epic as one of love, and as in Sappho's fragments, she and her beloved will be remembered through her poetic revision. Helen's revised poem embraces what she claims male-written epic missed:

> the million personal things,
> things remembered, forgotten,
>
> remembered again, assembled
> and re-assembled in different order
> as thoughts and emotions,
>
> the sun and the seasons changed,
> and as the flower-leaves that drift
> from a tree where the numberless
>
> tender kisses, the soft caresses,
> given and received; *none of these*
> *came into the story,*
>
> *it was epic, heroic and it was far*
> *from a basket a child upset*
> *and the spools that rolled to the floor.* (289, emphasis added)

Out of these forgotten memories of private, intimate moments and that eternal moment of the *hieros gamos* (sacred marriage) under Achilles' cloak, a new child, Euphorion, is born.

H.D. turns Euphorion, the son that Helen and Achilles engender in some versions of their myth, into a conflation of the young Achilles in Chiron's cave before he learns of war and the young Helen before Theseus comes to take her. H.D.'s androgynous figure is a melding of the two children at the moment of their dramatic change, just before their loss of innocence. Its birth allows an adult Achilles to remember his promise to his mother to work for peace and forget the lure of *aretē* and *kleos*; it also allows an adult Helen both to redeem herself as a mother for abandoning her daughter when she left Sparta and to craft a narrative of herself and her experiences, not as others have remembered, but as she wants to remember. In the end, "the heart accepts, / encompasses the whole / of the unde-cipherable script" (86). This understanding moves beyond Homer's, Stesichorus's, and Euripides's portrayals of Helen, whose identity was based on external reputa-tion, as H.D.'s Helen realizes that she does not need *an* answer to "the riddle" of who she is (31). She answers Achilles's question concerning which memories are real and which are not by saying that "they were one," and she accepts the various accounts of her life as containing kernels of truth; none needs to be rejected or accepted entirely (238). In her notes for a recording of *Helen in Egypt*, H.D. explains, "through her contact with Achilles, [Helen] finds reality." "Reality" does not mean that Helen has found a definitive, core self. Rather, it means an embrace of Helen's commitment to introspection and intuition, and an acceptance of her innate multiplicity. By the end of the poem, Helen has realized that what matters is her own perception. Helen's *anagnorsis*, her journey toward and arrival at self-awareness, comes through a recasting of gender roles embodied in a love so profound that it becomes the source of *kleos*, the reason why, as Sappho wrote, "someone will remember [them] . . . even in another time" (Fragment 147).

H.D.'s re-writing of *kleos* mythology came at a significant moment in history when women's roles in the family, workforce, and society were about to come under radical reconsideration. Her questioning of *kleos* performed a subversive function; it suggested that a woman could reject what she had always been told that she was, what had been spoken about her, and could reinvent herself. While Achilles does not speak at the end of the poem, the sequence implies that Helen has led him beyond the confines of his epic, as well. Although H.D. wrote out of her own "out of time, eternal" experiences with Ezra Pound, the *anagnorses* that Achilles and Helen undergo extend beyond H.D.'s personal quest to understand who she and Pound had become; they prefigure the cultural *anagnorsis* of the nascent second-wave of feminism. Through a continued engagement with Homer, Stesichorus, Euripides, and Sappho, H.D. embraced the tradition of classical revisionist mythmakers and became a model for later women poets to join in the tradition. She relied on cultural and literary foundations for her poetry, and "made it new" by animating female characters like Helen with a fresh mind and voice. *Helen in Egypt* anticipated the second-wave feminist scholarly and literary project of challenging the male high modernist criteria for the appropriate use of the classics and of revising male-authored literature and history. In H.D.'s poem, Helen has an active mind that yearns to interpret her own past. In one of the poem's most profound moments, Helen begins, "draw nearer, draw nearer; / do you hear me? do I whisper? / there is a voice within me, / listen—let me speak" (175). Like Helen, feminist writers of the next several decades would challenge the mythological literature recorded by men and would speak anew.

CHAPTER TWO

Sylvia Plath's Complex Electra

The Myth of Real Life

During a psychotherapy session in 1958, Sylvia Plath's doctor urged her to ask, "Who am I angry at?" Plath answered in her therapy journal that evening,

> it is my mother and all the mothers I have known who have wanted me to be what I have not felt like really being from my heart and at the society which seems to want us to be what we do not want to be from our hearts: I am angry at these people and images. I do not seem to be able to live up to them. Because I don't want to. (*Journals* 437)

Despite Plath's assertion, "I don't want to," and despite her frustration with social and gender inequalities, she had internalized the pervasive messages and images that attested to the incompatibility of independence and happiness, of autonomy and family. Her poetry and prose fiction, which often mirror language and ideas from her journals, abound with characters unable to cope successfully with the cultural pressures of domestic womanhood. Adrienne Rich explains that during the 1950s, "in a reaction to the earlier wave of feminism, middle-class women were making careers of domestic perfection" (*BBP* 173). In Plath's essay "America! America!," written a month before her suicide in 1963, she writes of her need to fit into "the cherished Norm" (*Johnny Panic* 55). Indeed, throughout her adult life, her journals and letters indicate that she vacillated between her desire to fulfill traditional "feminine" roles and her rage against the social constructs that she feared would keep her from realizing her artistic potential.

It was not until 1958–1959, when she turned to the classical literary models of Aeschylus's *Oresteia* and the *Electra* plays of Euripides and Sophocles, that a consistent framework for the poetic expression of her depression and anger emerged in her work. Plath's extremes of rage and manic depression manifested in her profession of "lust" and "love" for her father, who died when she was only eight, and her fury at losing him (*Journals* 230). In truth, they had not had a close relationship. According to biographer Paul Alexander, Sylvia interacted very little with her father, especially as his health deteriorated (28). He wrongly diagnosed himself with lung cancer. In fact, he had a treatable form of diabetes mellitus, but had put off treatment for too long. After undergoing the amputation of a gangrened left leg, he contracted pneumonia and died shortly thereafter. On the other hand, Plath did have a loving relationship with her mother, Aurelia, even while Plath was writing some of her most hostile journal entries about her. The biographical and cultural reasons behind Plath's fascination with multiple ancient sources for the Electra and Clytemnestra myth illuminate what drove her to close identification with the wretched, abandoned daughter and, in the final year of Plath's life, with the venomous, vengeful wife.

Plath's choice of Electra as a mythic model allowed her a lens through which to view her life. Electra interested her for a number of reasons: one was her anger at "all the mothers." This admission of hers demonstrates how Plath's frustration and depression led her to scapegoat other women. Betty Friedan tells us that the feminine mystique imposed sexual suppression and denial and fueled feelings of inadequacy and rage. Despite her categorization of her mother, Aurelia Plath, as complicit in society's attempts to limit her daughter's options, Plath acknowledged her mother's own frustration with the idealized "angel" of literature and popular lore. In 1950 she wrote in her journal, "When you catch your mother, the childhood symbol of security and rightness, crying desolately in the kitchen . . . it kind of gets to you" (19). In fact, Aurelia Plath was a professor and a widowed mother who fought to give Sylvia and her brother Warren the best of educations and opportunities; she hardly fit into her daughter's negative categorization of "mothers."[1] Plath's anger at "all the mothers," instead of at the patriarchal system that limited women's options, is striking.

Plath recognized that the customs enforced by "the mothers" highlighted gender imbalances in her culture. As a student at Smith College, she wrote,

> I have too much conscience injected in me to break customs without disastrous effects;
> I can only lean enviously against the boundary and hate, hate, hate the boys who can

dispel sexual hunger freely, without misgiving, and be whole, while I drag out from date to date in soggy desire, always unfulfilled. The whole thing sickens me. (*Journals* 20)

In this revealing passage, Plath creates a strange dialectic: women are unfulfilled and not "whole" if they do not have sex at the end of a date, but the taboo against premarital sex makes fulfillment risky; men, on the other hand, are "whole" because they can have sex without guilt. "Date to date" suggests that the person she is with matters less than the actual accomplishment of the sexual act, and her "soggy desire" emphasizes the animal nature of the sexual drive more than any romantic wishes for a partner. In a later journal entry she refers to "delicious animal fire" as "a refined hedonism" (*Journals* 105). Plath's feelings of disappointed longing, and fear of the "disastrous effects" of that longing would become manifest in her Electra poems.

Perhaps as a product of her cultural indoctrination, Plath was incapable of accepting her frustrations as legitimate. Instead, she hoped that she could overcome them. Her private papers reveal a constant battle, not against her status as woman, but against her distaste for that status. "I am at odds," she wrote. "I dislike being a girl, because as such I must come to realize that I cannot be a man. In other words, I must pour my energies through the direction and force of my mate. My only free act is choosing or refusing that mate. And yet, it is as I feared: I am becoming adjusted and accustomed to that idea" (54). As another Smith College student from the 1950s, Gloria Steinem, remembers, "At Smith, you were attempting to do some good work to fill the time before you got married. Your only real life-changing mechanism was marriage, and then after that you assumed your husband's existence" (quoted in Alexander 71). Plath wondered, "why do I hate what I am being drawn into so inexorably?" (*Journals* 98). She decided that because she chose "the physical relationship of intercourse as an animal and releasing part of life" and because she needed "to capture a mate" to look after her when she was older, she would have to marry. To remain single was inconceivable. Plath wrote in a January 26, 1958 journal entry of "the sterile forced pathetic smell of a woman without a man, pitied, yet despised for the very lack which constitutes her tragedy" (319).

Plath's frustrations were not only social and sexual, but also artistic. She knew that women poets were not esteemed as highly as their male counterparts, and her journals detail the conflict between femininity and artistic ability. She was torn between wanting to be the good girl and wanting to be an autonomous artist. She often wrote about her fears: "After a while I suppose I'll get used to the idea of marriage and children. If only it doesn't swallow up my desires to express myself in a smug, sensuous haze. Sure, marriage is self expression, but if only my art, my writing, isn't just a mere sublimation of my sexual desires which will run dry once

I get married" (*Journals* 21). Here, Plath suggests that her artistic creativity is a release of sexual aggression, of "soggy desire," which, when fulfilled, will not make her "whole," as she suggested in an earlier entry, but deficient in artistic imagination. In 1956 she wrote, "Some day when I am stumbling up to cook eggs and feed milk to the baby and prepare dinner for my husband's friends, I shall pick up Bergson, or Kafka, or Joyce, and languish for the minds that are outleaping and outskipping mine" (*Journals* 225). Plath struggled with these issues throughout her life. Even while Plath dated several men and considered marrying a few of them, she hoped that her artistic ambition would be too strong ever to accept the kind of annihilation that she thought would have to accompany marriage.

In 1956 while she was a student at Newnham College in Cambridge, Plath met Ted Hughes at a party, an encounter that led her to question whether she "desire[d] the things that [would] destroy [her] in the end," or if she and Hughes could have a mutually productive relationship. When he leaned in to kiss her at the end of the evening, she bit his cheek, actually drawing blood. Here was the "animal fire" she had been hoping to share with a man. She married Hughes only four months after their meeting and quickly subsided into what she considered to be a well-balanced, "proper" marriage. After Hughes published his first book of poems, she exclaimed, "I am so glad Ted is first. All my pat theories against marrying a writer dissolve with Ted: his rejections more than double my sorrow and his acceptances rejoice me more than mine" (*Journals* 271). When she was with Hughes, Plath believed in a sexual hierarchy. Although she still wrote her own poems, she invested an increasing amount of time in typing his poems for him, inquiring at journals, and sending out his work. She enjoyed her role as helpmate and adapted happily at first to the domestic life that accompanied marriage. This was certainly a far cry from her 1952 journal entry:

> Will I be a secretary—a self-rationalizing, uninspired housewife, secretly jealous of my husband's ability to grow intellectually and professionally while I am impeded—will I submerge my embarrassing desires and aspirations, refuse to face myself, and go either mad or become neurotic . . . Masks are the order of the day—and the least I can do is cultivate the illusion that I am gay, serene, not hollow and afraid. (151)

Her concerns proved eerily prescient.

During this time, before Plath settled on the figure of Electra as an emblem of her situation, she often used a mythic framework based on Robert Graves's *White Goddess* to explain her own condition. Without naming specific figures, Plath wrote several moon goddess poems and made gestures towards mythic types.[2] For instance, in a journal entry of January 18, 1953, she described coming out of a depression: "I have gone through my winter solstice, and the dying god of life and fertility is reborn. In fact, my personal seasonal life is two months ahead of the spring equinox this year!" (158). During this time, Plath wrote several poems based on the Demeter and Persephone myth. Hughes, too, was part of Plath's mythic landscape and became a god-creature. She mused,

> He sets the sea of my life steady, flooding it with the deep rich color of his mind and his love and constant amaze at his perfect being: as if I had conjured, at last, a god from the slack tides, coming up with his spear shining, and the cockleshells and rare fish trailing in his wake, and he trailing the world: for my earth goddess, he the sun, the sea, the black complement power: yang to yin. (*Journals* 287)

These beautiful though hyperbolic exclamations indicate the ease with which Plath moved between "real life" and myth, and foreshadow her adoption of the Electra and Clytemnestra models.

Her meeting with the young poet Adrienne Rich at a reading at Harvard in April, 1958 caused Plath to adopt a more specific mythic framework (the house of Atreus) that offered a way to express previously hidden emotions. She admired Rich's poetry, although she wrote several times in her journals that she found her own poetry "richer." After Rich and Hughes read, they dined with Plath and Rich's husband, Al Conrad. Plath was impressed. She described her fellow poet as "little, round & stumpy, all vibrant short black hair, great sparking black eyes and a tulip-red umbrella: honest, frank forthright & even opinionated" (371, 368). As she read more of Rich's poetry, she began to find fault with her own lack of "philosophy." She wrote, "finished her book of poems in half an hour: they stimulate me: they are easy, yet professional, full of infelicities and numb gesturings at something, but instinct with 'philosophy,' what I need . . . How odd, men don't interest me at all now, only women and womentalk" (466). In February of 1959, Plath admitted, "I must get philosophy in. Until I do I shall lag behind ACR" (469). She began to use Rich's work as a poetic and social model and described herself as

> Pulled. To the neat easy ACRich lyricism, to the graphic description of the world. My main thing now is to start with *real things: real emotions*, and leave out the baby gods, the old men of the sea, the thin people, the knights, the moon-mothers, the mad maudlins, the lorelei, the hermits, and get into me, Ted, friends, mother and brother and father and family. *The real world. Real situations*, behind which the great gods play the drama of blood, lust and death. (italics mine, 471)

Despite her determination, Plath moved from one world of fantasy to another, from the White Goddess to the Classical Greece of Electra and, later, Clytemnestra.

Although it seems contradictory, the mythic House of Atreus became Plath's "real world" in terms of the "real emotions" that the myth conveyed. On January 3, 1959 Plath confessed,

> As usual after an hour with R[uth] B[euscher], digging, felt I'd been watching or participating in a Greek play: a cleansing and an exhaustion. . . . What do I expect or want from mother? Hugging, mother's milk? But that is impossible to all of us now. Why should I want it still. What can I do with this want. How can I transfer it to something I can have? A great, stark, bloody play acting itself out over and over again behind the sunny façade of our daily rituals. (455–456)

She gave up trying to avoid mythic identification and urged herself to "Immerse self in characters, feelings of others—not to look at them through plate glass. Get to the bottom of deceptions, emotions" (519). When Plath wrote that she needed to write about "real situations," she used Electra as the model for the emotional reality she wanted in her poetry—the anger against her mother and grief for her father—and she located "reality" in the emotional connection she felt with the Greek daughter.

Plath resumed psychotherapy, which she had undergone in 1953–1954, to explore her extremes of depression. Plath was led to believe that her lifelong struggle related to her lack of a relationship with her father and anger towards her mother. Part of the tragedy of her therapy with Ruth Beuscher was the doctor's inexperience, which led her to encourage Plath's excessive and damaging identification with Electra. When Beuscher was assigned to Plath, she was only a psychiatric resident, and Plath was one of her first patients. Psychiatrist Karen Mardona interviewed Beuscher in 1998 and elicited a quite candid admission:

> But why would [Olive] Prouty and Aurelia Plath, Sylvia's mother, allow Sylvia to be treated by a trainee? When I asked Ruth this, she responded, "I don't think they knew I was that inexperienced. It was McLean and I was the doctor assigned to her. That was it." Furthermore, while the body of Sylvia Plath literature refers to Ruth Barnhouse [Beuscher] as her "analyst" or "psychoanalyst," she was not a psychoanalyst. She received psychoanalytically oriented training and supervision during her residency at McLean, but did not go through analytic training.

Plath's experience pushed her to reinterpret and re-narrativize herself. In a quote that clearly draws from Eliot's language in "*Ulysses*, Order and Myth," Plath called her own mythical method "a way of ordering and reordering the chaos of experience" (448). She acknowledged, however, that she identified too fully with her reading, and perhaps the increasingly confused boundaries of identity between herself and Electra created more psychological chaos than they "order[ed]" (199).

Unlike several of the other poets in this book who take on mythic themes and characters to challenge traditional representations of women, Plath found a myth in which she recognized emotions, and began, with Beuscher's encouragement, to apply it to her life, often claiming certain experiences of Electra's as her own and making damaging statements about women in the process.[3] In February of

1958, Plath was teaching several Sophocles plays in her English course at Smith College when she wrote in her journal, "I myself am the vessel of tragic experience" (*Journals* 334). She accepted this epiphany and determined to shape her life into mythology. Until the final *Ariel* poems, her poetry about her father adopts the trope of Electra mourning the death of Agamemnon. Although there are obvious differences between the circumstances under which Plath and Electra lost their fathers, Plath felt a connection to the Greek daughter's anger. Her cultural frustrations with pressures from "all the mothers," her interest in Adrienne Rich, her experience in psychotherapy, and her teaching of Sophocles appear to have focused Plath's rage onto this particular myth, which not only validated her anger but actually shaped her perception of her problems.

Electra's and Clytemnestra's Ancient Pasts

Plath's "To Do" list in her March 6, 1956 journal entry includes "read all Electras" (224–225). By these, she meant Aeschylus's trilogy, *The Oresteia*, Sophocles's *Electra*, and Euripides's *Electra*, three different accounts of the myth.[4] It is worth noting the similarities and differences between the plays in order to understand which details Plath used and which she ignored.[5]

The first play from Aeschylus's *Oresteia*, *Agamemnon*, produced in 458 B.C.E, depicts Clytemnestra's murder of the king upon his return to Argos after the Trojan War. He brings with him his slave Cassandra, the Trojan princess, daughter of Priam. Clytemnestra, who has been ruling Argos with her lover, Aegisthus, during her husband's absence, kills Agamemnon and Cassandra upon their arrival to avenge Agamemnon's sacrifice of their daughter, Iphigenia, ten years earlier. Artemis had demanded the sacrifice to compensate for the future deaths of children at Troy.[6] Clytemnestra never forgave Agamemnon for murdering their daughter. In *Agamemnon*, she avenges Iphigenia's death by stabbing the king in his bath.

From the play's opening, it is clear that Clytemnestra's pursuit of justice drives her vengeance. While the chorus of old men discusses the violence of the war at Troy, Agamemnon's slaughter of his daughter haunts the background. Several dualities work within the structure of the trilogy: the heroic violence of war that upholds patriarchy versus the domestic violence that threatens patriarchy; the Furies versus the legal process; mother-daughter versus father-son. In the play, Clytemnestra is sardonic and intelligent as she ensnares Agamemnon, playing on his hubris and inability to hear her double entendres as she flatters him even while she condemns him for their daughter's murder and warns of his impending death. After slaying Agamemnon, the proud Clytemnestra glories in her kill and chastises the chorus, who want to cast her into exile, for not having banished the king when he killed their daughter. She is sure of her right to avenge her daughter's murder and proud to have carried out a "masterpiece of Justice" (l.1430). Her references to law and judges foreshadow the trial decision in the *Eumenides*.

The second play in the trilogy, *The Libation Bearers*, bounds ahead several years, as Agamemnon and Clytemnestra's son Orestes returns to avenge his father's death, and his sister, Electra, urges him on. Orestes tells Electra that Apollo sent him to kill Clytemnestra and threatened to send Agamemnon's Furies to hound Orestes if he fails. The audience knows that his mother's Furies will pursue him after he kills her. A disguised Orestes, urged by the chorus to remember his bond to his father and reject his mother's supplications, finally kills both Clytemnestra and her lover, Aegisthus.

In all three tragedians' accounts of the myth, Clytemnestra's plea for her life involves her motherhood, suggesting the larger problem of a mother's legitimate bond to her children. In *The Libation Bearers*, when Clytmenestra recognizes Orestes, she bares her breast in a plea that he respect the love she gave to him. Once he resolves to kill her, Clytemnestra asks, "You have no fear of a mother's curse, my son?" to which Orestes responds, "Mother? You flung me into a life of pain" (ll. 899–900). Clytemnestra believes that she acted appropriately based on what she understands as the laws of retribution under which she, as mother of her slain child, must avenge the death.

The gods answer Orestes's questions concerning his mother's plea. In the final play of Aeschylus's trilogy, *The Eumenides*, Apollo proclaims to the court that a woman is "not the parent, just a nurse to the seed" (l.667). He declares, "The *man* is the source of life—the one who mounts. / She, like a stranger for a stranger, keeps / the shoot alive unless god hurts the root" (ll.669–671, original italics). Kathleen Komar explains the historical significance of Apollo's speech: "At this moment in cultural history, the ancient traditions of Mother Right based on blood relationships give way to a new order founded on legal relationships and on the subjugation of women" (39). Froma Zeitlin connects Komar's argument to marriage: "the basic issue in the trilogy is the establishment in the face of female resistance of the binding nature of patriarchal marriage where wife's subordination and patrilineal succession are reaffirmed" (149). Clytemnestra represents the male nightmare—the violent and unruly wife who murders her husband upon his return from war and who values her position as mother over wife. Clytemnestra's rebellious nature threatens the patriarchal order and must be eliminated. She becomes the symbol for the need to contain women legally.

Of the three plays in the trilogy, *The Libation Bearers* is the only one in which Electra figures. In fact, it is the first time that she appears in extant Greek literature. In the fan-shaped *theatron,* the grave mound was the focus of the audience's perspective. Aeschylus's Electra is at her father's grave pouring libations when Orestes reveals himself to her. She is unrelenting in her desire for vengeance and says to the chorus, who have just told Orestes of his father's "mutilation," "You tell him of father's death, but I was an outcast, / worthless, leashed like a vicious dog in a dark cell. / I wept—laughter died that day . . . / I wept, pouring out the tears behind my veils" (ll.433–436). Aeschylus's Electra is self-obsessed, referring continuously to the effect of her father's death and Clytemnestra's rule on herself. She does not mourn her father's death as much as her own wasted life. In so doing, she unintentionally links herself to her sacrificed sister, Iphigenia, in her willingness to sacrifice her future to support her father's legacy. She is helpless to do this on her own, however, and needs Orestes to act out her anger. Batya Casper Laks writes that the play, "dramatizes the revolutionary potential of frustrated and entrapped women" (18).

Sophocles's *Electra* draws on the rage and self-obsession of Aeschylus's heroine. His Electra weeps about her sad lot as an outcast in her father's house. The chorus suggests, "Do you not see?—the mischief / Is your own self-tourture / . . . / you must not make / Evil more evil still" (75). After a defiant speech, she justifies her own "evil" as simply a mirror of the evil that surrounds her. While Orestes murders his mother offstage, on stage, Electra cries, "Strike her again, strike!" (Sophocles 113). Her murderous rage mirrors Aeschylus's furious Electra. When Orestes is about to kill Aegisthus, she urges him on with a focus on her own suffering. Even if Electra's violence and anger are "appropriately" directed at her mother, as opposed to Clytemnestra's inappropriate murder of her husband, they are no less disturbing. Electra cannot acknowledge that like her mother she boils with stifled rage.

Sophocles's Clytemnestra is less ambiguous than Aeschylus's heroine, particularly in her relief when she hears false reports of Orestes's death. She refers to her motherly feelings of sorrow and guilt, but acknowledges that she is comforted to be safe from retribution. There is more interaction between mother and daughter than in Aeschylus's play, and the dialogue is bitter on both sides. Electra correctly claims to be hated by her mother. Perhaps unfairly, Electra suggests that lust for Aegisthus, not motherly love, drove Clytemnestra to kill Agamemnon, an accusation that Clytemnestra denies. Like Aeschylus's Clytemnestra, Sophocles's murderess claims to have Justice on her side in avenging her daughter's death, but Sophocles is less ambivalent about staging her cruelty.

Euripides's Electra differs from the previous two in that she is married to a Mycenaean peasant, and the marriage is unconsummated. This Electra mourns her diminished social standing. But like Aeschylus's and Sophocles's Electras, Euripides's heroine is irrational and self-obsessed. She is jealous of her mother's economic status and consumed with the effect of her father's death on herself.

Clytemnestra's role as a mother is central to Euripides's play. Electra must pray upon Clytemnestra's maternal sentiments to lure her mother to her country home. She sends word that she has given birth to a son and needs her mother to make the traditional sacrifices for the newborn. Clytemnestra's excuse for exiling Electra is that she saved her from death by removing her to the countryside; however, her vile treatment of her daughter not only belies her stated motive for getting rid of Electra, but also for slaying Agamemnon as revenge for Iphigenia. The mother-daughter struggle and the lack of loyalty exhibited by Clytemnestra centers the play. In fact, she admits not only to needing to avenge Iphigenia's murder, but also to her jealousy over Agamemnon's adultery, defending herself with the excuse, "Women are silly creatures" (202). Clytemnestra's admission to jealousy removes the audience's potential sympathy for a grief-stricken mother and the legitimacy of Clytemnestra's claim to be defending the law of blood-right.

Electra's loyalty to patriarchy is as problematic as Clytemnestra's lack of loyalty. In Aeschylus and Sophocles, Electra is consumed by rage; in Euripides, her anger gives way to guilt only once Orestes commits the murders. This Electra, whose hatred is exorcised, had not previously been portrayed on stage. After Orestes kills Aegisthus, Electra warns Orestes, "that gloating over the dead invites reprisals" (Euripides 197). She has more agency than in the other plays, not relying solely on Orestes to enact her vengeance, but admitting, "My hand was on the sword with yours" (208). Where she initially urged Orestes to attain manhood by killing, she feels incredible guilt after her mother dies: "What a fall of tears, my brother, / and I am the cause. / My anger was a furnace / Against my own mother" (207). This admission of Clytemnestra's legitimate role as mother calls Apollo's decree (with which an Athenian audience would be familiar) into question.

"Father, bridegroom": Plath's Tragic Identification

Plath not only alluded to the classics in her creative work; she began to write of herself in her therapy journals as if she were Electra. She did so in the journals, however, without making the comparison overt, which suggests the degree to which she had incorporated her alter ego. She stormed, "I rail and rage against the taking of my father, whom I have never known; even his mind, his heart, his face, as a boy of 17 I love terribly. I would have loved him; and he is gone . . . I lust for the knowing of him" (230). In 1958 Plath wrote of her intense hatred for her mother, despite their seemingly loving relationship:

Me, I never knew the love of a father, the love of a steady blood-related man after the age of eight. My mother killed the only man who'd love me steady through life: came in one morning with tears of nobility in her eyes and told me he was gone for good. I hate her for that. I hate her because he wasn't loved by her. He was an ogre. But I miss him. He was old, but she married an old man to be my father. It was her fault. Damn her eyes . . . So mother never had a husband she loved. She had a sick, mean-because-he-was-sick, poor louse, bearded-near-death "Man I knew once." She killed him (The Father) by marrying him too old, by marrying him sick to death and dying, by burying him every day since in her heart, mind and words. (431)

She goes so far as to say that her attempted suicide in August of 1953 was a deferred attempt to murder her mother:

> I feel guilty, feel I shouldn't be happy, because I'm not doing what *all the mother figures* in my life would have me do. I hate them then. I get very sad about not doing what everybody and *all my white-haired old mothers* want in their old age. So how do I express my hate for my mother? In my deepest emotions I think of her as an enemy: someone who "killed" my father, my first male ally in the world. She is a murderess of maleness. I lay in my bed when I thought my mind was going blank forever and thought what a luxury it would be to kill her, to strangle her skinny veined throat which could never be big enough to protect me from the world. But I was too nice for murder. I tried to murder myself. (432–433, italics mine)

In these passages, Plath modeled her world on Aeschylus's *Oresteia* and Euripides's and Sophocles's *Electra* plays, with her mother as the murderous Clytemnestra and father as the murdered Agamemnon. The story resonated so deeply for her, not literally in its events, but in its emotional intensity, that she did not challenge the myth but actually attempted to embody it. Most extraordinarily, in her journals she depicted herself as the violent, rage-filled Electra of all three tragedians without ever referring to Electra specifically, without ever using simile to describe the obvious connection to the classical model.

If such intense anger at her mother seems strange, her repeated references to "all the mother figures" help to explain it. She conflated her "hate" for her mother over her father's death with her "guilt" and "sadness" at not doing what "all my white-haired mothers" wanted. She aligned her cultural frustrations as a woman with the removal of a male "ally." Plath's friend Paul Roche argues in his "Introduction" to Euripides's *Electra* that the title character "is motivated as much by envy of her mother as by devotion to her father" (165). Indeed, Plath's mother embodied all of the pressures that Sylvia felt incapable of living up to. In 1951 she had agonized, "I have none of the selfless love of my mother" (*Journals* 98). Plath taught Sophocles during the academic year of 1957–1958. By late 1958, she was delving into her emotions in therapy and looking to find a way to write "real emotions" into her poetry: all of these factors explain her assumption of Electra's identity.

While several analysts, from Carl Jung, who coined the phrase "Electra Complex" in 1913, to Karen Horney in the 1940s, vociferously challenged Freud's theories of sexuality, Ruth Beuscher and Plath did not. Beuscher relied on the fashionable "blame the mother" theory popular at that time and encouraged Plath's interest in Freud and her self-deluded identification with Electra. Of course Freud structured his ideas on the male-authored, male-centered Greek myths. When Plath returned to those myths to express anger at her own culture's gender limitations, she did so, initially, with a surprising lack of reflective awareness. Plath's realization that she could never literally kill her mother was crucial. As Plath confessed, she turned all of the rage inward. In this way Plath embodied Electra's self-centeredness and assumption that she was the real victim of her father's death.

On March 9, 1959 Plath visited her father's grave for the first time and wrote of her "temptation to dig him up" (*Journals* 473).[7] The following week she composed her first Electra poem, "Electra on Azalea Path," in which the speaker imagines her own metaphoric extinction as a result of her father's death:

> The day you died I went into the dirt
> Into the lightless hibernaculum
> Where bees, striped black and gold, sleep out the blizzard
> Like hieratic stones, and the ground is hard.
> It was good for twenty years, that wintering—
> As if you had never existed, as if I came
> God-fathered into the world from my mother's belly:
> Her wide bed wore the stain of divinity.
> I had nothing to do with guilt or anything
> When I wormed back under my mother's heart.
>
> Small as a doll in my dress of innocence
> I lay dreaming your epic, image by image.
> Nobody died or withered on that stage.
> Everything took place in a durable whiteness.
> The day I woke, I woke on Churchyard Hill.
> I found your name, I found your bones and all (117)

The setting, the father's grave, mirrors the scene from Aeschylus's *Libation Bearers* in which Electra appears for the first time in Greek literature; it becomes, too, the first place where Plath's speaker manifests as Electra. In this modern Electra saga, the speaker realizes that during her psychological hibernation, she invented a problematic mythology to avoid the truth of her father's death. This is particularly ironic given that Plath was just beginning to invent her own mythology. Plath's imagery and ideas in the poem are not consistent. At first she claims that for twenty years she deliberately acted as if she did not have a father, "as if [he] had never existed." Her idea changes without explanation: "I lay dreaming your epic, image by image." Now Plath's speaker says that she had turned her father into a hero in an epic, then into a character in a play: "Nobody died or withered on that stage." She had lived in a state of "wintering," of "whiteness," with no "guilt."

The father's imagined godliness or heroism shatters when Plath's speaker visits her father's tomb and confronts the reality of her loss—her father is no god; the bones prove his mortality. As she contemplates the red color bleeding from the plastic flowers on the grave next to his, she continues,

> The stony actors poise and pause for breath.
> I brought my love to bear, and then you died.
> It was the gangrene ate you to the bone
> My mother said; you died like any man.
> How shall I age into that state of mind?
> . . .
> O pardon the one who knocks for pardon at
> Your gate, father – your hound-bitch, daughter, friend.
> It was my love that did us both to death. (116–117)

Here the speaker/ "hound-bitch" (reminiscent of Aeschylus's Electra who is "leashed like a vicious dog in a dark cell") admits her struggle to accept what "[her] mother said," implying that her mother may have had reason to lie about her father's cause of death. Euripides's Clytemnestra urged Electra to realize that her father was not heroic, "hatching [plots] against his nearest and dearest" (201). Plath's speaker implies that her mother also defaced the godlike image the girl had of her father. As she tries to "age into that state of mind" in which she believes that her father "died like any man," that "gangrene ate [him] to the bone," she contemplates his "bones and all." The repetition of the word "bone," and the physicality that the word connotes, suggests a paternal presence that is, in fact, missing. There is a notable absence of the father's spirit in both *The Libation Bearers* and Plath's grave poem. Agamemnon's spirit never appears, and there is no sense in either scene that there is real communication after death, only silence. Plath's Electra begs her father's "pardon" and accuses herself, in the end, of being the cause of his death. How her love is responsible remains unclear; she gets no reply. She gave up her own happiness to be "married" to death, to her father's memory. As Plath's speaker declares in another poem, "The Beekeeper's Daughter," "Father, bridegroom . . . / The queen bee marries the winter of your year" (118). Plath's Electra carries out this "self-torture," as Sophocles's chorus calls Electra's behavior, and ultimately blames herself and her love for killing him.

Plath's speaker identifies with the way in which marriage is associated with death in this myth through her reference to Agamemnon's sacrifice of her sister Iphigenia. She admits,

Another kind of redness bothers me:

> *The day your slack sail drank my sister's breath*
> *The flat sea purpled like that evil cloth*
> *My mother unrolled at your last homecoming.* (117, original italics)

Plath never wrote as Iphigenia, but here, her speaker acknowledges herself as a type of victim who, like this murdered sister, has sacrificed a part of herself. Iphigenia thought that she was to be married and was, instead, killed. She functions as the speaker's double, embodying the betrayal by Agamemnon that Plath's Electra can barely acknowledge. The brief reference hints at a latent understanding that Plath would manifest years later: that it is, indeed, the father and, to play on her statement about mothers, "all the fathers" who are responsible for the state of things. The Iphigenia reference is telling, but it is as if Plath's speaker cannot come to grips with the full implications of the reference. She returns to herself as culprit, stating definitively, "It was my love that did us both to death." After finishing "Electra on Azalea Path," Plath determined to continue to work out her father-worship through use of the Electra myth, declaring, "Must do justice to my father's grave" (*Journals* 477).

Plath had been reading Freud, particularly *Mourning and Melancholia*, which discusses the problems that can arise from inadequate mourning for a serious loss in childhood, and she felt that his theories might help her to understand her anger.[8] She wanted to write a story based on her own experiences that would be "an analysis of the Electra complex" (*Journals* 512). On October 4, 1959, she mentions reading about "a supposedly loving but ambitious mother who manipulated the child" in "Jung case-history," about which she writes, "All this relates in a most meaningful way my instinctive images with perfectly valid psychological analysis. However, I am the victim . . . My 'fiction' is only a naked recreation of what I felt, as a child and later, must be true" (*Journals* 514). Plath had first discussed hatred of her mother with Beuscher almost a year earlier, and in fact, her interest in this line of thought may well have sparked her first visit to her father's grave.

In her poem "The Colossus," Plath continues to delve into what she called "the old father-worship subject" (518). The poem's speaker searches to reclaim her lost father. She laments,

> I shall never get you put together entirely,
> Pieced, glued, and properly jointed.
> Mule-bray, pig-grunt and bawdy cackles
> Proceed from your great lips.
> It's worse than a barnyard.

Perhaps you consider yourself an oracle,
Mouthpiece of the dead, or of some god or other.
Thirty years now I have labored
To dredge the silt from your throat.
I am none the wiser. (129)

The daughter/speaker, who will later in the poem compare herself to Electra, unsuccessfully attempts to gain understanding from this father/god/statue. He is not entirely absent, as he was in "Electra on Azalea Path," but instead of prophecy, wisdom, or pardon, the speaker only gets undecipherable grunts and cackles, no revelatory information. She tries to put his great being together again, but continually fails:

Scaling little ladders with gluepots and pails of Lysol
I crawl like an ant in mourning
Over the weedy acres of your brow
To mend the immense skull-plates and clear
The bald, white tumuli of your eyes.

A blue sky out of the Oresteia
Arches above us. Oh father, all by yourself
You are pithy and historical as the Roman Forum.
. . .
My hours are married to shadow. (129–130)

The speaker's father is the Colossus.[9] He is Agamemnon. She is the worshipping and dutiful daughter obsessed with getting "back, back, back to you. / I thought even the bones would do" ("Daddy" 224).

Plath drew particularly from Euripides in her construction of her speaker's relationship to marriage. Euripides's play takes place on the day of the festival of Hera, the goddess of marriage and family. Froma Zeitlin notes that the festival "is a time when the bonds of social solidarity are strengthened and reaffirmed among the citizens" (263). In the play, Electra's refusal to participate in the celebration and involve herself in civic life derives from her frustration with her own unconsummated marriage to a peasant. Plath was interested in the idea of a stifled and angry woman's reaction to a marriage that feels like a death. While she would later use Clytemnestra as the embodiment of the betrayed and enraged wife, she had not yet made the switch from daughter to mother.

Complications arose in Plath's identification with the Electra myth when she started to transfer her father-worship onto her husband. Even before meeting Hughes, Plath knew what she wanted in a mate. In a January 1953 journal entry, she used imagery that she would later re-employ in her father poems: "Do I want to crawl into the gigantic paternal embrace of a mental colossus? A little, maybe" (163). She confessed in a 1955 entry, "I <u>do</u> want to have husband, lover, father, and son, all at once . . . And I cry so to be held by a man; some man, who is a father" (199, original underline). She admitted in another entry, "let's face it, I am in danger of wanting my personal absolute to be a demigod of a man . . . I want a romantic nonexistent hero" (182). Plath described Hughes's voice on their first encounter in February of 1956 as "colossal" (211). "He is my life now," she exclaimed, "my male muse, my pole-star centering me steady and right" (365). In typical mythic terms she saw "[her] own father, the buried male muse & god-creator risen to be [her] mate in Ted" (381). Plath's use of the Electra myth was a symptom of a cultural problem of the 1950s, that girls dutifully devoted their lives first to father then husband, often without consciously acknowledging their sacrifice. Plath wanted to marry her father as Electra, but, according to the myth, Clytemnestra is Agamemnon's wife. Plath initially did not acknowledge the implications of this shift in character from daughter to wife. She still wished to be the adoring and dutiful Electra to Hughes. As Plath seems to have become increasingly frustrated in her marriage, however, her identification with the myth changed, and this change helps to illustrate and explicate the psychological transformation that Plath experienced as she became disillusioned with her father and husband, and by extension, with her culture's repressive misogyny.

During the time in which Plath began to write of herself as Electra, her writing offers the first hint of discomfort with her marriage, a frustration that would gradually lead her to abandon the Electra character that she recently had adopted and, in 1962, take on Clytemnestra as her new persona. In her December 1958 journals, she sketches a new story "of an 'advanced' couple, no children, woman with career, above sewing on buttons, cooking. Husband thinks he agrees. Fight over sewing on buttons. Not really fight about that. Fight about his deep-rooted conventional ideas of womanhood, like all the rest of the men, wants them pregnant and in the kitchen. Wants to shame her in public" (443–444). In the same entry in which Plath plots her new story, she admits that Hughes told their friends that she refused to sew buttons on his shirts. The following month she spoke with her therapist "of Victorian women who fear men: men treat women as brainless chattels: have seen so many romances end in this sort of thing, waste of a woman, they don't believe marriage can work without woman becoming maid, servant, nurse, and losing brain" (461). She admitted to her doctor, "I have hated men . . . because they would degrade me, by their attitude: women shouldn't think, shouldn't be unfaithful (but their husbands may be), must stay home, cook, wash" (461–462). As she thought more about women's subordinate position in society, family, and the literary world, she pulled away from Hughes slightly, indicating more and more during 1959 her desire not to show her work to or share ideas with him.

Increasingly influenced by her reading of Adrienne Rich, Plath determined to define herself apart from Hughes. She wrote, "I can build up my own inner life, my own thoughts, without his continuous 'what are you thinking? What are you going to do now?' which makes me promptly and recalcitrantly stop thinking and doing. We are amazingly compatible. But I must be myself—make myself & not let myself be made by him" (401). In November of 1959 she revealed her fear that it was "dangerous to be so close to Ted day in day out. I have no life separate from his, am likely to become a mere accessory" (524). She had written in 1951 that she was scared that after being married, "One fine day I would float to the surface, quite drowned, and supremely happy with my newfound selfless self" (*Journals* 99–100). She now worried that this fear might have proved prescient, except that she was not happy.

As Plath's marriage unraveled and as she became more interested in writing by socially conscious women, she grew dissatisfied with the Electra model, which she had used for a little over a year. Plath increasingly realized that her mother and "all the mothers" were not the only source of her problems. Her culture's double standard had always frustrated her, but where she initially attacked the women who enforced society's rules, now she blamed her own complicity with the patriarchal system that demanded devotion and compliance from girls and wives.

"Too nice for murder": Plath's Tragic Failure

Plath's final poems mark one of the first mainstream demonstrations of a woman's vengeance poetry. Ted Hughes said after Plath's death that her final *Ariel* poems indicate the "successful integration" of the anger she had previously tried to repress (quoted in Middlebrook 218). Much of that anger seems targeted at him. During the summer of 1962, Ted Hughes began an affair with Assia Gutmann Wevill, which corresponds chronologically to the metamorphosis of Plath's poetic speaker from Electra into Clytemnaestra. Plath had become so involved in the mythic clan of Agamemnon that when the circumstances changed, although there were characters such as Medea who might have also fit the "slighted wife" scenario, she chose to remain within the Atrean family, tapping into Clytemnestra's rage. Plath's poetry changed dramatically in her final and most famous 1962–1963 *Ariel* poems, in which her Electra undergoes a mythic transformation from adoring daughter to murderous wife. In 1958, when she was beginning to identify with Electra, Plath revealed the latent violence that would burst forth years later; she wrote, "I am, at bottom, simple, credulous, feminine & loving to be mastered, cared for—but I will kill with my mind, my ice-eye, anyone who is weak, false, sickly in soul" (361). Once Hughes revealed what Plath considered to be weakness and perfidy, she determined to kill his mythic counterpart in her poetry.

Plath transformed her poetic images that she had previously used to show subordination into images of power. Her poem "The Applicant" suggests her resentment about what she had lost in her marriage to Hughes. Her persona still resembles the figure from "Electra on Azalea Path" who was "small as a doll in [her] dress of innocence," only now she is her husband's doll instead of her father's:

> Come here, sweetie, out of the closet.
> Well, what do you think of *that*?
> Naked as paper to start
>
> But in twenty-five years she'll be silver,
> In fifty, gold.
> A living doll, everywhere you look.
> It can sew, it can cook,
> It can talk, talk, talk.
>
> It works, there is nothing wrong with it.
> You have a hole, it's a poultice.
> You have an eye, it's an image.
> My boy, it's your last resort.
> Will you marry it, marry it, marry it. (221–222)

Plath writes with a sardonic distance that is missing from the original father poem. The doll / wife is an "it" entirely designed for the man's benefit. A similar transformation of imagery occurs in her poem "Daddy," which begins, "You do not do, you do not do / Any more, black shoe / In which I have lived like a foot" (222). The speaker conjures the father figure from "The Colossus," "Ghastly statue with one grey toe / Big as a Frisco seal," but no longer tries to glue him together. Rather, she admits, her drive to recover him led to her failed suicide attempt, after which others "stuck [her] together with glue" (224). But the girl is "through" (224). In a dramatic turn away from Plath's previous identification with Electra, her "Daddy" speaker determines, "Daddy, I have had to kill you" (222). She also kills her Hughes figure: "a model of you, / A man in black with a Meinkampf look / and a love of the rack and the screw" (224). As Plath acknowledged the sickness of her complicity with her father and husband, she began to revise her use of myth, while admitting to the perversity of her initial acceptance of the mythic role of Electra. The girl is not only "through" with self-denial, but also with being an accepting daughter/lover figure ("Daddy, daddy, you bastard, I'm through"). That "I" is finished, dies, to be reborn as an autonomous female figure who can no longer live within the confines offered by the patriarchal structure. The shoe no longer fits the foot.

Plath shed her former identity in favor of a more potent, vengeful one. She was fascinated with resurrection, as her poem "Lady Lazarus" suggests:

Dying
Is an art, like everything else.
I do it exceptionally well.

I do it so it feels like hell.
I do it so it feels real.
[. . .]
Herr God, Herr Lucifer,
Beware
Beware.

Out of the ash
I rise with my red hair
And I eat men like air. (246–247)

Of her first suicide attempt, Plath wrote, "Being dead, I rose up again, and even resort to the mere sensation value of being suicidal, of getting so close, of coming out of the grave with the scars" (February, 1956, *Journals* 199). Once Plath takes on Clytemnestra as a model, she can transfer her rage from her mother to Hughes, as she would reject her initial "marriage" to her father-"bridegroom" as a sacrifice of her own life. Her resurrected self accepts her potent mission to destroy those who once rendered her powerless.

Plath's new self, a queen, bursts to life in a series of bee poems that illustrate her speaker's transformation from victim to avenger and tie the queen bee to Aeschylus's Clytemnestra. Initially, she is the wintering bee, an image of her "marriage" to her dead father underground and to Hughes (Plath's father had been an apiarist, and in the summer of 1962, Plath and Hughes began keeping their own bees). In "The Arrival of the Bee Box," Plath's speaker is the "sweet God" who will set the bees free, for, "The box is only temporary" (213). This liberation from the box is an image of resurrection of the soul from the body, which surfaces again in "Stings":

It is almost over.
I am in control.

[...]

. . . I
Have a self to recover, a queen.
Is she dead, is she sleeping?
Where has she been,
With her lion-red body, her wings of glass?

Now she is flying
More terrible than she ever was, red
Scar in the sky, red comet
Over the engine that killed her –
The mausoleum, the wax house. (214–215).

This lioness, a conflation of Robert Graves's White Goddess and Aeschylus's Clytemnestra, emerges ready for vengeance against her oppressor. Graves wrote about a bee goddess with glass wings in *The White Goddess,* a book Plath knew well. In Aeschylus's *Agamemnon,* Cassandra perfects her description of Clytemnestra: "she is the lioness, / she rears on her hind legs, she beds with the wolf / when her lion king goes ranging" (ll.1272–1274). Cassandra uses this metaphor just before Clytemnestra unleashes her vengeance, killing both Cassandra and Agamemnon.[10] Clytemnestra awakens, or is reborn, "more terrible than she ever was," in Plath's speaker. In "Wintering" Plath's speaker exclaims, "The bees are all women, / Maids and the long royal lady. / They have got rid of the men" (218). The queen bee recalls the royal Clytemnestra with her entourage of Furies. In "Elm" Plath writes, "Now I break up in pieces that fly about like clubs. / A wind of such violence / Will tolerate no bystanding: I must shriek" and "I am terrified by this dark thing / That sleeps in me; / All day I feel its soft feathery turnings, its malignity" (192). Plath's poetry increasingly dealt with an avenging female figure killing a man or men.

In Classical mythology, Clytemnestra's desire for bloody revenge raises the question of whether women had any acceptable options for punishing cheating men. In Euripides's version of the myth, Clytemnestra cries:

When a husband goes a-roaming
And neglects his nuptial bed,
The wife is apt to copy her husband and get herself a lover.
Then what a burst of scandal flares up around her,
While the real culprit, the man, goes off without a blotch. (202)

Electra responds,

You plead justice,
And your plea is a sham—utterly unjust.
A woman, in everything, if she has any sense,
Should yield to her husband. (202)

As a woman in the early 1960s, Plath dealt with a surprisingly similar dilemma and often vacillated internally between Clytemnestra's and Electra's viewpoints. As Bennett points out, Plath "lived at a time when women received no cultural support for their feelings of rage and no help from society to break through their isolation and oppression" (109). Hughes confessed to his affair with Assia during the summer of 1962, and by October of that year, he had moved out permanently.

He became, for Plath, the model of the modern Agamemnon, and she rejected her previous Electra-like excuses for men's behavior. In "Purdah," written during the same month of Hughes's move, her speaker is Clytemnestra, watching as Agamemnon, "the bridegroom[,] arrives" (242). She promises,

> And at his next step
> I shall unloose
>
> I shall unloose—
> From the small jeweled
> Doll he guards like a heart—
>
> The lioness,
> The shriek in the bath,
> The cloak of holes. (243–244)

The doll becomes lioness; Electra becomes Clytemnestra. Plath channeled her anger into a mythology that allowed her a means of fictional vengeance.

Plath's growing sense of social injustice and gender imbalance made her identify more with the slighted wife of myth: she wanted Clytemnestra to be avenged. She was developing her cultural and feminist awareness and working towards what she hoped would be a socially powerful poetry like that of Adrienne Rich. Between 1962 and 1963, according to Hughes, she was voraciously reading literature by women. In her rage at his adultery, Plath burned all of Hughes's manuscripts and letters that she could find, as well as her own manuscript for a second novel. Her mother later wrote, "All Sylvia would say was that the manuscript had symbolized a period of joy that now proved to have been built on false trust—the character of the hero was dead to her—this had been his funeral pyre" (quoted in Middlebrook 175). In her poem "Burning the Letters," Plath's "merciless" fire is like "dogs . . . tearing a fox," "A red burst and a cry / That splits from its ripped bag and does not stop / With the dead eye / And the stuffed expression, but goes on" (205). She imagines that her "immortal" fire that makes her "veins glow" destroys, "kills," the "papers that breathe like people" (205, 204). Her poem corroborates her mother's assertion that for Plath, burning Hughes's letters was a type of deferred murder.

Unlike Clytemnestra, however, Plath would not kill her unfaithful husband. As her speaker confesses in "The Jailer," "I wish him dead or away. / That, it seems, is the impossibility" (227). Plath reserved that manifestation of her rage for herself. As she had suggested that her previous suicide attempt was a deferred desire to kill her mother, so now she turned her hatred for Hughes on herself. In truth, although her symptoms were aggravated by external circumstances, Plath battled clinical depression and a morbid fascination with suicide and death throughout her life.

In early 1963, she wrote to her psychiatrist in Boston, "I can feel my mind disintegrating again" (quoted in Middlebrook 207). She hired a live-in nurse to help her manage her two children and she began taking antidepressants. After a severe bout with the flu, with her spirits at one of their lows, Plath committed suicide on February 11, 1963 by inhaling gas from her kitchen oven.

Plath used Greek tragedy throughout her poetic career to artistically render what she called her own "tragic experience" (*Journals* 334). In the first poem from *Collected Poems*, "Conversation Among the Ruins," written in 1956, the speaker addresses the image of her dead father: "While you stand heroic in coat and tie, I sit / Composed in Grecian tunic and psyche-knot, / Rooted to your black look, the play turned tragic" (21). A modern-day father haunts his ancient daughter's home. In a conflation of contemporary and ancient, real and mythic, Plath's speaker exists in a liminal realm in which she is dogged, not only by this father and his "wild furies," but also by the trouble she has in articulating the devastation of her situation. As the crumbling surroundings indicate, this daughter has been ruined by her father's death. But, how can she express the tragedy? She asks, in the poem's final line, "What ceremony of words can patch the havoc?" Plath's answer comes in the next seven years of poems: a poetry that depends upon allusion to ancient Greek tragedy was the best way she knew to create order from life's chaos.

In what was perhaps her final poem, "Edge,"[11] Plath returns back to the woman from "Conversation Among the Ruins," only, now that the woman is dead, she has the answers that the young speaker did not. Plath celebrates her own "ceremony of words," her career as poet, indicating her certainty that her writing was her greatest accomplishment:

> The woman is perfected.
> Her dead
>
> Body wears the smile of accomplishment,
> The illusion of a Greek necessity
>
> Flows in the scrolls of her toga,
> Her bare
>
> Feet seem to be saying:
> We have come this far, it is over. (272)

This dead woman wears a toga whose folds resemble scrolls. Through this metaphor, Plath enshrouds the woman in the receptacle of her thoughts and writings—the scrolls. The body also "wears the smile of accomplishment." The body's state of perfection, what it has achieved, then, is connected to the other "garment" it wears, the scroll-like toga. Through this image, the woman's accomplishment is linked to her writing. Completion, perfection, and death are all tied, in this final poem, to the ancient Greek model.

Had Plath lived out the year, she would have witnessed the publishing of *The Feminine Mystique* and the ensuing development of a women's movement. She might have found solace in the revelation that there was an entire community of women ready to band together and demand the social and legal transformations that the next several decades would bring. In a letter to her mother dated January 16, 1963, less than one month before her suicide, Plath wrote, "I just haven't felt to have any *identity* under the steamroller of decisions and responsibilities of this last half year, with the babies a constant demand" (495). While her depression may have been chemical or biological in origin, her social frustrations were certainly real. Plath's poems indicate a nascent feminist consciousness. In "When We Dead Awaken" (1971), Adrienne Rich writes,

> It strikes me that in the work of [Sylvia Plath] Man appears as, if not a dream, a fascination and a terror; and that the source of the fascination and the terror is, simply, Man's power—to dominate, tyrannize, choose, or reject the woman. The charisma of Man seems to come purely from his power over her and his control of the world by force, not from anything fertile or life-giving in him. . . . It is finally [Plath's] sense of *herself*— embattled, possessed — that gives the poetry its dynamic charge, its rhythms of struggle, need, will, and female energy. Until recently this female anger and this furious awareness of the Man's power over her were not available materials to the female poet, who tended to write of Love as the source of her suffering, and to view that victimization by Love as an almost inevitable fate. (*OLSS* 36)

Plath ultimately rejected this image of the suffering, love-struck heroine. She had lived that life of "victimization by Love," as both daughter and wife. In her identification with Electra, she described herself as a daughter who hated her mother and "all the mothers" for their demand that she sacrifice her identity. By the last year of her life, she had transformed her speaker from victim to avenger. As Clytemnestra, Plath's persona becomes one of the most hated mothers in literary history, who avenges the sacrifice of her daughter. Plath's use of the Electra and Clytemnestra characters provides a window into her battles with socially controlled gender roles and limited resources and options for women.

If Plath could not benefit from her own poetic innovations, women poets who outlived the oppressive 1950s and witnessed the advent of the second wave of feminism certainly would. Plath's divided self, manifested in her Electra/ Clytemnestra split, destroyed her. As she fell deeper into despair, and particularly during the manic last period of her life when she was writing sometimes two or three poems a day, she used the foundations of an existing mythology to blow apart the cultural myth of the self-sacrificing daughter/wife in a previously unmatched female poetics of vengeance.

The Mysteries of Adrienne Rich's Radical Feminism in *The Dream of a Common Language*

The Book of Myths

Like most of the women in this study, Adrienne Rich grew up copying the subjects and styles of the male poets whom she admired, but unlike many of her female contemporaries, she eventually rejected classical allusion. During the surge in feminist interest in matrifocal cultures and goddess worship in the 1970s, however, Rich adopted the *Homeric Hymn to Demeter* and the Eleusinian Mysteries, which celebrated the Greek goddess Demeter's search for and reunion with her daughter Persephone, as relevant to her own life. Her prose work *Of Woman Born* (1976) and her volume of poems *The Dream of a Common Language* (1978) delineate what she gradually came to see as the crucial problem of patriarchal cultures—the fractured relationship between mother and daughter, woman and woman. Unlike Sylvia Plath's choice to reinvent the tension-fraught mother/daughter relationship from the Electra/Clytemnestra myth, Rich worked from the joyous reunion of Demeter and Persephone in the myth that symbolized for her the essential connection for which contemporary women must strive.

Rich grew up reading the canonical male poets and believing that in order to be taken seriously as a poet herself, she would have to reject or hide "feminine" aspects of her thoughts or style. She writes in "When We Dead Awaken: Writing as Re-Vision" (1971), "I had been taught that poetry should be 'universal,' which meant, of course, nonfemale" (*OLSS 44*). Her poetic evolution would coincide with her feminist evolution, and her interest in the matrifocal Eleusinian Mysteries reflects a rejection of patriarchy in all its forms, including the men who shaped her writing and her early perception of herself as an artist. Rich's father, Arnold Rich, played a significant role in his daughter's literary education. He instructed her on what subjects and styles were acceptable to the great male writers. In *Of Woman Born,* Rich acknowledges that by making her copy the styles of Blake, Keats, Rossetti, and Tennyson he taught her how to write metered and rhymed verse. In *Snapshots of a Daughter-in-Law* (1963), she appropriates mythic personalities, as did many of the male poets she grew up reading. Her speaker is Prometheus or Antinous; even when she takes on the feminine voice of Odysseus's nurse Euryclea, it is to wonder at the relationship between father and son, Odysseus and Telemachus. These mythic allusions carry no feminist consciousness and are not yet politically charged, as her later mythic revisions would be.

Prestigious male poets acknowledged Rich, as they had H.D., as a promising young poet. When she was twenty-one, for example, W.H. Auden nominated Rich for the Yale Younger Poets Series. His now famous introduction to her first book, *Change of World* (1951), describes her poems as "neatly and modestly dressed, [they] speak quietly but do not mumble, respect their elders but are not cowed by them" (11). He and modernist poets such as Eliot, Pound, and Yeats were standard reading in Rich's poetry courses at Radcliffe College. In "When We Dead Awaken: Writing as Re-Vision," Rich admits that her early verse, including her 1954–1962 *Snapshots of a Daughter-in-Law,* "strikes me now as too literary, too dependent on allusion; I hadn't found the courage yet to do without authorities" (45). This statement indirectly responds to Eliot's assertion in his 1920 essay "Tradition and the Individual Talent" that "[n]o poet, no artist of any art, has his complete meaning alone. His significance, his appreciation is the appreciation of his relation to the dead poets and artists. You cannot value him alone; you must set him, for contrast and comparison, among the dead." Rich, on the other hand, explains the significance of "do[ing] without authorities":

> Every group that lives under the naming and image-making power of a dominant culture is at risk from this mental fragmentation and needs an art which can resist it. [. . .] But at the middle of the fifties I had no very clear idea of my positioning in the world or even that such an idea was an important resource for a writer to have. [. . .] I had been taught a particular version of our history, the version of the propertied white male; and in my early twenties *I did not even realize this.* (175, emphasis added)

Once she does realize how biased her education had been, however, she writes, in "The Stranger" (1972), "my visionary anger cleans[ed] my sight" (*DW*, 19).[1] Where Plath's anger consumed, Rich's anger "cleansed"; unlike her contemporary, Rich was able not only to challenge the prescribed models of femininity and literary legitimacy, but also to overcome them.

While T.S. Eliot's conception of an artist working within Tradition corresponds on one level to what Rich is doing as a poet, her agenda contrasts starkly with Eliot's. In "Tradition and the Individual Talent" Eliot argues,

> What happens when a new work of art is created is something that happens simultaneously to all the works of art which preceded it. The existing monuments form an ideal order among themselves, which is modified by the introduction of the new (the really new) work of art among them. The existing order is complete before the new work arrives; for order to persist after the supervention of novelty, the *whole* existing order must be, if ever so slightly, altered; and so the relations, proportions, values of each work of art toward the whole are readjusted; and this is conformity between the old and the new. Whoever has approved this idea of order, of the form of European, of English literature, will not find it preposterous that the past should be altered by the present as much as the present is directed by the past. And the poet who is aware of this will be aware of great difficulties and responsibilities. (original italics)

Rich's bold revisions of the Demeter myth seem to conform to the longstanding tradition of mythic revision that alters the past through the introduction of a fresh take on old themes. But Rich does not wish to subtly shift the existing monuments; her agenda is more violent. For example, in response to Eliot's articulation of the poet's struggle to incorporate into Tradition, Rich writes in "When We Dead Awaken,"

> Re-vision—the act of looking back, of seeing with fresh eyes, of entering an old text from a new critical direction—is for women more than a chapter in cultural history: it is an act of survival. Until we can understand the assumptions in which we are drenched we cannot know ourselves. And this drive to self-knowledge, for women, is more than a search for identity: it is part of our refusal of the self-destructiveness of a male-dominated society . . . A change in the concept of sexual identity is essential if we are not going to see the old political order reassert itself in every new revolution. *We need to know the writing of the past, and know it differently than we have ever known it; not to pass on a tradition but to break its hold over us.* (*OLSS* 35–36, italics mine)

In this extraordinary passage, Rich explains her reasons for engaging in literary revision and suggests that it is an essential act in a woman's "drive to self-knowledge," enabling her to break the hold of Tradition.

Rich determined to create poems that mixed politics and art (*BBP* 178). In "Toward a More Feminist Criticism" (1981), she argues, "*All* art is political in terms of who was allowed to make it, what brought it into being, why and how it entered the canon, and why we are still discussing it" (*BBP* 95, original italics). In "In the Evening" (1966), she declares, "The old masters, the old sources, / haven't a clue what we're about, / shivering here in the half-dark 'sixties" (*CEP* 287). The "old masters" were no longer viable as models. Rich's lines are a direct response to Auden's "Musée des Beaux Arts," in which the speaker claims, "About suffering they were never wrong, / The old masters." Rich's reaction against her literary and biological fathers was violent. In 1969, she imagined a fierce overthrow of her father's canon:

> . . . I'd rather
> taste blood, yours or mine, flowing
> from a sudden slash, than cut all day
> with blunt scissors on dotted lines
> like the teacher told. (*CEP* 323)

Her poetry would no longer be "neat and modest," would no longer cut bluntly, safely, ineffectually, but would slash and draw blood.

The Greco-Roman mythic tradition was part of the androcentric literary world that Rich addressed. She writes in "Planetarium" (1968) of "Galaxies of women, there / doing penance for impetuousness" (*CEP* 361). When the poem's speaker looks at the sky, she can "reconstruct" her body and mind by changing the image of a "woman in the shape of a monster / a monster in the shape of a woman." She writes, "What we see, we see / and seeing is changing." This fresh perception allows for the destabilization of once accepted and acceptable mythic images. More often than not, female poets during the 1960s and 1970s used myth to expose gender assumptions in the ancient myths themselves or in their own culture's perpetuation of gender stereotypes. This mythic-poetic endeavor was part of the larger second-wave project of challenging the male canon and conventional representations of women in literature, religion, and art, and rewriting or recreating those women from a feminist perspective.

Once Rich determined to engage in "re-vision," she concentrated on marriage and motherhood, a focus that became inseparable from her belief in the political value of lesbianism as a means of battling a culturally ingrained hatred of women. Like Sylvia Plath, Rich became a wife and mother during what she calls "the family-centered, consumer-oriented, Freudian-American world of the 1950s" (*OWB* 25). She remembers, "In a high-school yearbook of my generation, one of the most brilliant students listed as her ambition: 'to be married to a great man,'" which is reminiscent of Plath's desire for a "demigod" husband (*OWB* 70, *Journals* 182). While Rich was horrified by this desire, she acknowledges,

I did not then understand that we—the women of that academic community—as in
so many middle-class communities of the period—were expected to fill both the part
of the Victorian Lady of Leisure, the Angel in the House, and also of the Victorian
cook, scullery maid, laundress, governess, and nurse. I only sensed that there were false
distractions sucking at me, and I wanted desperately to strip my life down to what was
essential. (*OWB* 27, emphasis added)

She insists that "[f]or centuries no one talked of these feelings," and explains that
"even . . . the most independent of us, those who seem to lead the freest lives"
were oppressed by engrained cultural beliefs (*OWB* 25, 34). The ensuing rage
often fueled "revisionist mythmaking" or what Rich called "writing as re-vision."
Paula Bennett posits a tradition of "rage poetry" that was a literary backlash against
prescribed social roles. Sylvia Plath's *Ariel* poems certainly embody this anger, as
do Rich's poetry and prose.

Rich put her poetry in dialogue with her prose and used both toward her revi-
sionist agenda. In an archetypal underwater journey, the speaker in "Diving into
the Wreck" (1972) explores the "wreck" of herself and of women's history: "the
wreck and not the story of the wreck / the thing itself and not the myth" (*DW* 23).
She finds that she has read "a book of myths / in which / our names do not appear."
Rich believed that the act of "seeing" or "re-reading," for which she argues in her
prose and poetry, would force dramatic social and cultural change.

Rich's poetry from the 1960s and early 1970s reveals her initial wish to include
men in the possibility for a "change[d] world." In "The Stranger" her persona
becomes "the androgyne" who declares, "I am the living mind you fail to describe /
in your dead language" (*DW* 19). "The Phenomenology of Anger"'s speaker indi-
cates her hope that men will join in the movement for radical change:

When I dream of meeting
the enemy, this is my dream:
white acetylene
ripples from my body
effortlessly released
perfectly trained
on the true enemy

raking his body down to the thread
of existence
burning away his lie
leaving him in a new
world; a changed
man (*DW* 29)

These "androgyny" poems, both written in 1972, engage with H.D.'s use of Achilles in *Helen in Egypt*. Rich's "changed man" resembles the "New Mortal" Achilles after he sleeps with Helen; the product of their union is Euphorion, the perfect melding of male and female that represents a return to cultural innocence before individuals adopt dangerous gender stereotypes.

Rich's initial acceptance of androgyny, as in her declaration "I am she: I am he" from "Diving into the Wreck," eventually developed (by the time she was writing *Dream of a Common Language* in 1974) into a belief in the necessity for lesbianism, which she viewed as a return to mother-love and self-love. She called for lesbian eros as a means to break the literary and cultural tradition of patriarchy, "two women, eye to eye / measuring each other's spirit, each other's / limitless desire, / a whole new poetry beginning here" (*DCL* 76). She realized that the "changed man" was not feasible. Why, she wondered, did she and other women spend time conceiving of him when they should have focused on women? Rich wrote in "Natural Resources" (1977):

> The phantom of the man-who-would-understand,
> the lost brother, the twin—
>
> for him did we leave our mothers,
> deny our sisters, over and over?
>
> did we invent him, conjure him
> over the charring log . . . (DCL 62)

That perfect male counterpart, Rich posits, was a female mythic creation just as dangerous for women to believe in as the goddesses and whores that men created. The fantasy of the perfect man drove women apart.

As Rich came to believe that men could not be included in her vision for a "changed world," she defined manhood anew:

> . . . another kind of being
> was constructing itself, blindly
>
> —a mutant, some have said:
> the blood-compelled exemplar
>
> of a "botched civilization"
> as one of them called it
>
> children picking up guns
> for that is what it means to be a man

. . .

> There are words I cannot choose again:
> *Humanism androgyny* (*DCL* 62–63, 66, original italics)

The poet whom Rich dismisses as "one of them" is Ezra Pound, who wrote of "a botched civilization" in "Hugh Selwyn Mauberly," a poem concerning modern society's inferiority to ancient Greece. The poem also offers a condemnation of WWI, a war in which so many good men died, Pound argued, "For an old bitch gone in the teeth / For a botched civilization." In her condemnation of a different kind of "botched civilization," one that excludes women as valuable, participating members, Rich includes Pound as one of the "mutant beings," who openly fought for the exclusion of women's work from historical memory, specifically in his efforts to prevent women poets from publishing in respected journals. Pound and other male poets like Auden or teachers like her father were the embodiments of patriarchy, "father rule." She had to break their hold over her.

In order to free herself, Rich rejected the need to incorporate masculine traits and values in her movement. Of the words "humanism" and "androgyny," she writes, "their glint is too shallow, like a dye / that does not permeate / the fibers of actual life / as we live it, now" (66). In other words, while the concepts may have been appealing, they were unrealistic and implausible in real life, and it was too damaging for women to waste time waiting for these fantasies to become realities. In an interview with Elly Bulkin in 1977, Rich explains:

> the idea of androgyny which is so seductive somehow as a liberal solution [is] essentially the notion that the male will somehow incorporate into himself female attributes – tenderness, gentleness, ability to cry, to feel, to express, not to be rigid. But, what does it mean for women? The "androgyny" people have not faced what it would mean in and for society for women to feel themselves and be seen as full human beings. (quoted in Markey 205n)

Not only should women stop hoping for men to "become" tender or "feminine," but women are, Rich explains, whole in and of themselves. They do not need to incorporate any masculine qualities to become full human beings. Rich's speaker in "Love Poem IV" (1974–1976) expresses "incurable anger, my unmendable wounds" because men love wars and violence "and they still control the world" (*DCL* 27). Why, Rich asks, would women want any part of those traits? The desire for androgyny only diminishes what women actually are.

Once she realized that the concept of androgyny was flawed, and as she began to develop a radical feminist ideology, Rich cast her lot with women only. She asserts,

My heart is moved by all I cannot save:
so much has been destroyed

I have to cast my lot with those
who age after age, perversely,

with no extraordinary power,
reconstitute the world. (*DCL* 62–67)

Among the central tenets of radical feminism are "that the personal is political; that patriarchy, or male-domination—not capitalism—is at the root of women's oppression; that women should identify themselves as a subjugated class or caste and put their primary energies in a movement with other women to combat their oppressors—men; . . . and that the women's mode [of culture] must be the basis of any future society" (Donovan 156). Some radical groups, such as Ti-Grace Atkinson's The Feminists, called marriage "a primary formalization of the persecution of women" (116). In "The Feminists: A Political Organization to Annihilate Sex Roles" from their *Notes From the Second Year* (1970) they argued, "we consider the rejection of this institution both in theory *and in practice* a primary work of the radical feminist" (116, original italics). Also appearing in 1970, were Kate Millet's *Sexual Politics*, which argues that "patriarchal ideology is that of male supremacy, which conditions women to exhibit male-serving behavior and to accept male-serving roles" (Donovan 159); and Shulamith Firestone's *The Dialectic of Sex: The Case For Feminist Revolution*, which urges feminists to end "the tyranny of the biological family" (11).

In the same year (1970), Rich rejected her marriage "both in theory and in practice." She left her husband of seventeen years for political as much as personal reasons. She declares in "Tear Gas" (1969): "The will to change begins in the body not in the mind / My politics in my body, accruing and expanding with every act of resistance and each of my failures" (*CEP* 420). Like Plath, Rich conceived of her new identity in terms of her separation from husband and father. In "Sources VII" from *Your Native Land, Your Life* (1982) she describes the experience of dismissing her father's hold over her:

> For years I struggled with you: your categories, your theories, your will, *the cruelty which came inextricable from your love*. For years all arguments I carried on in my head were with you. I saw myself, the eldest *daughter raised as a son*, taught to study but not to pray, taught to hold reading and writing sacred: the eldest daughter in a house with no son, she who must overthrow the father, take what he taught her and use it against him. All this in a castle of air, the floating world of the assimilated who know and deny they will always be aliens.

> After your death I met you again as the face of patriarchy, could name at last precisely the principle you embodied, there was an ideology at last which let me dispose of you, identify the suffering you caused, hate you righteously as part of a system, the kingdom of the fathers. I saw the power and arrogance of the male as your true watermark; I did not see beneath it the suffering of the Jew, the alien stamp you bore, because you had deliberately arranged that it should be invisible to me. It is only now, under a powerful, womanly lens, that I can decipher your suffering and deny no part of my own. (9, italics mine)

While she admits that she used the concept of patriarchal injustice to categorize him and his treatment of her, and that he, too, suffered as an outsider, she does not indicate remorse or forgiveness.

The culture, of which her father was a representative, separated mother and daughter. Plath offers a classic example of this division: she hated her mother because of her father's death and the sacrifices that her mother made to raise Plath well. In "Re-forming the Crystal" (1973), Rich's speaker declares:

> Tonight I understand
> my photo on the license is not me,
> my
> name on the marriage-contract was not mine.
> If I remind you of my father's favorite daughter,
> look again. The woman
> I needed to call my mother
> was silenced before I was born. (*FD* 117)

Her reference to her own father and mother signals her larger shift from patriarchy to matriarchy. The indoctrinated hatred of the maternal and the feminine dismayed Rich. As the lesbian theorist Charlotte Bunch argued in "Not for Lesbians Only" (1975), heterosexuality was "a cornerstone of male supremacy" (68). Rich echoes Bunch's sentiments in her essay "Compulsory Heterosexuality and Lesbian Existence" (1980), in which she argues that compulsory heterosexuality is a "political institution" (*BBP* 35). Rich's woman-centered vision involved uniting women, allowing for a reconciliation between women who had been kept apart by cultural ideology, who had been wrenched from their initial love of their mothers and "forced" into loving men. Her mythic model for this phenomenon and its reversal was the *Homeric Hymn to Demeter* and the Eleusinian Mysteries.

Homeric Hymn to Demeter and the Eleusinian Mysteries

In the 1970s, there was a surge of scholarly interpretations of the Demeter and Persephone myth that corresponded to the renewed interest in goddess worship evoked by second-wave feminism. The principal version of the myth is the 7th century B.C.E. *Homeric Hymn to Demeter.*[2] At the beginning of the *Hymn*, Zeus gives Hades permission to abduct Persephone, his daughter with Demeter, and drag her down to the underworld to be his bride. A grief-stricken Demeter wanders the earth searching for Persephone. Hekate, who in later interpretation and literature becomes "the crone," is the first to reveal to Demeter that an immortal god stole her daughter. Furious at Zeus's brash disregard for her wishes as a mother, Demeter leaves Olympus, determined to retrieve her abducted daughter. While an ancient audience would certainly have recognized Zeus's right, as patriarch, to marry his daughter to whomever he pleased, the myth does not shy away from equating marriage with a kind of death for girls. Demeter's withdrawal from Olympus does not constitute defeat, however; she has a plan. She travels to Eleusis, where she disguises herself as an old woman and asks the daughters of the chief prince there if they will help her to find a job as a maid. The girls' mother, Metaneira, recently gave birth to a son for whom Demeter takes over nursing responsibilities. While it may seem strange that Demeter chooses to nurse a boy when she has just lost her daughter, she does not seem to be looking for a surrogate child. Her plan is to make Metaneira's son immortal, and to do so, she places him in the fire each night to burn away his mortality. Her motive may be to make an immortal son, loyal to her, who will be strong enough to fight Zeus. One night, however, Metaneira discovers Demeter placing her son into the fire, and understandably terror-stricken, she unwittingly ruins the goddess's plan.

Despite her frustration that her plan has failed to create a son to overthrow Zeus, Demeter hatches another plot. She establishes her Mysteries at Eleusis and orders: "let all the people build me a great temple / . . . / I myself will lay down the rites so that hereafter / performing due rites you may propitiate my spirit" (16). She then causes a universal famine until Zeus, missing his sacrifices (Zeus's weakness is the aroma of burning fat that rises to Olympus), sends Hermes to tell Hades that he must let Persephone go. Mother and daughter joyously reunite, but because Persephone ate a pomegranate seed, symbolizing consummation of the marriage, she must return to Hades for one third of every year. Zeus had sent other gods to attempt to reason with Demeter, but now he sends Rhea, Demeter's mother. Once Rhea urges her daughter to rejoin the Olympians, Demeter agrees. She first shows men the sacred rites "that are not to be transgressed, nor pried into, / nor divulged. For a great awe of the gods stops the voice," and then returns to Olympus (26). Despite Zeus, Demeter claims her power as a mother and cre-ative, life-giving force.

The *Homeric Hymn to Demeter* explains the origin of the Eleusinian Mysteries, which celebrated the life cycle of the grain and the earth's fertility. The Mysteries centered on Demeter, "Grain mother," who was associated with the ripe grain, and her daughter Persephone, also called Kore, "Maiden," associated with the newly planted seed. The *Hymn* promises blessedness to individual initiates: "Blessed is the mortal on earth who has seen these rites, / but the uninitiate who has no share in them never / has the same lot once dead in the dreary darkness" (26). In the *telestrion* (great temple) the hierophant, "he who shows holy things," would chant and then "amid profound silence [would display] an ear of newly mowed grain . . . Embodied as plant, the gift of her mother to humans and gods alike, the Kore sprout has been harvested and from the harvest comes not death, not finality, but the seedcorn for the ongoing cycle of life" (Carlson 44).[3] During the stage of *epopteia*, "the seeing," the Hierophant showed the grain to the initiate, "in the state of having seen." Agha-Jaffar explains that through participation in and witnessing of a reenactment of Demeter's loss of, search for, and reunion with her daughter, "initiation into the mysteries constituted a means for addressing the perennial concerns of humanity: the meaning of life, loss, grief, suffering, death, and renewal" (12).

One of the first major works on Demeter in the second half of the twentieth century was Carl Kerényi's *Eleusis: Archetypal Image of Mother and Daughter* (1966), based upon earlier studies such as J.J. Bachofen's *Mother Right* (1861), James Frazer's *The Golden Bough* (1893), Jane Harrison's *Prolegomena to the Study of Greek Religion* (1903), Carl Jung's work on archetypes, and the Jungian Erich Neumann's *The Great Mother* (1955). Their ideas about matriarchal or matrifocal societies and religions challenged people to think about religion and culture in radically different ways.[4] This first wave of goddess scholarship influenced and inspired feminist works such as Mary Esther Harding's *Woman's Mysteries* (1971), Mary Daly's *Beyond God the Father* (1973), Merlin Stone's *When God Was a Woman* (1976), and Rich's own *Of Woman Born* (1976).

A correspondence developed between second-wave feminism and interest in the goddess as women questioned the foundations of both patriarchal thought and societies. One of the most obvious of these foundations was monotheistic religion. In her essay "The Politics of Women's Spirituality," Charlene Spretnak explains, "Christianity, Judaism, Islam . . . all combine male godheads with proscriptions against women as temptress, as unclean, as evil" (394). Political groups and women's spirituality movements sprang up in the late 1960s and 1970s: NOW, the New York Radical Feminists, Carol Christ's Rising Moon, the New Age movement, neo-paganism, witchcraft and wicca. Christine Downing explains the appeal of the Goddess during this period: "we felt that the rediscovery of these ancient images of female power as sacred and transformative could be transformative in our own lives, both individually and socially. We hoped that the discovery of a prepatriarchal world might help us imagine forward to a postpatriarchal one" (104). Women's spirituality groups challenged traditional images of God "as male, disembodied, and separated from the changing world" (Christ, *She Who Changes*, 1). The New Age and Women's Spirituality movements of the 1970s and 1980s preached empowerment, observance of ritual to communicate with the sacred, reverence for nature (Goddess or Mother Earth), and questioning of gender structures.[5]

The Demeter myth, which contains each of these elements, appealed to second-wave feminists. Carol Christ writes, "To know ourselves as of this earth is to know our deep connection to all people and all beings. All beings are interdependent on the web of life. This is the distinctive conception of nature and our place in it found in Goddess religion" (*Rebirth* 113). Many women have used the Demeter myth as a model for the beauty of the mother/daughter relationship; others have focused on Hades' rape of Persephone and Zeus's connivance with this violation as representative of patriarchy and the institution of marriage; some are moved by the collaborations and friendships between women and goddesses as representative of what Agha-Jaffar calls "female mentoring" (73).[6] She explains, "This collaborative sharing of skills and resources in a non-competitive environment in which each part works for the betterment of the whole . . . differs from the traditional leadership style that is hierarchical and characterized by the Western model of power *over* another" (Agha-Jaffar 74, original italics). She characterizes this "collaborative sharing" as particularly female. Carol Christ agrees, "Power over is domination. Power with is cooperation, partnership, and mutuality" (*SWC* 93). Some read Demeter as representative of the power within women to fight for what they believe in and for those who cannot fight for themselves.[7] The positive union at the end of the myth of maiden, mother, and crone, resonated with many of the second-wave writers, including Adrienne Rich, as representative of the stages of life that all women experience. Downing sums up several aspects of the myth that resonated deeply with women because of

> its hints of the world-view of matristic cultures, its representation of the patriarchal conquest of a woman-centered world, its valorization of the love
> that connects mothers and daughters and in a more extended way all women,
> its recognition of women's vulnerability to male violence, its providing the
> basis for several female rites of passage, its relevance to our hopes for creating
> a postpatriarchal world in which concern for the earth might again become
> a central value. (101)

The wide range of interpretations of the myth by contemporary women attests to its enduring power to provide an interpretative framework for female experience.

"Old Songs With New Words": Adrienne Rich's Eleusis

In her volume of poetry *The Dream of a Common Language* (1978)[8] and her prose work *Of Woman Born* (1976), Rich approached the Demeter myth as a vision of the rupture of the female bond. She writes, "The loss of the daughter to the mother, the mother to the daughter, is the essential female tragedy" (*OWB* 237). Erich Neumann writes in his influential book *The Great Mother*, which Rich sites several times in *Of Woman Born*, "the close connection between mother and daughter, who form the nucleus of the female group, is reflected in the preservation of the 'primordial relationship' between them" (305–306). He continues, "The one essential motif in the Eleusinian mysteries and hence in all matriarchal mysteries is the *heuresis* of the daughter by the mother, the 'finding again' of Kore by Demeter, the reunion of mother and daughter" (307–308). For Rich, the central problem of contemporary culture was its loss of a relationship to the Mother. In "Transcendental Etude" Rich writes,

> Birth stripped our birthright from us,
> tore us from a woman, from women, from ourselves
> so early on
> and the whole chorus throbbing at our ears
> like midges, told us nothing, nothing
> of origins, nothing we needed
> to know, nothing that could re-member us.
>
> Only: that it is unnatural,
> the homesickness for a woman, for ourselves (*DCL* 75)

Rich saw this ruptured relationship as one that women in patriarchal cultures throughout history must have mourned. She explains, "Each daughter, even in the millennia before Christ, must have longed for a mother whose love for her and whose power were so great as to undo rape and bring her back from death. And every mother must have longed for the power of Demeter, the efficacy of her anger, the reconciliation with her lost self" (*OWB* 240). Rich used this historical longing for *heuresis*, for finding again or reunion, as a way to highlight what she saw as her contemporary culture's hatred of women. Her poem's lines, broken by short phrases such as "from a woman, from women, from ourselves," enact the women's separation, while the repetition of the words "from" and "nothing" demonstrate the connectedness of the separated bodies through shared experience. Women may have been torn from one another, but the repeated words indicate something shared that will eventually allow them to find one another again—to piece the disjointed fragments into a whole.

Heavily influenced by the *Homeric Hymn to Demeter*, Rich fills *Dream of a Common Language* with examples of physical, mental, and cultural rifts between women. In "Splittings" Rich describes the pain of separation from her lover who is in another city. The Pain speaks:

> I am the pain of division creator of divisions
> it is I who blot your lover from you
> and not the time-zones nor the miles
> It is not separation calls me forth but I
> who am separation And remember
> I have no existence apart from you (10)

But Rich's Mind responds to the Pain:

> I will not be divided from her or from myself
> by myths of separation
> …
> I am choosing
> not to suffer uselessly and not to use her
> I choose to love this time for once
> with all my intelligence. (11)

Physical distance separates these women, embodied through the spaces within the structure of the poem itself. The speaker and her lover cannot be fully living, the speaker posits, until they stop loving in secret and accept their lives openly. Only then can she "call [their experience] life" (9). The physical distance between time-zones and miles is a metaphor for the emotional turmoil of living a secret.

The sonnet sequence "Twenty-One Love Poems" develops the personal relationship between the speaker and her lover, their partings, distances, and returns. The tension of the women's secret relationship leads to the speaker's meditation on intimacy and connection. She tells her lover,

> *I dreamed you were a poem,*
> *. . . a poem I wanted to show someone . . .*
> and I laugh and fall dreaming again
> of the desire to show you to everyone I love,
> to move openly together (II, 25, original italics)

She worries that environmental destruction, ravages of war, and other political crises are "mere emblems of that desecration of ourselves," a desecration caused by "the failure to want our freedom passionately enough" (VII, 28). In sonnet "XV" the speaker says,

If I lay on that beach with you
white, empty, pure green water warmed by the Gulf Stream
and lying on that beach we could not stay
because the wind drove fine sand against us
as if it were against us
if we tried to withstand it and we failed—
if we drove to another place
to sleep in each other's arms
and the beds were narrow like prisoners' cots
and we were tired and did not sleep together
and this was what we found, so this is what we did—
was the failure ours?
If I cling to circumstances I could feel
not responsible. Only she who says
she did not choose, is the loser in the end. (32–33)

Rich's speaker does not want the winds and sands of cultural circumstances to make the lovers complacent in their separation: "And this was what we found, so this is what we did." The lovers must choose to withstand these storms. In sonnet "XVI," the speaker feels a connection to her lover, despite the physical separation, "Across a city from you, I'm with you." Rich plays on the narrow bed image from the previous sonnet to reconcile the two lovers, "This island of Manhattan is wide enough / for both of us, and narrow" (33). This marks not only a determination to reject the cultural restrictions that keep them apart, but also harkens back to "Splittings," in which the speaker worries about physical separation and suffers from her lover's absence. In sonnet "XVI" the suffering is gone, even though, as she says in sonnet "XIX," "two women together is a work / nothing in civilization has made simple" (35). Throughout the volume, Rich wrestles with the extraordinary difficulty women face in their drive to connect to one another.

Cultural and class-based distances also threaten women's understanding of one another. In "Hunger" Rich's speaker admits, "I live in my Western skin, / my Western vision, torn / and flung to what I can't control or even fathom" (12). She posits a connection between a black lesbian, a white prostitute, a starving woman of genius, and women from all over the world who are starved in various ways by "that male god . . . that male State" (13). Rich writes:

Something that kills us or leaves us half-alive
is raging under the name of an 'act of god'
. . .
yes, that male god that acts on us and on our children,
that male State that acts on us and our children (*DCL* 13)

Rich makes a correlation between the male god and male State and pits those against women and children. In this poem she urges women to fight against the "terrorist of the mind": "The decision to feed the world / is the real decision. No revolution / has chosen it. For that choice requires / that women shall be free" (13). She argues that "Until we find each other [daughters, sisters, lovers], we are alone" (14). Women must seek *heuresis*.

Rich's speaker determines to use poetry as her way of attempting to reconcile these divided groups of women. She calls poetry "The drive / to connect. The dream of a common language" ("Origins and History of Consciousness" 7). Instead of speaking the "so-called common language," the phallogocentric, accepted language, "The syllables uttering / the old script over and over," "living in the formal network of the lie," she will write a poetry, she claims, that connects women in a new common language of truth (18–19). Themes of frustrated power, separation, and the need for reconciliation abound, and Rich attempts her reunion through poetry. She meditates on women isolated by marriage, childbirth, cancer, and death, and on women's efforts to connect, despite the odds against them. The various historical and fictional female speakers form a chorus to condemn the patriarchal civilization in which they are forced to live. Men, for Rich, are "that kind of being [that] has lain in our beds / declaring itself our desire / requiring women's blood for life / a woman's breast to lay its nightmare on" ("Natural Resources" 63). Rich's speakers turn away from the men in their lives and call, in "limitless desire," to the women from whom they have been driven (76).

Through this tapestry of separations and reconciliations, the *Hymn to Demeter* binds the entire volume; even when not referenced directly, its themes inform every poem. Rich interweaves direct references to the Demeter myth and the Eleusinian Mysteries with the voices of women who either mourn the loss of a relationship with a woman or rejoice at the connection with another woman. She writes in *Of Woman Born*, "The separation of Demeter and Kore is an unwilling one; it is neither a question of the daughter's rebellion against the mother, nor the mother's rejection of the daughter" (240). She viewed Zeus's deal with Hades, which severed the bond between mother and daughter, as representative of the forces that drive women from each other into unwanted relationships with men. In *The Homeric Hymn to Demeter: Translation, Commentary, and Interpretive Essays*, Helene Foley writes, "Adrienne Rich's *Of Woman Born* inaugurated the feminist re-appropriation of the myth" (167). Christine Downing attests to the popularity of Rich's interpretation among lesbian feminists: "The love between Demeter and Persephone has been felt by many to symbolize *not only the mother-daughter bond but more generally the intense, intimate connections among women* whose loyalty to one another takes precedence over their relationships with men" (136, italics mine).[9] Susan Stanford Friedman affirms, "for Rich, reconstitution of a mother-centered world is inseparable from lesbianism" (*CL* 242). Rich used the myth in her prose and poetry as a way for women to recognize the violation, which was not only familial, but cultural, and to repair it.

In number VI of her "Twenty-one Love Poems," Rich's speaker compares her lover's body to "the Eleusinian cave." Caves were sacred spaces in goddess worship, representing the fertile womb of the earth and female sexuality. She repeatedly posits her lover as the rich and mysterious earth that she will become initiated into understanding. This initiation would represent a return to the sacred feminine that, Rich believed, was lost to our culture. Downing explains, "Even though women's lovemaking with women is not biologically connected to reproduction, experiencing it touches on that mystery through a mutual return to and mutual departure from the gate of our origin" (145). Thus, Rich used the myth and its accompanying Mysteries as a way to express the extraordinary spiritual and physical bond between women.

Although Rich often wrote specifically about her partner, she saw a return to a woman-centered life as necessary between women in various types of relationships. Downing writes, "all close bonds among women inevitably conjure up memories and feelings associated with our first connection to a woman, the all-powerful mother of infancy. They remind us of a time in which one neither required the phallus nor rebelled against its power, when it was merely irrelevant" (144). Rich desires to return to the point when only the mother and child exist and there is no knowledge yet of the patriarch. In "Sibling Mysteries" she draws upon the notion of woman-centered mysteries to address her estranged sister:

> Remind me how we loved our mother's body
> our mouths drawing the first
> thin sweetness from her nipples
>
> our faces dreaming hour on hour
> in the salt smell of her lap
> . . .
> and how we thought she loved
> the strange male body first
> that took, that took, whose taking seemed a law
>
> and how she sent us weeping
> into that law
> . . .
> hold me, remind me
> of how her woman's flesh was made taboo to us. (*DCL* 48–49)

Recognition of the extent to which patriarchy rips women apart happens when they can speak of that violation together, and it is essential, Rich posits, to "remind" one another of the possibility of an alternate world that was once and can again be available.[10] Rich's speaker joins the tradition of women bonding against their husbands and fathers: "beneath / the strange male bodies / we sank in terror or in resignation" (49). She concludes,

> The daughters never were
> true brides of the father
>
> the daughters were to begin with
> brides of the mother
>
> then brides of each other
> under a different law
>
> Let me hold and tell you. (*DCL* 52)

Rich asks her female readers to learn of this past and to acknowledge what they have lost. Only then can they work to reconstruct it. "Not Somewhere Else, but Here" attests to the destruction in the city, walls caving in, "Bad air in the tunnels," dirt and blood. In the midst of the destruction, Rich's speaker asserts her "Courage / to feel this To tell of this to be alive" (39). The radical feminist movement gave Rich a vocabulary with which to attack patriarchal and heterosexual culture. Indeed, she played an integral part in developing that vocabulary.

In "Upper Broadway," while Rich adapts the Mysteries to initiate her speaker on a personal level, through this individual transformation comes group initiation into collective understanding. She writes,

> The leafbud straggles forth
> toward the frigid light of the airshaft this is faith
> this pale extension of a day
> when looking up you know something is changing
> winter has turned though the wind is colder
> Three streets away a roof collapses onto people
> who thought they still had time Time out of mind
>
> I have written so many words
> wanting to live inside you
> to be of use to you

The catastrophe of people dying, "who thought they still had time," makes Rich's speaker think of her relationship with her lover. She had wanted "to live inside" the woman, linking her to the house whose roof collapsed. Clearly there has also been some sort of "collapse" in the speaker's relationship. As in Demeter's mysteries, where initiates learn of the cyclical nature of renewal out of death, in "Upper Broadway," humans' finite time is set against "natural" time; the leafbud emerges out of winter; new life forms to become part of the continuing cycle. The poem's phrase "though the wind is colder" indicates that despite the current bleakness, "winter has turned," there will be a spring and rebirth.

The juxtaposition of human and natural time makes the speaker think about her own temporality:

Now I must write for myself for this blind
woman scratching the pavement with her wand of thought
this slippered crone inching on icy streets
reaching into wire trashbaskets pulling out
what was thrown away and infinitely precious

I look at my hands and see they are still unfinished
I look at the vine and see the leafbud
inching towards life

I look at my face in the glass and see
a halfborn woman (*DCL* 41)

Initially, the speaker watches a leafbud emerging out of winter, a "pale extension of a day," and laments that she had tried to write to her lover without a recognition that time passes, that their relationship might be ephemeral. During the process of writing, however, and while watching the new life moving towards the light, the "crone" that she thought she had become is rejuvenated through understanding: she, like the leafbud, is "inching towards life," as she acknowledges that she is only "halfborn." After collapse comes reconstruction. Unlike the people who were killed by the collapse, this speaker's life is "extended." She still has more time. Her transformation is not physical but psychological: she realizes that even old age is formative in itself. Through her images of crone, woman, and leafbud, she plays on the Eleusinian images of crone, mother, and maiden (new grain), and embodies all of these aspects within herself. The modern speaker's potential for growth and transformation comes through her identification with the ancient Mysteries, during which initiates would gain an understanding of the process of death and life, wasting away and rejuvenation. Rich's speaker is similarly initiated, and her "rebirth" comes through the recognition that she must write for herself, not for her lover, in order to experience renewal.

Rich shares her epiphanies with her readers, who then participate in the transformative power of the Eleusinian Mysteries that is alive in Rich's poetry. In "Cartographies of Silence" Rich admits,

> If from time to time I envy
> the pure annunciations to the eye
>
> the visio beatifica
> if from time to time I long to turn
>
> like the Eleusinian hierophant
> holding up a simple ear of grain
>
> for return to the concrete and everlasting world
> what in fact I keep choosing
>
> are these words, these whispers, conversations
> from which time after time the truth breaks moist and green. (*DCL* 20)

Through her writing, she is as powerful as Demeter's hierophant. Rich's words are the *sacra*, the sacred objects that will enlighten readers, the initiates. There will be no visual epiphanic moment, but her poetry is comparable to the new grain; it brings rejuvenation and new life out of the old. In fact, in a miraculous moment, the words and grain are one, and will, as "time after time" suggests, continue to sprout truths as long as she continues to write. In another poem, Rich imagines her lover's hands:

> piec[ing] together
> the fine, needle-like sherds of a great krater-cup
> bearing on its sides
> figures of ecstatic women striding
> to the sibyl's den or the Eleusinian cave. (*DCL* 28)

These images of women, either creating or piecing together images, fragments, and memories, allude to the Eleusinian Mysteries as a way for Rich to frame her dialogue about how to transform women's lives in a patriarchal world.

The evocation of feminine power within patriarchy is particularly evident in her poem "Mother-Right." With a title taken from J.J. Bachofen's 1861 book and Jane Alpert's feminist theoretical essay of the same name, Rich places the poem in the tradition of "studies" of matriarchal myths and histories.[11] The poem begins: "Woman and child running / in a field A man planted / on the horizon" (*DCL* 59). Whereas in the Demeter myth, both mother and child are associated with various stages in the life of the plant—the mature and young grain—here mother and child are fluid, moving, and it is the man who is "planted." The play on the word "plant" suggests man's distance from nature in this scene, whose field recalls Persephone's place of abduction. He does not enter the field, the natural space that contains the mother and child, but remains on the outskirts. The "planted" man is, in fact, not rooted: "The man is walking boundaries / measuring He believes in what is his / the grass the waters underneath the air // the air through which child and mother / are running." This image serves as a microcosm of the world as Rich sees it: men believe that they own the earth, which includes women and children, whereas women are a part of the natural environment, not separate from it. Rich highlights this idea through repetition of "the air." The first time she uses the image, the air "belongs to" the man; next, it is an open space through which mother and child move away from the man's oppressive power.

Rich wanted women to resist feelings of guilt or necessity that might drive them to remain in a patriarchal framework that they would otherwise abandon. It is no coincidence that Rich chose H.D.'s words to begin her volume of poems that looked to an ancient model of female bonding and strength. *The Dream of a Common Language* opens with a quote from H.D.'s long poem *The Flowering of the Rod* (1946):

> I go where I love and where I am loved,
> Into the snow;
>
> I go to the things I love
> With no thought of duty or pity.

Rich uses H.D. as a model of a woman who successfully created a strong community of women and who, after leaving her marriage to Richard Aldington, had a long-lasting love relationship with Winifred Bryher and raised a daughter, Perdita, without shame or guilt. In her essay "What Does a Woman Need to Know?" (1979), Rich asks what a woman must do "to become a self-conscious, self-defining human being" (*BBP* 2). As if in anticipation of this question, she had written eight years earlier in "When We Dead Awaken," "to be a female human being trying to fulfill traditional female functions in a traditional way *is* in direct conflict with the subversive function of the imagination" (*OLSS* 43, original italics). H.D. was an example for Rich of a self-conscious, self-defining human being.

Rich's allusion to H.D.'s long poem is more complex than H.D.'s biographical appeal; H.D.'s late long poems, including *The Flowering of the Rod*, attest to her dream for an inclusive common language among women, a dream that Rich pursues in her own poetry. H.D. was fascinated with religious syncretism and often conflated mythic and religious figures to demonstrate recurring principles throughout religions. Deanna Polson argues that H.D.'s reading of Sir Arthur Evans's essay, "The Earlier Religion of Greece, in the Light of Cretan Discoveries," shaped her interpretation of goddess figures in *The Flowering of the Rod*. In his essay, Evans describes vessels that "represent offerings intended for the Goddess on the Epiphany of the infant God" and rings that portray Minoan goddesses as mother figures (Polson 52). Evans notes, "Nothing could be more remarkable than the parallelism that this whole scene presents with the Adoration of the Magi" (281). He finds other relations to Anatolian and Syrian goddesses. His essay lists several examples of iconographic and narrative syncretism.

In *Flowering of the Rod*, as in *Helen in Egypt,* H.D. plays with similarities among various representations of the Great Goddess: "Isis, Astarte, Cyprus / . . . /he might re-name them / Ge-meter, De-meter, earth-mother" (30). H.D. tells a story about the jar of myrrh with which Mary Magdalene anointed Jesus's feet. Mary is one of the narrative voices in the poem, and she offers an alternate female story to those male versions of events available in the Bible. If Mary is a manifestation of the Great Goddess, as is Demeter, then the poetic voice from the excerpt that Adrienne Rich uses could be not only Mary's, but Demeter's as well. The complete poem is as follows:

> I go where I love and where I am loved,
> Into the snow;
>
> I go to the things I love
> With no thought of duty or pity;
>
> I go where I belong, inexorably,
> As the rain that has lain long
>
> In the furrow; I have given
> Or would have given
>
> Life to the grain;
> But if it will not grow or ripen
>
> With the rain of beauty,
> The rain will return to the cloud;
>
> The harvester sharpens his steel on the stone;
> But this is not our field,
>
> We have not sown this;
> Pitiless, pitiless, let us leave
>
> The-place-of-a-skull
> To those who have fashioned it. (8–9)

Chisholm explains, "*The Flowering of the Rod* is not a 'tale' so much as a collection, collation, analysis, shelving or resolving of 'fragmentary ideas, apparently unrelated' but eventually 'found to be part of a special layer or stratum of thought and memory' which we, the readers, are invited to piece together skillfully in collaboration with the writer" (61). The story of Jesus's resurrection that took place after his crucifixion at Golgotha (Place of a Skull) was recorded by male writers. H.D. imagines Mary's perspective, but in so doing, conjures another female character devastated by the loss of a loved one—Demeter. The reader must "piece together skillfully" the multiple character possibilities for H.D.'s speaker. Mary (who later appears with her flowering branches of myrrh—an epiphanic vision of resurrection) is also Demeter (whose hierophant holds up the grain as a vision of regeneration and rebirth), who goes into the winter snow to retrieve her lost daughter with no thought of what she is "supposed" to do: give life to the grain. She thinks only of recovering what has been lost to her.

When her words open Adrienne Rich's volume of poems, H.D. becomes a prophetess who beckons to women to pursue what they love, regardless of societal pressures, regardless of consequences.[12] Rich's chorus of voices throughout the volume sings its response to H.D. The voices are many, but they sing in a common language.

During the 1970s, Rich struggled, as H.D. had before her, to find a way to use male-written myths in a feminist way, to "sing [. . .] old songs / with new words" (*DCL* 31). She argued,

> For the first time in history, a pervasive recognition is developing that the patriarchal system cannot answer for itself; that it is not inevitable; that it is transitory; and that the cross-cultural, global domination of women by men can no longer be either denied or defended. When we acknowledge this, we tear open the relationship at the core of all power-relationships, a tangle of lust, violence, possession, fear, conscious longing, unconscious hostility, sentiment, rationalization: the sexual understructure of social and political forms. (*OWB* 56)

In her poem "Translations" (1972), she underscores this idea that patriarchy is not inevitable and that women must tear open the sexual understructure. She writes that the "grief" that women experience as a result of patriarchy "is shared, unnecessary / and political" (*DW* 41). Rich viewed the Eleusinian Mysteries as "a final resurgence of the multiple aspects of the Great Goddess in the classical-patriarchal world" (*OWB* 240). She used them as a model for how to address women's strengths and powers in her own patriarchal world. Rich believed that her use of this myth, which records a goddess's refusal to bow to male rule and celebrates the power of life and rejuvenation associated with women, would be a way to have her "name" appear in "the book of myths" that she and other likeminded women would have radically altered. She returned to a story of female power within the patriarchal Greek mythological tradition to suggest that women can find ways to assert themselves within the current system.[13]

"Cutting-away of an old force": Rich's Rejection of Classical Mythology

Despite her use of mythic images of female strength and unity, after *Dream of a Common Language*, Rich decided that classical mythology, as a tradition of repression, evoked too much anger in her. In "Twenty-One Love Poems," Rich hints at her ensuing decision to stop using Greek mythology:

> I can see myself years back at Sunion,
> hurting with an infected foot, Philoctetes
> in woman's form, limping the long path,
> lying on a headland over the dark sea,
> looking down the red rocks to where a soundless curl
> of white told me a wave had struck,
> imagining the pull of that water from that height,
> knowing deliberate suicide wasn't my métier,
> yet all the time nursing, measuring that wound.
> Well, that's finished. The woman who cherished
> her suffering is dead. I am her descendent.
> I love the scar-tissue she handed on to me,
> but I want to go on from here with you
> fighting the temptation to make a career of pain. (*DCL* 28–29)

Rich's sonnet references the Greek Philoctetes, whom the Greeks, on their way to Troy, abandoned on the isle of Lemnos after his foot became horribly infected. Sunion was the place where Aegeus threw himself into the sea when he saw black sails on his son Theseus's ship. Upon his return from slaying the Minotaur, Theseus forgot his promise to change the black sails to white to indicate a successful mission. Aegeus committed suicide believing that his son was dead. In her sonnet, Rich's speaker conflates the characters of Philoctetes nursing his wound, which is also his wounded pride and his anger at being betrayed by the Greek forces, and Aegeus contemplating suicide at the loss of his son. But her character is "in woman's form," leading us to imagine all of the angers, betrayals, abuses, and losses women have undergone. While the speaker is a descendent of this composite character, she wants to move beyond her ancestor's "career of pain." This poem offers a strange combination of unrelated myths and foregrounds the paradox of Rich's desire to break from the past, while finding herself engrossed in it. In other words, she used myth to explain why she would no longer use myth. She began to view the tradition of feminist mythic revision as a participation in the role of victim and of the oppressed, and she wondered if her use of classical mythology actually validated the power of the tradition she wished to devalue.

Rich also grew discouraged with factions inside the feminist movement and worried that there might be a danger in the idealization of motherhood. In 1986, she wrote in her new "Introduction" to *Of Woman Born*:

> . . . I find myself dubious about the politics of women's peace groups, for example, which celebrate maternality as the basis for engaging in antimilitarist work. I do not see the mother with her child as either more morally credible or more morally capable than any other woman. A child can be used as a symbolic credential, a sentimental object, a badge of self-righteousness. I question the implicit belief that only 'mothers' with 'children of their own' have a real stake in the future of humanity. (xxiv)

Rich did not want to value mothers over other women. She had meant her portrait of the mother/child relationship in the Demeter myth to be a metaphor for women's relationships with one another, not a glorification of motherhood.

Breaking from Greek mythology, the bedrock of the poetic tradition, was not an easy task. In "Transcendental Etude" Rich explains,

> No one who survives to speak
> new language, has avoided this:
> the cutting-away of an old force that held her
> rooted to an old ground
> the pitch of utter loneliness
> where she herself and all creation
> seem equally dispersed, weightless, her being a cry
> to which no echo comes or can ever come. (*DCL* 75)

Rich was just beginning to wrestle to extricate herself from a tradition of immense cultural power. Whereas Sylvia Plath was unable to channel her anger into a rejuvenating poetics that would help her to live in a society in which she felt frustrated and pressured to fit particular gender roles, Adrienne Rich used her poetics of rage to free herself. Once Rich could look at the world through her "womanly lens," she came to reject her early poetry as too absolute and orderly. By the late 1970s, after *Dream of a Common Language*, Rich turned away from the classical tradition, finding the foundational stories undesirable and unnecessary for her poetry. She had involved herself in the dialectic between the feminist poet and the canonical text, and she concluded, as Alice Templeton writes, that "resistance ironically implies inclusion" (72). In "Conditions for Work" (1976) Rich declares:

> Feminism begins but cannot end with the discovery by an individual of her self-consciousness as a woman . . . Feminism means finally that we renounce our obedience to the fathers and recognize that the world they have described is not the whole world . . . *Feminism implies that we recognize fully the inadequacy for us, the distortion, of male-created ideologies, and that we proceed to think, and act, out of that recognition.* (*OLSS* 207, italics mine)

Rich's recognition led her to appropriate, attack, and then transcend male-authored mythologies.

In 1971 Rich had written, "We need to know the writing of the past, and know it differently than we have ever known it; not to pass on a tradition, but to break its hold over us" (*OLSS* 35). By the end of the decade, her prose had influenced Goddess theory, the Feminist Spirituality movement, and Radical Feminist theory, and her poetry about the Eleusinian Mysteries had shown how women could radically change the ways in which they engage with other women. Although she did not return to classical models after *Dream of a Common Language*, this volume offers a lens into a particular aspect of feminist and poetic history. In 1986 Paula Bennett wrote, "for Rich, as for feminist writers generally, this outpouring of rage has been the necessary first step in the creation of a verifiably woman-centered vision, a feminist poetic" (218). Rich's ultimate rejection of Greek mythology raised the question of whether women poets would, or even should, move past the "poetics of rage" that she and Plath helped to create and continue to engage with the classical tradition in new ways.

CHAPTER FOUR

Margaret Atwood's Transformed Circe

Living on the Margins

During the same years in which Adrienne Rich was experimenting with mythology, only to turn away from it as too representative of oppression to use in her writing, Margaret Atwood also wrestled with how to make it meaningful for a modern audience. Much like Rich, she sought to expose the dangerous gender constructions within the existing stories that she felt had become so engrained that they not only reflected human behavior but influenced her contemporaries' actions, ensnaring them in limiting and dehumanizing roles. She wanted to shatter the belief that archetypes are inflexible, that the familiar endings to stories are fixed, that the gender roles assigned to the sexes through the ages are inevitable. But unlike Rich, she would not give up on mythology. When Odysseus washes up on Circe's island in Atwood's twenty-four-poem sequence "Circe/Mud Poems" (1974), he is ready to relive the same story to which he has been bound for millennia. Atwood's Circe challenges him to break free of the myth that keeps them locked in a cycle of violence and abandonment, to envision an alternate life in which the two characters defy their ascribed roles. Through Circe, Atwood challenges mythology's failings, even while she embraces *The Odyssey*'s affirmation of Odysseus's choice of mortality over immortality. Ultimately, through her revisions Atwood upholds a principal theme of Homer's epic: the need for humans to rediscover the essence of their humanity.

When Margaret Atwood was young, she did not feel social or familial pressures restricting opportunities for her sex. Until 1950, when she turned eleven, Atwood spent six to seven months each year in the Canadian bush in northern Ontario and Quebec, where her father, an entomologist, did research. Her parents taught her to fish, camp, and survive in the wild, and she watched them share the jobs of cooking and cleaning. Her mother, Margaret Killam, came from a long tradition of strong-minded, educated women who defied convention by balancing family and career. Atwood was primarily homeschooled until she was eleven, when she began to attend school full-time. Her unconventional upbringing had a profound, lifelong effect on her. This outsider's perspective was critical in forming her ideas about gender and literary authority, as she was not raised to think that traditional roles or cultural conventions were natural.

Unlike Rich, Atwood did not have parents who treated her as a son because of her propensity for reading; unlike Plath, Atwood did not feel torn between being "a good girl" and being an intellectual. Atwood attributed much of her strength to her mother: "I've . . . concluded that life doled out to me the perfect mother, although being the perfect mother was, I suspect, never one of her goals . . . So when I think of my mother, I don't think of lipstick and feathers or the little woman or furniture polish or even five-course dinners" (quoted in Cooke 51). Atwood's father explained, "We didn't intentionally raise Peggy in any specific way. The marriage market just didn't make sense. Independence and freedom rate very high with us" (quoted in Sullivan 68). Her parents' attitudes rubbed off. Atwood declared, "I don't give a piss about generalized 'roles.' Never have. If I'd believed in 'roles,' espec. the ones being doled out in the 50's, I never would have been a writer. Would have been Betty Crocker instead" (quoted in Cooke 49).

Atwood's particular relationship to social roles meant that her approach to mythology would be quite different from that of her contemporaries who used it to lash out at patriarchal forms of oppression. She believed that mythic impulses shape our relationships with other humans, with animals, and with the earth. Linda Wagner-Martin writes that Atwood "wanted poetry to move beyond the personal and toward the 'unconscious mythologies' that motivate most human beings" (32). This concept of "unconscious mythologies that motivate most human beings" underlies all of her poetry and is particularly relevant in her approach to the Circe and Odysseus relationship.[1]

By demonstrating that myths not only record a particular culture's fears, desires, and values, but become so ingrained as to actually motivate the repetition of behaviors across cultures, Atwood hoped to move men and women beyond unconscious impulse. To address this effect of myth is to bring the subconscious patterns to the surface. Carl Jung's archetypes, reflections of the "collective unconscious," are the recurrent images from cultures the world over upon which myths are built. Archetypes are timeless. On the other hand, if myths encode and justify values or practices of a specific culture, they would need to adapt to reflect societal change. If they do not adapt, the culture is living by, or subconsciously re-enacting, a dead mythology. Changing a mythology's hold over a culture is certainly harder than just rewriting the stories, but Atwood believed that when writers expose the no-longer-viable representations of gender in the myths and challenge other humans to actively interrogate the mythologies by which they live, real change becomes possible.

While attending Victoria College at the University of Toronto, Atwood observed the growing academic interest in mythology in the critical work of Northrop Frye, Robert Graves, and Joseph Campbell. She had loved Greek mythology and fairy tales since her childhood and was eager to pursue her interest.[2] She studied the *Bible* under Frye, a star professor at Victoria who published *Anatomy of Criticism* (1957) while she was there. He wrote that the poet must resolve "the perennial technical problem of transmuting the substance of myth into the form of immediate experience" (43–44).[3] He was one of several influences on Atwood's study of myth, although she has said that he was not the primary source of inspiration. Other professors at Victoria College also engaged in myth studies, and Atwood's most beloved professor Jay Macpherson wrote a collection of poetry, *The Boatman* (1957), which taught her student how to parody myth in poetry.

Robert Graves was also an important model. Atwood read his work, *The White Goddess* (1946), which influenced the moon-goddess imagery in her poetry and fiction, although she disliked his idea that the female muse is destructive. Her first chapbook, *Double Persephone* (1961), is a series of seven poems dealing with Graves's double vision of the goddess: Persephone is seducer and destroyer, maiden and wife, daughter and extension of the mother goddess, Demeter. It did not take long, however, for Atwood to question the concept of the woman as a seducer and destroyer of men. She joked, "All this sounded a little strenuous, and appeared to rule out domestic bliss" (quoted in Sullivan 109). She continued to challenge and revise Graves's moon goddess imagery in her poetry and fiction.[4] From the "Snake Poems" of *Interlunar* to the Persephone of *The Robber Bride* to the triple-goddess of *Survival*, Atwood has continued to work throughout her career with goddess imagery.[5] Her myth-laden education has influenced virtually every piece of her writing.

Atwood's Victoria College English department hired female professors, and Atwood has said that she took for granted women who were "not only supporting themselves, but thinking" (quoted in Cooke 58). While in college, she focused her study on 19th-century women writers, reading the Bröntes, George Eliot, Jane Austen, and Emily Dickinson. It never occurred to her, she said later, that women were not supposed to write. The obstacle for Atwood was that she was Canadian, not that she was a woman. She remembers noticing that no Canadian writers were taught in her literature courses. Atwood thought that if she could overcome the "Canadian writer" challenge, she would be taken seriously. When she arrived at Harvard for graduate school in 1962, however, she was bombarded by a new set of cultural assumptions about literary authority.

At Harvard, there were no female professors in the English department, female students were not allowed to use the Lamont Library, which housed the modern poetry collection, and it was the first time, Atwood has said, that she connected people's shock at her desire to be a writer with her gender. She wrote, "I had no idea, for instance, that I was about to step into a whole set of precon-ceptions and social roles that had to do with what poets were like and how they should behave" (quoted in Sullivan 67). Atwood noted that in courses at Harvard, American women writers were often "treated as honorary men" (Sullivan 122). One of her only available models, she said, was "Suicidal Sylvia" (quoted in Cooke 231). In the 1950s and 1960s, poets produced a body of "confessional" poetry that dealt with rage, madness, revenge, and suicide. Atwood hoped to defy the notion that she would have to die or live in depression or rage, hiding her femininity, in order to be a great writer.

While Harvard offered a rude awakening for Atwood in terms of American ideas about women, it was also the place where she began to recognize the politi-cal potential in literature, and she determined to link that potential to existing mythologies. Because of her outsider's perspective, Atwood recognized a gendered power struggle even before second-wave feminism took hold in America. Once it had established itself, she wrote in a January 18, 1971 letter to her friend Margaret Laurence that the new movement comforted her: "It's really hard to go the way you know is . . . right for you and have everyone else (everyone else, not just men) think you're immoral or some kind of freak. What a relief to discover that there are those who think you may be right" (quoted in Sullivan 246). Atwood has said that she lives a life that exemplifies what the feminist movement strives for: "If feminism is deal-ing with women as independent entities, then I'm a feminist . . . What the hell, why not?" But in her 1976 essay "Paradoxes and Dilemmas: The Woman as Writer," she wrote, "no good writer wants to be merely a transmitter of someone else's ideology" (quoted in Rosenberg 148). Atwood may be better defined as a human rights activist in that she believes in feminism as a part of a larger struggle for equality and justice, as exemplified by her years of work with Amnesty International.

Even after the transformations of the 1960s, Atwood believed that relationships between men and women were still about power, domination, and submission. She had read her mythology and knew that women were usually the victims. This bored her. She wasn't interested in perpetuating those roles through her writing. Rather, she wanted to confront head-on the ways in which contemporary men and women were "acting out unconscious myths" (Sullivan 196). In her collection *Power Politics* (1971), written during the beginning of the dissolution of her marriage to James Polk, Atwood uses mythology to discuss individual and political motivations for human action; she draws a correlation between private battles and the violence of public conflicts. In a discussion of the book, she describes poetry as "a lens through which the human universe can see itself, an aural focusing through which human languages can hear themselves" (quoted in Sullivan 248). In her next collection, *You Are Happy*, she uses mythic poetry to show her readers how they are "acting out unconscious myths." As H.D. challenged the archetypal figures of the warrior Achilles and temptress Helen, Atwood explores the iconic, mythic types, Circe and Odysseus. Both writers believed that men and women first have to realize the impact myths have had in shaping gender identities and roles. Once they acknowledge the gravity of myth's impact on contemporary culture, they have to work together to break from the mythic constraints. This decision to rewrite the myths that underlie human action became explicit in Atwood's revision of the Circe and Odysseus relationship in *You Are Happy*.

The Origins of the Stereotypes

In Book 10 of Homer's *The Odyssey*, Odysseus and his men wash ashore on Aiaia, an island inhabited by Helios's daughter Circe. Thoroughly disoriented and exhausted, the crew spots smoke rising from a chimney in the distance. Wary of strangers after several disastrous encounters, Odysseus sends half of his crew to find out who lives in the house. What the men find dazzles and terrifies them. Outside of Circe's palace, Odysseus later recounts, were bewitched wolves and lions, and inside, the men could hear Circe "singing in her beautiful voice" (148). All of Odysseus's men but one, Eurylochus, enter the palace, and Circe drugs them "to make them lose all memory of their native land . . . And when they had emptied the bowls which she had handed them, she drove them with blows of a stick into the pigsties. Now they had pig's heads and bristles, and they grunted like pigs; but their minds were as human as they had been before" (149). Circe is called *polypharmakon* (powerful with many herbs and charms) and her magic powers are transformative. Justifiably terrified, Eurylochus escapes back to the ship to tell Odysseus what has happened. When the hero determines to confront Circe himself, he sets the stage for a transformative experience of his own.

Scholars from Karl Kerényi to Judith Yarnall have convincingly argued for Circe's beginnings in Great Goddess figures such as Cybele, Artemis, and Aphrodite. The "*Potnia theron*," the Mistress of wild animals, is remembered in Circe's throngs of tamed lions and wolves outside of her palace.[6] Unlike other human men who were often destroyed by their contact with the Great Goddess, Odysseus meets Circe's potential threat and evades danger. On his way to her palace, he encounters Hermes, who gives him the moly plant to "make [him] immune from evil" (150). Hermes warns Odysseus that when Circe strikes him with her stick, he must draw his sword

> and rush at her as though you mean to kill her. She will shrink from you in terror and invite you to her bed. You must not refuse the goddess's favors, if you want her to free your men and look after you. But make her swear a solemn oath by the blessed gods not to try any more of her tricks on you, or when she has you stripped naked she may rob you of your courage and your manhood. (150–151)

Circe is an archetypal threat to the hero; she has power literally to unman him, to make him inhuman.

When Circe realizes that Odysseus has not succumbed to her magic, however, the relationship shifts from one that is potentially dangerous and dehumanizing to one that ultimately allows the hero a return to humanity. Circe proclaims, "I am sure you are Odysseus, that resourceful man; the man whom the Giant-killer with the golden wand always told me to expect here on his way back from Troy in his swift black ship. But now put up your sword and come with me to my bed, so that in making love we may learn to trust one another" (151–152). From this point on, Circe's relationship with Odysseus is one of respect. She addresses him as "Heaven-born son of Laertes, resourceful Odysseus" and he calls her "Lady" and "goddess." In her book *Transformations of Circe*, Yarnall comments, "it is as if she has been waiting all along for her 'defeat' at the hands of Odysseus. What is actually defeated in their encounter, however, is the notion that one of them must have clear dominance over the other" (21). After Circe swears not to harm Odysseus, she is no longer witch-like, Marina Warner argues in her article "The Enchantments of Circe"; rather, "she takes the part of storyteller, a wise teacher, a sibyl" (3). As Odysseus has the power of logos, Circe's most significant gift is "her voice and its command of experience through language" (2). Her most common epithet is *audeessa* (human-voiced). In fact, Odysseus's men hear her singing before they see her. Atwood will draw on the power of Circe's voice in depicting the struggle between Circe and the hero.

Once Circe and Odysseus sleep together, she frees his men from their pig form. They live with her for one year until Odysseus's men, bewildered at their commander's lack of initiative, beg him to leave. Circe agrees not to keep him against his will and tells him he must travel to Hades to consult Tiresias. Odysseus learns in Hades that he will have to return to Aiaia to bury his comrade, Elpinor.

The arrival on Circe's island, departure to Hades, and subsequent return frames one of the most significant exchanges in the epic, between Odysseus and Achilles, who chose to die young and give up a long, happy life in exchange for *kleos,* everlasting glory. In Hades, Odysseus tells Achilles, "you are the most fortunate man that ever was or will be! For in the old days when you were on Earth, we Argives honored you as though you were a god; and now, down here, you have great power among the dead" (173). Achilles responds, "I would rather work the soil as a serf on hire to some landless impoverished peasant than be King of all these lifeless dead" (173). *The Odyssey*'s first word in the Greek is *andra* (man), which indicates immediately that Homer is dealing with a different kind of hero from the godlike Achilles in *The Iliad*; Achilles had struggled against his mortality. In the conversation in Hades, Odysseus learns the importance of his humanity. He even refuses the immortality offered to him by Calypso later in his journey. Unlike traditional Greek heroes, who are usually half mortal, half immortal, Odysseus is fully human.

When Homer first introduces Odysseus in Book V, he is with the nymph Calypso. She offers him immortality if he stays with her on her island. Her name, "I shall conceal," resembles one of Hades's epithets, "the invisible" or "the concealer," suggesting paradoxically that immortality is like death; it also emphasizes the necessity that Odysseus reject immortality. Calypso is, in essence, concealing Odysseus from the world. Just as Achilles's self-imposed isolation in *The Iliad* removes him from humanity, Odysseus is not himself until he can return home to those who make him a full man—king, husband, son, and father. If he were to choose immortality, it would mean remaining isolated, far from other men. Whereas *The Iliad* shows the hero's movement towards death, *The Odyssey* shows the hero's movement towards life.

Even the opening lines of Book V indicate how crucial it is that Odysseus rejects immortality: the book begins with an image of Eos, Dawn, having risen from the bed where she sleeps beside her lover Tithonus. Every other reference to "rosy-fingered dawn" leaves out mention of Tithonus, but he is included before the Calypso scene for a reason. He was Eos's mortal lover. She begged Zeus to grant him immortality, which he did. She forgot, however, to ask for eternal youth. Tithonus grows older and older and eventually withers away into a cicada. The temptation of immortality is dangerous for humans, and Odysseus must not succumb. In a similar vein, Atwood's Circe tells Odysseus to choose a finite but vital life outside of the story that has entrapped him.

In Homer, Odysseus's adventures represent a crucial psychological cleansing that washes off the savagery of war and allows the hero to return to civilization, to make a choice of life over death. After the sack of Troy, Odysseus and his men first come to the land of the Cicones, a peaceful people whom Odysseus's men rape and kill. Odysseus mentions this as a terrible act when he recounts his story at the court of Alcinous. The land of the Cicones is the last place he reaches in the known world before he is thrust out into the lands of the adventures, where he will need to reject barbarism and all that is uncivilized before he can successfully reintegrate into Ithacan society. Each adventure marks a departure in one way or another from what it is to be civilized. The Greeks believed in proper marriage, appropriate sacrifice, the cooking of meat, guest/host friendship (*xenia*), agriculture, and involvement in a community as the marks of a civilized people. Odysseus and his men encounter brothers who marry their sisters (Aeolus), sacrifice of immortal cattle (Isle of Hyperion), hosts who want to eat their guests (Cyclopes, Laestragonians), communities that do not practice agriculture (Aeolus, Cyclopes), hosts who want their guests to forget their homes and community (Lotus-Eaters, Circe), monsters who lure men to their deaths (Sirens).

Circe's involvement with Odysseus frames his descent into Hades, a journey that highlights Odysseus's liminal status as one not fully living. To the Greeks "living" would mean Odysseus's involvement in politics on Ithaca, connection to family as a husband, father, and son, and ability to tell his story and have people sing his praises. Ultimately Odysseus's physical journey is also a psychological one, and his adventures symbolize a shedding of the warrior mindset and a reintegration into humanity, into a Greek civilized society. When he meets Circe he is emotionally as well as physically lost and battered. She helps to set him back on the course toward his life, in every sense of the word, on Ithaca.

After the descent to Hades, Odysseus and his men return to Circe's island, where the goddess allows them to feast and drink. She and Odysseus talk of his experience in Hades, and she warns him about his imminent adventures including the Sirens, the wandering rocks, Scylla and Charybdis, and the cattle of Hyperion. Yarnall highlights a small but significant detail about this interaction:

> Her message is very much about the boundaries of heroism. When Odysseus wants to know how to fight off Scylla, she again teasingly addresses him as [obstinate fool] and asks if he must always engage in battle. All his bronze-sworded valor, she says, will be powerless against this immortal monster. The best course for him and his men will be to bend to the oars, flee. The exchange . . . beautifully illustrates the perspective, constant in Homer, against which the glory of heroism is seen. Her divine knowledge makes military prowess appear as a limited thing. (17)

Once Circe warns Odysseus of his potential future, she sends a "friendly escort of a favorable wind," and Odysseus and his men depart (Homer 183). She never indicates that she wants him to stay with her and fail to fulfill what she knows will happen; rather, she tells him what to expect as if she knows that there is no alternative to Odysseus's fated return to Ithaca. Odysseus will be a hero who lives a long, glorious life, but that life does not include her.

Over the centuries, Circe underwent numerous transformations as writers revised her character, stripping her of the complexity of Homer's goddess, and turning her into a stock figure of lovesick dejected female, vengeful slighted lover, or temptress whose goal is to seduce a hero away from his chosen path. The Roman poet Ovid tells three Circe tales in his *Metamorphoses*, written around the turn of the first millennium. The sketch in which Circe encounters Ulysses strays little from Homer's narrative, although it is highly simplified. The other stories suggest a jealous and bitter character. "No one," Ovid writes, "had a heart more susceptible to love than Circe" (311). But Ovid's Circe remains unrequited. When she finds her love for Glaucus slighted, "In her rage at finding her love rejected, she straightway ground together certain evil herbs, whose juices contained horrid powers" (312). As a result, Scylla, the object of Glaucus's affections, is transformed into a monster. In another story, Circe is gathering herbs on a mountainside when she falls in love with Picus. Alas, he loves Canens and refuses Circe, who, out of revenge, turns Picus into a bird and all of his comrades into wild beasts. Ovid's Circe embodies the dangerous vengeance of a woman's unrequited passion.

Ovid's categorization stuck with Circe throughout the ages. Virgil is uninterested in her and mentions only briefly in his *Aeneid* (written in the 20s B.C.E.) that unlike the weaker Odysseus, Aeneas is able to avoid the evil temptress entirely. When Renaissance writers revise her character, she is "no longer the self-sufficient goddess or the irresistible succubus reclining in her lair, she is merely a deviant but lovelorn female in need of masculine direction and control" (Yarnall 145). By the time she appears in Atwood's poems, Circe wavers between extremes. She is dominant and passive; architect of her own situation and victim of the whims of a sometimes tender, sometimes violent man. She orders him to leave and begs him to stay. Unable to live in these prescribed roles any longer, Atwood's Circe finally declares, enough! The question is whether her hero will agree.

If Circe could not transform Odysseus in *The Odyssey*, centuries of writers after Homer would. In fact, the character that Atwood's Circe encounters has changed so radically from his Homeric beginnings, has been battered about so thoroughly on the pages of literature that he washes to this modern Circe's shore barely recognizable. How did this happen? What had he become?

The classical playwrights Euripides and Sophocles exposed in Homer's champion the ruthless brutality of war heroes. Euripides's tragedy *The Trojan Women*, written in 415 B.C.E. during the Peloponnesian War, attests to the barbarism of war. His lead, Hecuba, bound to be Odysseus' slave, calls the Homeric hero:

> That loathsome, perfidious beast,
> That enemy of every right,
> A monster who knows no law:
> A twister with a double-tongue
> Who lies and breaks his promises
> And turns all friendship into hate. (470)

Euripides, whose plays often bemoan the horrors of war, wrote the play as Athens, already at war with Sparta, was about to launch a campaign against Sicily. What better way for the playwright to expose Athens's underbelly than to vilify one of its most beloved warriors?

Only six years later, in his tragedy *Philoctetes*, Sophocles used Odysseus to depict the moral failings of the physically powerful. In an archetypal battle of might versus right, Achilles's son, Neoptelemus, is torn between Odysseus and Philoctetes. Does he collude with Odysseus, despite his moral beliefs, to trick the wounded and abandoned Philoctetes into giving up Heracles's bow and joining the expedition at Troy? His conscience pulls him in another direction. Odysseus urges the young warrior to lie and deceive in order to be successful. When a perplexed Neoptholemus asks whether Odysseus thinks it wrong to lie, an unphased Odysseus simply reiterates that it is justified if the success of a mission depends upon it. Philoctetes calls Odysseus a "worthless creature, shrewd of tongue and cunning" and a "foul villain, making God's word a lie to shield [his] practices" (196–197). Instead of inspiring awe and delight in others for his cunning ability with language, the Classical Odysseus inspires contempt and despair.

In admiration for his forefathers, the Trojans, the Roman writer Virgil thrashes the Achaean warriors for the conniving way in which they sacked Troy. In Book II of *The Aeneid*, Virgil places Ulysses front and center in the Trojan Horse scheme—it was his idea. For this ruse, Ulysses is "unpitying" and "merciless" (51, 59). According to Virgil, Greeks were not to be trusted.

Dante, who did not read the Greek texts, models his Ulysses on Virgil's villainous liar in his *Inferno* (written in the early 1300s). In Canto XXVI, with Virgil as his guide, Dante finds Ulysses in the eighth circle of Hell with other frauds. Before they meet, Dante assures his readers that he is telling the truth about his next encounter, that he will "force / [His] art to make its genius more restrained / than is [his] usual bent, lest it should run / Where virtue doesn't" (ls. 21–24). Dante will not lie, will not be un-virtuous; he will not, in other words, be like Ulysses. Dante follows Virgil in blaming Ulysses for the conception of the Trojan Horse, but also invents a new side of the hero: the tireless wanderer who is willing to sacrifice family and friends in pursuit of experience. Dante's Ulysses speaks:

Not fondness for my son, nor any claim
Of reverence for my father, nor love I owed
Penelope, to please her, could overcome

My longing for experience of the world,
Of human vices and virtue. (ls. 91–95)

He and his men sail past the Pillars of Hercules, "beyond which men were not to sail" (l. 104). Dante illustrates Ulysses's recklessness as he urges his men onward despite the knowledge that they may die as a result: "You were not born to live as a mere brute does, / But for the pursuit of knowledge and the good (ls. 114–115). In fact, his urging leads them to their death, as a storm swells over their ship, and they drown.

In the nineteenth century, Alfred Lord Tennyson, clearly under Dante's influence, envisions an elderly Ulysses, in his poem of that name, who cannot be content with a family life on Ithaca. He is the antithesis of Homer's character, whose return home is his goal. Tennyson's Ulysses declares,

I cannot rest from travel: I will drink
Life to the lees: I am become a name;
For always roaming with a hungry heart
Much have I seen and known;
. . .
How dull it is to pause, to make an end,
To rust unburnish'd, not to shine in use!

And this gray spirit yearning in desire
To follow knowledge like a sinking star,
Beyond the utmost bound of human thought.
. . .
for my purpose holds
To sail beyond the sunset, and the baths
Of all the western stars, until I die.

Like Dante's Ulysses, Tennyson's hero is ready to abandon family and country for experience.

In his later incarnations, Homer's hero is transformed into a symbol, an archetype. He *is* the brutality and immorality of war; he *is* the wanderlust in every man. He is the quintessential adventurer/warrior. This is the shell of a hero who, in 1974, after centuries of transformations, washes, lost and battered, onto a fed-up Circe's shore.

"Escaped from these mythologies?": Heroic Transformations

Atwood's use of mythology in the sequence "Circe/Mud Poems" from her tenth book of poems *You Are Happy* (1974) is far less autobiographical than that of H.D., Plath, or Rich. She saw the Circe myth as highlighting subconscious forces in human nature and society that drive the ways in which men and women engage with one another. As in the meeting of Helen and Achilles in H.D.'s *Helen in Egypt*, in "Circe/Mud Poems," two archetypal figures meet—the love-lorn seductress and wandering warrior. Atwood wrote her sequence at a time when domestic violence was just beginning to be addressed as a social issue, and she was at the cutting edge of discussions in literature about this pervasive, culturally ingrained problem. The poetic sequence is a social commentary on the precarious line between dysfunction and "normal" practice in relationships.

Atwood's characters drag the entirety of their history with them into the sequence. It is critical therefore that Atwood never names the man whom Circe addresses. To Circe, he is "you," neither Odysseus nor Ulysses, but both. To name him would be to fix his character as one or the other; refusal to name allows for the spectrum of his attitudes and experiences. This composite character ultimately will have to choose which hero he wants to be. Can he make that return, that *nostos*, back to what he once was, to the potential that Circe, representative of women and progressive modern culture itself, acknowledges in him?

The ancient world offers many heroes, and it is worth asking why Atwood chose her character (as opposed to Achilles or Heracles, for example). To read her sequence as an attack on *The Odyssey* would miss her point and would indicate a misreading of Homer's epic. Homer's culture in Archaic Greece embodied many values that modern readers find immoral or difficult to accept, slavery and sub-ordination of women among them. While these differences from modern culture are significant, there is a compelling intricacy in Homer's character development and a playful joy at the human ability for emotional connection that intrigued Atwood. In her poem, she does not rail against Homer's Circe and Odysseus; indeed, she begs for a return to the complexity of these characters in light of what has happened to them since Homer. For this reason and for convenience's sake, I call her hero Odysseus, for that is the core character still present under all of the other layers. Even as Atwood dramatizes Circe's submission to the pre-established feminine role assigned to her by literature after Homer—that of a sexual object and abandoned woman—she constructs an untraditional plot. After playing her part in the dysfunctional relationship for most of the sequence, Circe suggests to Odysseus that they leave behind the current story and write themselves a new one that includes *The Odyssey*'s embrace of humanity in a way that incorporates equality for the couple.

In Atwood's sequence, Circe reflects in a non-linear way on the power struggle between her and Odysseus, his seeming passivity, her desire to "save" him, the psychological violence of the seduction, his eventual boredom and desire to leave, and her plea that he break out of his story. Through most of the sequence, she is caught up in the courtship, at once aware of the destructiveness and perversity of her relationship and yet incapable of extricating herself. Like Homer's Circe, Atwood's heroine tries to teach Odysseus the boundaries of heroism and the limits of military prowess. She will challenge him to shed the role of the questing hero. Whereas it was essential for Homer's hero to overcome obstacles preventing his return home, a feat that Circe helped him achieve, this Circe attests to the perils of Odysseus's mythic journey, urging him to forego departure for a life with her.

This variation can be disconcerting for anyone familiar with *The Odyssey*. In Homer's text, the desire to return to Penelope drives Odysseus, and his rejection of immortality stems, in large part, from his longing for his wife. This backdrop would make Atwood's Circe the "other woman" who asks Odysseus to abandon his marriage, and her frustrations at his inability to commit to her would seem petty compared to his devotion to his wife. Atwood has something else in mind. She recasts Penelope as a lure for Odysseus that keeps him locked into his mythic story. Penelope is, therefore, dangerous to his growth as a man. Circe mentions Odysseus's "other woman" only once in the sequence in poem twenty:

> When you look at nothing
> what are you looking at?
> Whose face floats on the water
> dissolving like a paper plate?
>
> It's the first one, remember,
> the one you thought you abandoned
> along with the furniture.
>
> You returned to her after the other war
> and look what happened.
> Now you are wondering
> whether to do it again.
>
> Meanwhile she sits in her chair
> waxing and waning
> like an inner tube or a mother,
> breathing out, breathing in,
>
> surrounded by bowls, bowls, bowls,
> tributes from the suitors
> who are having a good time in the kitchen

waiting for her to decide
on the dialogue for this evening
which will be in perfect taste
and will include tea and sex
dispensed graciously both at once.

She's up to something, she's weaving
histories, they are never right,
she has to do them over,
she is weaving her version,

the one you will believe in,
the only one you will hear. (65)

Initially, Circe can only think of Penelope as an "it": "*It*'s the first one," a paper plate, an inner tube. Circe neither names Penelope nor calls her Odysseus's wife. She, like Circe, is a woman whom Odysseus abandoned. It is essential to his story that he did so. But his previous return to her was not a fairytale ending: he left her again, and now contemplates another return that Circe knows will not be permanent. Circe establishes his relationship with this "other woman" as part of his cyclical story. When Circe compares Penelope to an inner tube, she at once dehumanizes her and makes her the necessary prop to sustain a shipwrecked sailor, as Odysseus's memories of Penelope sustain him in *The Odyssey*. Circe's Penelope is not as virtuous as Homer's. She graciously dispenses tea and sex to her suitors.

As a woman trying to urge Odysseus out of his story, Circe is interested in Penelope's weaving and aware of it as a competing story that may tempt Odysseus back to his wife. If Penelope's story is "the only one [Odysseus] will hear," he will reject Circe's plea that he stay with her. She knows that in "the story" Odysseus will leave her, will return to his wife, will leave again to fight in another war, will, essentially live a life of thoughtless, cyclical violence. For this reason, while Penelope is a powerful draw, and, Circe admits, a complex and provocative character, she is, nevertheless, a part of "the story" that only perpetuates Odysseus's fulfillment of his myth.

Atwood's Circe conflates the mythic figure from Homer's *Odyssey* and her later incarnations with a modern speaker, suggesting the contemporary enactment of ancient patterns. In the first poem of the sequence, Circe sets the scene. Here is what Odysseus finds, she states squarely, when he lands on her "dry shore":

Through this forest
burned and sparse, the tines
of blunted trunks, charred branches
this forest of spines, antlers (46)

What has happened to Circe's island, to the fertile forests teeming with life? Myth happened. Her island becomes synonymous with culture itself. The reenactment of myth (for Circe, the story she has lived so many times that she can now recite it forwards and backwards) has destroyed it.[7] This Circe is larger than Homer's character or any one of her other manifestations in literature. We learn that Odysseus and his men have been to her island before, have used up its resources, left, returned again. They are apparently unaware that they are caught in the vicious story that binds them to perpetually repeat their actions. Circe, on the other hand, knows it and wants to end the cycle.

Like Atwood's Odysseus, Circe is a composite character with knowledge of creatures from other cultures' mythologies and of modern technology:

Men with the heads of eagles
no longer interest me
or pig-men, or those who can fly
with the aid of wax and feathers

or those who take off their clothes
to reveal other clothes
or those with skins of blue leather

or those golden and flat as a coat of arms
or those with claws, the stuffed ones
with glass eyes; or those
hierarchic as greaves and steam engines.

All these I could create, manufacture,
or find easily: they swoop and thunder
around this island, common as flies,
sparks flashing, bumping into each other,

on hot days you can watch them
as they melt, come apart,
fall into the ocean
like sick gulls, dethronements, plane crashes.
I search instead for the others,
the ones left over,
the ones who have escaped from these
mythologies with barely their lives;
they have real faces and hands, they think of themselves as
wrong somehow (47)

Atwood's speaker places a value judgment on mythology—it is at once boring and dangerous. Something is happening to these mythic men, though. They are falling apart. The stories can no longer sustain them. At the same time that "these mythologies" seem unreal and manufactured, they hold such power that they can threaten lives and make "real" people feel "wrong." Circe seeks to establish a community of people who have rejected the stories of what men should be and who have chosen instead to be "real."

Odysseus and his men attack these "real" people, whom Circe mentions briefly in poem four as "the silent ones." She identifies Odysseus as a colonizer-type who, with his men, has "assaulted daily, with shovels, axes, electric saws, the silent ones, the ones they accused of being silent because they would not speak in the received language" (49). On her island, the "received language" is myth. Odysseus and his men have stripped her island bare, have, in other words, killed what was real and alive. While in traditional stories about Circe, she turns men to swine, Atwood's Circe swears,

> it was not my fault, these animals
> who once were lovers
>
> it was not my fault, the snouts
> and hooves, the tongues (48)

She calls the pig-men who can no longer speak "wrecked words." In these lines, Atwood alters the traditional stories about Circe and posits that the men are responsible for their own transformation because they succumbed to the dehumanizing power of myth. She also contrasts "real" language with the language of myth. Circe spends her days "with [her] head pressed to the earth . . . collecting the few muted syllables left over" (49). The men who gave themselves over to their inhumanity, who have been dehumanized because of their involvement with "the story," have suffered the ultimate loss, the inability to formulate language, as their comparison to "wrecked words" indicates. Now, however, these men are "clamouring suppliants" who "come from all over to consult [her], bringing their limbs which have unaccountably fallen off, they don't know why . . . They offer [her] their pain, hoping in return for a word, a word" (49). Without even understanding it, they are begging for a language that will allow them to heal themselves from the sickness that is literally destroying them.

Circe's request that Odysseus reject entrapment in the existing mythology also involves a power struggle over language. She succinctly demonstrates this point in a couplet that follows her description of the suppliant males: "Come away with me, he said, we will live on a desert island. / I said, I am a desert island. It was not what he had in mind" (49). "He" is Odysseus, introduced here as one who operates in clichés. How romantic it seems to offer to sweep a woman away to a place where the couple will be alone in their love! I *am* that very place, Circe tells him; you are there already. The hero clearly wants to avoid the truth of what he already has and prefers to live in a world of fantasy. Atwood's project in "Circe/Mud Poems" is to expose and subvert the tendency to believe in romantic delusion rather than reality. In the opening poem of the sequence, as Odysseus approaches her island, Circe says, "You move within range of my words / you land on the dry shore / You find what there is" (46). Circe's claim of lack of responsibility ("I made no choice / I decided nothing") is suspect, however, as she participates in and enacts the cultural script assigned to her (50). She at once mocks romantic clichés and is complicit in seeking them out.

Like all of the women in this study, Atwood revises a foundational myth from a female character's perspective and asks her readers to question their previous understandings of myth, gender, and language; like H.D., Atwood is not so reductive as to imply that everything male is evil and everything female is good. Her Circe is more complex. She derives pleasure from giving to a man who reciprocates little. In this masochistic relationship, she is willfully passive. She feels a perverse pleasure in abdicating her power to Odysseus. She tells him:

> There are so many things I want
> you to have. This is mine, this
> tree, I give you its name,
>
> here is food, white like roots, red,
> growing in the marsh, on the shore,
> I pronounce these names for you also.
>
> This is mine, this island, you can have
> the rocks, the plants
> that spread themselves flat over
> the thin soil, I renounce them.
>
> You can have this water,
> this flesh, I abdicate,
>
> I watch you, you claim
> without noticing it,
> you know how to take. (54)

She gives him her powers, her words. As Circe's powers were rendered impotent by Odysseus's moly plant in *The Odyssey*, so in "Circe/Mud Poems," Circe initially renounces the source of her strength: language. Atwood's character illustrates how self-destructive women can be in their relationships with men. Atwood uses the myth to highlight this culturally ingrained behavior: although Circe wants to free herself, she remains bound by the social formations of man as aggressor/subject and woman as victim/object.

The sequence is a meditation on the hold of the classical tradition and the power that it gives and takes. Atwood's outsider position in cultural and academic circles influenced her attack on the myths that motivate the behaviors that she saw as unnatural and unhealthy. Adrienne Rich stopped revising mythology in her poetry because she feared that even an insistence that the tradition is fundamentally flawed still shores up its continued power and influence; Atwood, on the other hand, chose to engage directly with human belief in the function of myth. She recognized that to enact real social change and to make her poetry politically relevant, she would need to make people believe that ancient archetypes do not have to function in a modern world, that the story can be altered, that the ending with which they are familiar is not inevitable.

Circe confronts Odysseus's inability to commit to her by telling him that she is tired of him living out the myth that has developed around him without challenging it. She asks him:

> Don't you get tired of killing
> those whose deaths have been predicted
> and are therefore dead already?
>
> Don't you get tired of wanting
> to live forever?
>
> Don't you get tired of saying Onward? (51)

She urges him not to accept this cyclical, never-ending life in myth. Like Homer's Circe, she directs the lost hero, attempting to act as a psychological guide who teaches the limits of the warrior/wanderer lifestyle. In *The Odyssey*, Odysseus and his men weep every time they hear that they will have to continue their adventure and prolong their return home. In contrast, Atwood's hero embodies the careless wanderlust of Dante's and Tennyson's Ulysses. In Homer, Odysseus recounts his interactions with Circe at the court of Alcinous. He introduces her in the past tense as someone he has already left behind. This gives Odysseus the power to define her as he wishes. In Atwood's poem, although he seems to have agency and control, the male hero merely fulfills the myth that others have written. Meanwhile, Circe reflects on the roles they play and tries to "escape from" the mythology by urging Odysseus to exist with her in the present and a yet-undefined future.

Atwood extends her argument regarding the difficulty of breaking with tradition to the difficulty her speaker has extricating herself from a threatening but intoxicating relationship. She connects fulfillment of mythic patterns with gendered violence. At the moment that Odysseus lands, he begins to exploit Circe's power. She says:

One day you simply appeared in your stupid boat,
your killer's hands, your disjointed body, jagged
as a shipwreck,
skinny-ribbed, blue-eyed, scorched, thirsty, the usual,
pretending to be—what? a survivor?

Those who say they want nothing
want everything.
It was not this greed
that offended me,
it was the lies.

Nevertheless I gave you
the food you demanded for the journey
you said you had planned;
but you planned no journey
and we both knew it.

You've forgotten that,
you made the right decision.
The trees bend in the wind, you eat, you rest,
you think of nothing,
your mind, you say,
is like your hands, vacant:

vacant is not innocent. (50)

Like many of Atwood's potentially dangerous male characters, Odysseus has an innocuous façade.[8] His acceptance of Circe's submission is not simply a passive action. He has his "boot on the boat prow / to hold the wooden body / under" (51). This vivid image of gendered violence recalls Plath's "boot in the face" from her poem "Daddy." There is another similarity between Plath's speaker and Circe: "Every woman adores a Fascist" (Plath). In Atwood's poem, Circe could be any woman who gives everything to a man while knowing that he neither appreciates nor reciprocates her generosity. She asks,

If I allow you what you say
you want, even the day after

this, will you hurt me?
If you do I will fear you,
If you don't I will despise you

To be feared, to be despised,
These are your choices. (53)

The image of the boot holding down the wooden body becomes Odysseus holding down Circe's body:

> Holding my arms down
> holding my head down by the hair
>
> mouth gouging my face
> and neck, fingers groping into my flesh
> [. . .]
>
> If I stopped believing you
> this would be hate. (55)

The violence of the sexual act that initially sounds like a rape becomes the thread that ties Circe to Odysseus. Her love is that of one complicit in her own suffering. Atwood presents the woman who plays the victim role. There is something insidious about Circe's pleasure in giving herself up to this man.

It was only in the late 1960s and early 1970s that the shroud of secrecy surrounding domestic and gendered violence lifted as the Women's Liberation Movement began to discuss publicly as a critical social issue what had previously been seen as a "private" affair.[9] It grew into a battered women's movement that, in conjunction with the newly-emerging anti-rape movement, urged women not to feel shame or responsibility for the abuse. Until then, many abused women believed that it was their wifely duty to endure and excuse the violence, a pattern that Atwood's Circe follows. The first national domestic violence organization, Women's Aid, was founded in 1974, the same year that Atwood published *You Are Happy*. It was not until the late 1970s and 1980s that the criminal and civil legal systems began to enact legislation to protect women. Atwood was one of the first poets to write about this newly exposed issue and to link gendered violence to the entire culture's ideas of appropriate gender behaviors in relationships, ideas that can be traced back to some of Western culture's defining myths.

During her violent encounter with Odysseus, Circe describes a shrunken fist that she wears around her neck, evidently a symbol of her magic power. A clenched fist also signifies a woman's power to fight back against her aggressor. It is a clear allusion to the fist inside the biological female symbol, an emblem of the Woman's Liberation Movement. But in front of Odysseus, "the fist stutters, gives up, / you are not visible / You unbuckle the fingers of the fist, / you order me to trust you" (57). He destroys Circe's means of self-defense. These "love" scenes are reminiscent of H.D.'s *Helen in Egypt*, in which the moment of violent anger (Achilles seizing Helen's throat) is the moment of the sexual act. As H.D.'s Achilles needs to abandon "The Iron Ring" and "The Command," patriarchal forces of killing and destruction, in order to become the "New Mortal," Circe will eventually ask

Odysseus to choose a life different from the one offered by the perpetual quest, so that both of them can break out of the violent cycle in which they are trapped.

Circe clarifies the implications of Odysseus's arrival into her world as she recounts a story that she once heard from another traveler:

> When he was young he and another boy constructed a woman out of mud. She began at the neck and ended at the knees and elbows: they stuck to the essentials. Every sunny day they would row across to the island where she lived, in the afternoon when the sun had warmed her, and make love to her, sinking with ecstasy into her soft moist belly, her brown wormy flesh where small weeds had already rooted . . . Afterwards they would repair her, making her hips more spacious, enlarging her breasts with their shining stone nipples.
>
> His love for her was perfect, he could say anything to her, into her he spilled his entire life. She was swept away in a sudden flood. He said no woman since then has equaled her.
>
> Is this what you would like me to be, this mud woman? Is this what I would like to be? It would be so simple. (61)

Here, man literally turns land into woman. In a tradition that runs from Pygmalion to Henry Higgins, these boys shape their perfect woman to suit their own purposes. Her headlessness is crucial: she can't talk back. When Circe asks Odysseus if he would want her to be one of these "invented" women, one who does only as her lover/creator desires, she realizes that it would be easier perhaps than to be a thinking woman, one with a head on her shoulders. This is not Homer's Odysseus who loves Penelope for her cleverness, who tells Nausicaa, "there is nothing better or finer than when two people of one heart *and mind* keep house as man and wife," who sleeps with Circe so that they "may learn to trust one another" (90, 152, emphasis added). Atwood's Odysseus has lost the tenderness and respect that Homer's character embodied. Circe is no mud woman, and she resents Odysseus's distance and ambivalence.

Women are not the only victims of patriarchy, however. Odysseus, too, has been dehumanized. Circe says,

> You stand at the door
> bright as an icon,
> dressed in your thorax,
> the forms of the indented
> ribs and soft belly underneath
> carved into the slick bronze
> so that it fits you almost
> like a real skin

You are impervious
with hope, it hardens you,
this joy, this expectation, gleams
in your hands like axes (53)

Circe's similes brilliantly depict what Odysseus has become. An icon is a counter-feit likeness to a real thing; it can also be an object of worship or admiration. The dual meaning here implies that Odysseus, as his character in Tennyson brags, has become a name. The stories about him and the acclaim that he has received for his ventures have eclipsed the man to the point that he is only a counterfeit of a human. In his armor, he is an insect with a "slick bronze" exoskeleton. His hope and joy have the violent potential to destroy Circe. While Circe does not liter-ally turn him into an animal, her words illuminate the gruesome transformation that has already happened because of the hero's unthinking joy at his fulfillment of his own myth.

Atwood recognizes the potential transformations into mud woman and insect (or pig) warrior that women and men can undergo if they allow themselves to be persuaded by the mythological structures that underpin modern culture. Her characters' (and modern men's and women's) transformations are not inevitable, however. Alicia Ostriker has argued that Circe

> is transformed in Margaret Atwood's "Circe/Mud Poems" into an angry but also quite powerless woman . . . Circe is "a desert island" or "a woman of mud" made for sexual exploitation, and her encounters with Odysseus are war games of rape, indifference, and betrayal, which she can analyze caustically, mounting a shrewd critique of the heroic ethos . . . But this is a passive, not active, resistance and cannot alter Odysseus' intentions. (222)

Her often-cited argument misses the critical point of Atwood's choice of mythic characters. Odysseus, more than any other character from Greco-Roman mythol-ogy, *will* be inclined to follow Circe onto her second island; and despite the strip-ping away that has happened to her over the centuries, Circe is no mud woman. By the last several poems of the sequence, Circe defies her categorization as a desert island and pulls away from her cyclical mythic role. Circe actively changes what she previously had been:

Now it is winter.
By winter I mean: white, silent,
hard, you didn't expect that,

it isn't supposed to occur
on this kind of island,
and it never has before (67)

In her self-imposed transformation, Circe claims her power to determine her own destiny, and in her council to Odysseus that he follow her out of the story, she reclaims her role as sibyl, as wise advisor to the lost and confused hero.

Circe looks in on the myth that has developed around them and, from a distance usually unavailable to a literary character, she confesses, "I worry about the future. In the story the boat disappears one day over the horizon, just disappears, and it doesn't say what happens then. On the island that is . . . Am I really immortal, does the sun care, when you leave will you give me back the words? Don't evade, don't pretend you won't leave after all: you leave in the story and the story is ruthless" (68). As Circe recognizes, the current story is "ruthless"; but what if the lovers could write themselves into a new story? The power struggle within the relationship parallels Atwood's struggle with larger issues of tradition and mythology. Circe acknowledges the power of the myth and worries that she will be hurt by its "ruthless" strength. Even so, she urges her lover not to shun an emotional relationship with her and tells him to break out of the traditional myth about them. In so doing, she challenges modern culture to reject the fixedness of archetypal characters and patterns and to revise ancient models to suit current cultural needs.

Throughout the sequence, Circe's impulse has been to reject the current myth for another one. As in H.D.'s *Helen in Egypt*, the sequence posits that multiple stories are possible and can co-exist:

> *There are two islands*
> *at least, they do not exclude each other*
>
> *On the first I am right,*
> *the events run themselves through*
> *almost without us,*
>
> *we are open, we are closed,*
> *we express joy, we proceed*
> *as usual, we watch for*
> *omens, we are sad*
>
> *and so forth, it is over,*
> *I am right, it starts again,*
> *jerkier this time and faster,*
>
> *I could say it without looking, the animals,*
> *the blackened trees, the arrivals,*
>
> *the bodies, words, it goes and goes,*
> *I could recite it backwards.* (69, original italics)

This mythology has developed around them. They can play it by rote. In it, each of them fulfills the roles prescribed to them: she gives, he takes; she gets hurt, he is ruthless. The alternative life is not as clearly defined, but Circe constructs the possibility for change. Odysseus only needs to accept it.

While Circe knows that an alternative story can be better than the current one, she does not pretend to know what it will entail. She and Odysseus will write it together:

> *The second I know nothing about*
> *because it has never happened;*
>
> *this land is not finished,*
> *this body is not reversible.*
>
> *We walk through a field, it is November,*
>
> *the grass is yellow, tinged*
> *with gray, the apples*
>
> *are still on the trees,*
> *they are orange, astonishing, we are standing*
>
> *in a clump of weeds near the dead elms*
> *our faces upturned, the wet flakes*
> *falling onto our skin and melting*
>
> *We lick the melted snow from each other's mouths,*
> *we see birds, four of them, they are gone, and*
>
> *a stream, not frozen yet, in the mud*
> *beside it the track of a deer.* (69–70, original italics)

Atwood allows that the traditional myths exist and cannot be ignored because they have played such a crucial role in dictating how men and women interact. At the same time, she alters them through her identification with Circe. The new story is not stagnant; it melts and cleanses and promises hope. Circe had initially abdicated the power of her words to Odysseus and worried in the previous poem whether he would give them back when he leaves her. But she did not lose them, as we see here. She takes them with her to the second island, regains the power of her voice, and creates a beautiful and fresh poetry. Circe has been known as a seer. Here she knows nothing about what the future holds. The four birds that once may have been interpreted as an omen now simply leave the scene without Circe attempting to read anything into their flight. The mud, like the birds, does not mean anything more than what it is. It is not anthropomorphized. It is not there for men to exploit. On the second island, it is freed from its mythic association with a woman's body.

Atwood's final image of "the track of a deer" marks the return to the moment in Homer before the couple's encounter and before any of the action unfolds that will set into motion the relationship between them. When Odysseus arrives on Circe's island in *The Odyssey*, his first action is to kill a stag to feed his men. The deer on Circe's second island is alive. Odysseus has not yet killed it, which indicates that none of the action in the mythic stories has happened yet. The couple has the opportunity to start fresh. The deer image also refers to the title poem in the first section of *You Are Happy* in which the speaker and her lover find, along their walk through snow, "In the ditch a deer / carcass, no head" (28). The live deer on Circe's second island is perhaps a symbol of the choice that Odysseus will make for life with her instead of a repetition that is synonymous with death-in-life. This is similar to Odysseus's choice in *The Odyssey* to embrace his humanity. Atwood's Circe does not make men inhuman; rather, she tries to make Odysseus *more* human.

For a Greek Odysseus, to be alive meant to be a part of a community where he is recognized for his connections to others (as father, son, king, husband). He could not choose an immortal life with Calypso, for he would have been kept from fulfilling what, in his culture, it meant to be human. Although our modern Circe asks Odysseus to live with her on her second island, her request is unlike Calypso's. The modern conception of what it is to be human, though so different from the Archaic ideal from *The Odyssey*, still encourages the shedding of the warrior mindset for a reintegration into humanity. Perhaps leaving behind those centuries of wandering will be Odysseus's final challenge. Circe has retained her power of transformation—it is here the power to change the story and transform the "stuck" hero into a man. She hopes that he will choose with her to abandon the immortal story preserved in myth. Odysseus will have to overcome the siren song of the mythic life and remember who he was in his first conception—a man willing to give up immortality and embrace humanity.

The "Circe/Mud Poems" sequence illustrates Atwood's attempt to transcend the static, damaging aspects of myth for a new mythology that is viable in the contemporary world. She dismantles the old mythic ideal by exposing what has, for thousands of years, been conceived as "normal" behavior. As she undermines the archetypal, eternal quality of mythology, she challenges her readers to reconstruct the existing mythologies so that there is no victim, no warrior, and no set gender roles. Circe does not pretend to know what the new stories will entail, but suggests that they can exist, somewhere, on that second island, and are waiting to be written. Atwood's readers, like Odysseus, need only accept that possibility of moving forward into the un-written future.

The True Story in the Book of Myths: Atwood's Dive into Rich's Wreck

In "Circe/Mud Poems" Atwood chose a potentially dangerous female model, not to destroy the hero, but to help him to create a better story with her. Critics such as Frank Davey have claimed that she deconstructs and transcends *The Odyssey* and that she disrupts and discredits the story. As Hilda Hollis has argued, however, Atwood's texts are not fully in line with deconstruction or postmodern irony: "Atwood's stance differs from some postmodern theorists in her insistence on the possibility of *bearing witness*. She deconstructs oppressive structures of power, but stops short of undermining *all* positions" (117, original italics). Rather than completely reject or discredit Homer's epic, Atwood takes from it the vital theme of the choice to live as rich and fully human a life as possible. For Atwood's contemporaries, this choice means first acknowledging that "unconscious mythologies" have driven our actions and choices and then rewriting them in order that cultural change can occur.

In 1972 Adrienne Rich wrote her famous poem "Diving into the Wreck" to investigate the damage done to men and women who had sought to find themselves in "the book of myths." Her speaker begins,

> First having read the book of myths,
> and loaded the camera,
> and checked the edge of the knife-blade,
> I put on
> the body-armor of black rubber
> the absurd flippers
> the grave and awkward mask.

She later declares her purpose:

> I came to explore the wreck.
> The words are purposes.
> The words are maps.
> I came to see the damage that was done
> and the treasures that prevail.
> [...]
> the wreck and not the story of the wreck
> the thing itself and not the myth

She concludes:

> We are, I am, you are
> by cowardice or courage

the one who find our way
back to this scene
carrying a knife, a camera
a book of myths
in which
our names do not appear. (22–24)

After finding "the thing itself and not the myth," Rich's speaker realizes that she has read "a book of myths / in which / our names do not appear." She finds the "real" thing, not the story of it, as if, beyond the false myths, there were a definitive truth available for those who search for it.

Almost ten years later in 1981, Atwood wrote what seems like a response to "Diving Into The Wreck" in her collection's title poem, "True Stories":

Don't ask for the true story;
why do you need it?

It's not what I set out with
or what I carry.

What I'm sailing with,
a knife, blue fire,

luck, a few good words
that still work, and the tide. (9)

In the poem's final section the speaker says:

The story lies
among other stories,

a mess of colors, like jumbled clothing
thrown off or away,

like hearts on marble, like syllables, like
butchers' discards.

The true story is vicious
and multiple and untrue
after all. Why do you
need it? Don't ever

ask for the true story. (11)

In her 1983 interview with Jan Garden Castro, Atwood explains, "nobody can claim to have the absolute, whole, objective, total, complete truth. The truth is composite, and that's a cheering thought. It mitigates tendencies toward autocracy" (232). The difference between the two poems is representative of the different ways in which the two second-wave poets dealt with mythology. Rich decided that it is a literature of lies and omissions and stopped using classical allusion entirely; Atwood declared that it contains truths and falsehoods, some to be embraced, some to be cast aside, but that ultimately, the "good words . . . still work."

CHAPTER FIVE

Eavan Boland's Aging Earth Mother

Theories of Myth and Aging

From W.B. Yeats's Kathleen Ni Houlihan to Seamus Heaney's Bog Queen, the poetic trope of land as woman pervades Irish literature. In traditional male poetry, the earth as an old hag, such as the Cailleach Beare, who turns into a young queen leaves no room for a woman's natural aging process. Since the feminist movement took effect in Ireland in the 1970s, women poets have questioned the images of woman as a cyclically barren and fertile mother earth that are so pervasive in Irish poetry and legend. When Adrienne Rich wrote of "a book of myths in which our names do not appear" in "Diving Into the Wreck," she highlighted the dearth of representations of "real" women in mythology. Using the Demeter and Persephone myth to undergird each poem in her subsequent collection, *Dream of a Common Language,* Rich set out to inscribe her own name and those of other women, calling for "a whole new poetry" based on feminine eros that would break the hold of Tradition. While Boland writes in *Object Lessons* (1995) about the profound influence Rich had on her understanding of her own position as a woman poet, she rejects Rich's "separatist thinking," which, she explains, "is a persuasive and dangerous influence on any woman poet writing today. It tempts her to disregard the whole poetic past as patriarchal betrayal. It pleads with her to disregard the complexities of true feeling for the relative simplicity of anger" (244–245). In the 1990s Boland chose instead to work from within the poetic and mythic traditions even while she sought to revise the representations of women as renewable creatures. In her collections *In a Time of Violence* (1994) and *The Lost Land* (1998), Boland reworks, not only the Mother Ireland motif, but another myth of cyclical renewal—that of the Greco-Roman grain goddess and mother, Ceres (or Demeter), and her daughter, Persephone.[1] It is not until her most recent volume, *Domestic Violence* (2007), that she seems to sympathize more with Rich's break with Tradition.

Boland's dismissal of Rich's anger as simplistic speaks to a fundamental shift in the poetic use of myth in the 1990s and 2000s. Revisionist mythmaking at the turn of the millennium often lacks the anger of the earlier revisionist movement. Boland, who is familiar enough with the revisionist tradition to reference Alicia Ostriker's book *Stealing the Language* in her memoir *Object Lessons*, joins other mythmakers through her appropriation of the Ceres/Persephone myth. The myth has been a particularly popular subject for mythic revision among contemporary women poets because of its range of potential meanings.[2] Several studies on the enduring importance of the Ceres myth were published in the 1990s-2000s when Boland was writing her own Ceres poems.[3] Particularly relevant to Boland's use of the myth were Jungian feminist studies, such as those by Christine Downing and Kathie Carlson, which describe the archetypal qualities of the mythic mother and daughter and urge women to relate to and enter the myth themselves.

Eavan Boland's revisionist mythmaking coincides with literary gerontology, a theoretical methodology, which grew in popularity during the 1980s and 1990s, that studies age and aging in literature.[4] Literary gerontologists argue that while feminist theorists have studied representations of race, gender, and class in literature, they often have overlooked the category of age as a marker of difference and oppression.[5] Young feminists of the early second-wave movement were rebelling against the older generation and could hardly imagine including its members in their ranks. The feminist movement largely ignored the subject until the 1980s, when many aging second-wave feminists began to write about cultural and literary representations of age and aging, which include decrepitude and loss of physical and mental ability. In the conclusion of *Age Matters: Realigning Feminist Thinking* (2006), Martha Holstein calls women to action: "The time is ripe for both feminists and gerontologists to affirm the materiality of the body" to "confront the rhetoric of agelessness and eternal youth" (326, 328). Eavan Boland, who has written about the tremendous impact that the American feminist movement has had on her, confronts the age-old rhetoric head-on.[6]

Like many of her contemporaries, Boland recognizes the archetypal qualities in the Ceres myth as they relate to her own roles as daughter and mother. She incorporates two feminist theoretical strands, revisionist mythmaking and studies of aging, into her revision of the Ceres myth to frame her questions about the place of aging women in literature and mythology that she had grappled with for several decades.

"What great art removes": Ephemeral and Fixed Bodies

Boland's interest in the Ceres myth grew from her awareness of the absence of aging women in poetry and mythology. Several poems from her first collection, *New Territory* (1967), address concerns that Boland would wrestle with throughout her career, such as the need to avoid poetic conventions that fix women into undying images. In the poem "From the Painting *Back From Market* by Chardin," the speaker questions the effect of great art: "I think of what great art removes: / Hazard and death. The future and the past" (*OLW* 18). Fifteen years later in "Domestic Interior" from *Night Feed* (1982) Boland depicts a painting of a bride who

> will stay
> burnished, fertile,
> on her wedding day,
> interred in her joy. (*OLW* 150)[7]

One could argue that Boland iterates a problem common to all art that imposes stasis on the world of time; however, though Chardin may portray women and their sphere in a positive light, Boland wants women to tell their own stories. She believes that the fixed images conceal women's involvement in the domestic life of "jugs and kettles" and "a sleeping child," and fail to include real, aging women. In fact, "Back From Market" seems to depict the domestic life that Boland suggests is missing—Chardin's woman leans to place breads on a table, while her other hand holds a market bag with chickens. On the table and floor are bottles and a jug. Indeed, Chardin has often been praised for his reverence of the women he paints and the beauty he finds in the domestic sphere. Boland would argue, however, that this idealized image of domestic life omits the hardships and toils of everyday women. According to Boland, the women in traditional art and poetry serve the purposes of their male creators; the real women of history or the real women behind the art objects are never seen. She wants to see women depicting *themselves* in poetry. She posits that even as objects in their own poems, women are also subjects, thinking and acting *inside* of the poems. Boland proposes a new poetic space for women—"a magnetic field where the created returns as creator" (*OL* 217).

Ireland's traditional songs and canonical poems simply cover up the wounds and crimes of the past, which, Boland argues, include the marginalization and subjugation of women. In 'Mise Éire,' from *The Journey* (1987), the speaker declares that

> the songs
> . . . bandage up the history,
> the words
> . . . make a rhythm of the crime. (*OLW* 156)

Rather than entirely reject the images, forms, and language of the tradition, Boland chooses to work within the tradition to challenge conventional portrayals of women. She acknowledges the command of language in many poems written by men and explains that as a poet she still finds them "beautiful and persuasive" (*OL* 236). As a young poet, she thought these poems "enabling and illuminating. As a woman [she] felt some mute and anxious kinship with those erotic objects which were appropriated; as a poet [she] felt confirmed by the very powers of expression which appropriated them" (*OL* 237–238). Through this seeming contradiction, Boland highlights the struggle that many revisionist mythmakers have felt between myth's power as a legitimizing force in the poetic tradition and its misogyny.

As a woman poet, Boland has had to negotiate a poetic and mythic canon filled with undying female images. Boland declares in "A Formal Feeling," "I am changing the story" (*LL* 66).[8] Her "formal feeling," or her compulsion to write in conventional forms and to use traditional myths, indicates her desire to enter into dialogue with poems and myths of the past and to transform them into something to which she relates. She also tries to reshape the poetic and mythic images of women by writing the aging body into poetry. Traditional poems by male writers fix women in "a terrible suspension of life," she argues, so that they are unable to age and die.[9] Any woman depicted by a man is an object. The only way to have female subjects in poems is for women to write them. In *Object Lessons*, Boland asks, "Suppose it were possible to encounter the poems of the past not as finished forms but as actions we could reverse" (216–217). In reversing these actions in her poetry, Boland can express her conflicted feelings about seeing her own body changing and aging.

"Words I can grow old and die in": A Menopausal Ceres

Boland's generalizations about myth, history, and poetry become focused in her adaptation of the Greco-Roman Ceres myth. In "What Language Did" from *In a Time of Violence*, Boland writes in terza rima, a traditional poetic form, about what traditional forms have done to women. She alludes to the Ceres myth to establish a paradigm for how women can rewrite myths from a patriarchal tradition.[10] The speaker begins with a lamentation on her own aging:

> I stood there and felt the melancholy
> of growing older in such a season,
> when all I could be certain of was simply
> in this time of fragrance and refrain
> whatever else might flower before the fruit,
> and be renewed, I would not. Not again. (*ITV* 63)

These lines allude to a 10th century anonymous Irish poem, "The Old Woman of Beare." The old woman laments her decrepit body: "Once again for ill or good / Spring will come and I shall see / Everything but me renewed." While the reference to the woman of Beare is clear, Boland draws our attention to her persona's action: she is searching for her daughter. The above lines, then, evoke the image of a menopausal Ceres, disconnected from the fertile natural world, the seasons, and the renewal in nature typically associated with the power of the goddess. She is the only aging element, looking "to pick out [her] child from the distance." Instead of the live girl whom she hopes to retrieve, she sees images of maidens and mermaids trapped by the myths that hold them in perpetual youth:

> I went nearer. They were disappearing.
> Dusk had turned to night but in the air—
> did I imagine it? – a voice was saying:
>
> *This is what language did to us. Here*
> *is the wound, the silence, the wretchedness*
> *of tides and hillsides and stars where*
>
> *we languish in a grammar of sighs,*
> *in the high-minded search for euphony,*
> *in the midnight rhetoric of poesie.*
>
> *We cannot sweat here. Our skin is icy.*
> *We cannot breed here. Our wombs are empty.*
> *Help us to escape youth and beauty.*
>
> *Write us out of the poem. Make us human*
> *in cadences of change and mortal pain*
> *and words we can grow old and die in.* (*ITV* 63–64, original italics)

The poem suggests that the poetry and mythology of the past lie through omission, since they do not include a woman's representation of her own aging and dying body. In *Object Lessons*, Boland explains, "I would have to reexamine and disrupt and dispossess [traditional images]" in order to make up for the paucity of dynamic, multidimensional women in poetry (29). The constellations of women allude to Adrienne Rich's "Planetarium" (1968), in which the transfixed speaker "sees" for the first time the revelation of "Galaxies of women, there / doing penance for impetuousness" (*CEP* 361). As the speaker comes to realize, "seeing is changing." When Boland's speaker "sees," becomes aware of the women trapped by conventional poetry and mythology, she hears her call to action: she must write change, aging, and dying into her poetry. Boland answers Rich's call for "re-vision" from "When We Dead Awaken" in that she conjures women who exist in male-written poems and myths precisely to "break [that tradition's] hold."

Boland's metrical and formal regularity emphasize the force of the patriarchal tradition that traps women. Her choice of the technical, crafted terza rima suggests her conscious use and manipulation of traditional forms to highlight the preservational quality of form and regular meter. In fact, although the lines are consistently nine to eleven syllables, a variation of rhythm plays in the lines themselves. Fragments like "Suddenly," or "Not again," and short statements such as, "We cannot sweat here. Our skin is icy. / We cannot breed here. Our wombs are empty," show Boland working against a regular meter and form, enacting the women's struggle to break free from the imprisoning lines. The women are fighting the form. This countering of the regular metrical flow through interruptions and pauses jolts her readers into a world of complex emotions, while the retention of form holds them at a distance and forces them to reflect on Boland's argument. Boland's choice of the Ceres myth, and the form in which she revises it, establishes the tension between patriarchal power, exemplified in the myth by Zeus and Hades, and female resistance and rebellion. Boland plays on the tensions within the myth itself and posits them as analogous to her own dilemma as a feminist poet who is both disrupting and maintaining the Irish tradition.

"Woman Painted on a Leaf" embodies the "awkward, jagged reality" that the voices from "What Language Did" tell us that they want in poetry (*OL* 218). The poem's speaker studies an ageless face painted on a leaf. Her meditation leads her to declare:

> This is not death. It is the terrible
> suspension of life.
>
> I want a poem
> I can grow old in. I want a poem I can die in.
>
> I want to take
> this dried-out face,
> as you take a starling from behind iron,
> and return it to its element of air, of ending —

so that Autumn
[. . .]

will be,
from now on,
a crisp tinder underfoot. Cheekbones. Eyes. Will be
a mouth crying out. Let me.
Let me die. (*ITV* 69–70)

Through the breakdown of language, which signifies the breakdown of the body, we see that "a fixed part of the Irish poem ha[s] broken free and become volatile" (*OL* 191). Boland disturbs the nature/woman correlation so pervasive in myth and poetry and frees the woman from the mythic/artistic prison. Male writers, Boland argues, have forced women's image onto nature. She wants that image to die.

"Woman Painted on a Leaf" is the final poem of *In a Time of Violence*, which emphasizes the weight of the speaker's epiphany. Echoing the phrase "words we can grow old and die in" from "What Language Did," the speaker responds to the women's calls that haunt the final stanzas of the first poem. It is also a powerful reversal of Yeats's "Sailing to Byzantium," in which he begs that his decrepit body, a "dying animal," be consumed away and that he be gathered "into the artifice of eternity." Boland, who grew up on Yeats's poetry, makes her speakers plead for the opposite. Her irregular rhythm, sentence fragments, and variable stanza length mark a correlation between the breakdown of form and the aging and ultimate decay of the body that she seeks to inscribe. The long lines embody the need to allow the image to go free, and not to hold it in. Though the long line wants to propel us forward towards the ultimate revelation, the fragments hold us back, forcing us to stop and see each haunting image fully: "Cheekbones. Eyes." The face changes to become fragmented and disjointed like the line in the poem. In "What Language Did" and "Women Painted on a Leaf," Boland shows how she can move from regular meter that "encodes information about a poem's relation to contemporaneous influences, traditions, and societal attitudes and to the poetic past and its supporting structures" to an irregular line in a free verse poem.[11]

While "What Language Did" and "A Woman Painted on a Leaf" attack the stasis of traditional art and enunciate the desire that poetry allow women to grow old and die, Boland admits to having trouble figuring out how to write that aging body into her poetry. Even a decade later in her collection *Domestic Violence*, Boland grapples with a similar problem. She declares, "To write about age you need to take something and / break it. // (This is an art that has always loved young women. / And silent ones.)" (77). It is one thing to declare the necessity for such a "break," but another thing to find a way to enact it without falling into essentialism. In "Anna Liffey," from *In a Time of Violence*, Boland writes,

I am sure
The body of an ageing woman
Is a memory
And to find a language for it
Is as hard
as weeping
[. . .]
An ageing woman
Finds no shelter in language.
She finds instead
Single words she once loved
Such as "summer" and "yellow"
And "sexual" and "ready"
Have suddenly become dwellings
For someone else. (*ITV* 57–58)

What language, then, can the woman poet use to write the body? Ingrid Arnet Connidis confirms Boland's speaker's fears about losing the possession of words that denote sexuality: "regardless of gender or sexual orientation, younger adults, who see sex as their domain, are uncomfortable with sex between older people" (123). But Boland admits that she has always felt uneasy with her body, that even when she was younger, it seemed "a strange and unrecorded part of [the tradition]" (*OL* 110). She feels, therefore, that, to use Rich's phrase, her name has never appeared in the book of myths.

Literary gerontology confirms (and favors authors who confirm) the positive aspects of aging. With her ambivalence toward aging, Boland indirectly challenges the concept that a writer must be pro-age to contribute to the conversation. She recognizes the dearth of aging women in poetry and wants to make up for that lack as she writes about her own life, but she also acknowledges how devastating aging can be and how hard it is to write about. Her poems indicate her struggle and her attempt to accept that which she grieves. Literary gerontologists may find fault with Boland in that while she articulates the words that she fears that she no longer possesses, she does not reclaim them. She does not celebrate her aging body with the kind of joie de vivre that many theorists argue is essential if we are to move beyond the stereotypes that link age with any number of negative associations like decay and decline. Boland would counter that her role as poet is to inscribe her personal truth, which includes grief and loss.

"Let me die" is the last line of "A Woman Painted on a Leaf," the final poem of *In a Time of Violence*; this line prefigures her next volume, *The Lost Land*, which explores how women can heal past afflictions and uses the story of Ceres to focus attention on a menopausal, middle-aged mother. In Boland's view, one way to reinterpret the old images of women is to bring them out of the shadowy world of myth by rewriting them from a woman's perspective and including in these revisions "cadences of change and mortal pain" (*ITV* 65).

While Boland does not abandon the correlation between land and woman that is pervasive in both Irish literature and Greco-Roman myth, she fills *The Lost Land*, not with images of the fertile earth, but with wounds and scars. In "The Scar," the speaker asks, "If colony is a wound what will heal it? / After such injuries / what difference do we feel?" (23). In her sequence, "Colony," Boland relates England's colonization of Ireland to men's subjugation of women through her own experience as an Irish girl living in England. Thus she adopts the comparison between land and woman, but by making the conventional image personal (in her story of her first scar), she connects her scars with Ireland's scars. She explains,

> I thought it vital that women poets such as myself should establish a discourse with the idea of the nation. I felt sure that the most effective way to do this was by subverting the previous terms of that discourse. Rather than accept the nation as it appeared in Irish poetry, with its queens and muses, I felt the time had come to rework those images by exploring the emblematic relation between my own feminine experience and a national past. (*OL* 148)

Boland's poems do not "bandage up the history," but rather let the wounds breathe so that she can determine the "difference" that she feels once the scar forms (22).

Myth is also a wound that she examines so that she can "find a language for," give voice to, the "memory" of "the body of an aging woman" (*ITV* 57). Women in traditional myths represent male fears and fantasies, not the reality of women's lives. Boland makes a correlation between myth and history—both are subjective, selective, and patriarchal. When Boland rewrites history and myth and attempts to include a female perspective, she does not claim to be objective. While she recognizes her own subjectivity, she believes that her personal experiences and memories can translate into shared experiences and memories. In this way, she reworks the old myths, which were, according to the Greeks, stories inspired by the daughters of Memory. As "myth" and "history" are slippery terms, "memory" itself becomes multivalent because Boland not only transcribes her own memories, but also invents a past, a memory of women she never knew. Boland is aware of the multiplicity of meaning latent in her terms. She seems not to want to define but rather to explore the various levels of meaning within myth, memory, and history. Her poem "Anna Liffey" suggests that "The body of an ageing woman / Is a memory" that needs to have its place in myth (57). Because there is currently no language for it, Boland must invent a new vocabulary, a revised mythology, which includes that memory, that aging body. She writes in her poem "Story," "I am writing / a woman out of legend. I am thinking / how new it is – this story. How hard it will be to tell" (*ITV* 62).

In both *In a Time of Violence* and *The Lost Land*, Boland tries to make the Greek mother/daughter myth relevant to twentieth-century women. Her interest in Ceres is not that she is an Earth goddess, but that she is a mother grieving the loss of her daughter, Persephone. "To Memory," from her 2007 volume *Domestic Violence*, addresses Mnemosyne, the Greek goddess of memory. The speaker tells the goddess, "My last childless winter was the same / as all the other ones. Outside my window / the motherless landscape hoarded its own kind" (47). Unlike Demeter who controls the earth's fertility, Boland's speaker looks at the landscape from a distance. She is inside, separate from the outside realm controlled by the mother goddess. Boland enters the myth through personal experiences that link her to Ceres: specifically, the grief of watching her daughter grow up and away from her. In her adaptation of the Ceres myth, however, she recognizes that she cannot fully relate to the goddess, because the way in which she experiences Time as a mortal mother is fundamentally different from how Ceres experiences it as an immortal goddess. Ceres never permanently ages. In the *Homeric Hymn*, Demeter transforms herself into a woman past childbearing years, but the key difference between the disguised goddess and Boland's speaker lies in Demeter's choice. She controls her outer appearance and is able to change back into her mother goddess form when she wishes.[12] *The Hymn* reads, "golden-haired Demeter / remained sitting apart from all the immortals, / wasting with desire for her deep-girt daughter," but once Persephone rejoins her mother, Demeter changes back from barren to fertile (16). The speaker in Boland's poems, on the other hand, watches herself growing older and knows that she cannot keep her daughter with her, for her daughter must experience life on her own.

The *Hymn* and other versions of the myth depict women of all ages. Demeter travels to Eleusis, where she disguises herself as "a very old woman cut off from childbearing / and the gifts of garland-loving Aphrodite," and sits at the *Parthenion*, the "maiden's" or "virgin's well" (6). When the maiden daughters of Keleos, chief prince of Eleusis, approach her, she asks, "dear children, . . .whose house [might I] come to, a man's / or a woman's, there to do for them gladly / such tasks as are done by an elderly woman. / I could nurse well a newborn child . . ." (8). The girls depart to find their mother Metaneira, who had been thought to be beyond child-bearing years, who is nursing her "late-born child, much prayed for" (10). At the end of the *Hymn*, when mother and daughter, Demeter and Persephone, joyously reunite, the crone, Hekate, joins the two, and Demeter's mother, Rhea, is instrumental in urging her daughter to rejoin the Olympians.

Scholars such as Polly Young-Eisendrath and Christine Downing have responded, in particular, to the characters Metaneira, Rhea, and Hekate, who highlight issues of motherhood, menopause, and middle and old age.[13] For example, Metaneira already has several teenage daughters by the time she gives birth to her "late-born child, much prayed for." Demeter's mother Rhea demonstrates the continued loving relationship between a mother and daughter, even after Demeter has a daughter of her own. Although not depicted as elderly in the *Hymn*, Hekate, who in later traditions becomes associated with the crone, signifies for modern readers the wisdom and guidance of an elder generation of women. Women and goddesses such as these potentially problematize Boland's argument, as they embody the moments in women's lives that Boland claims are absent from myth and literature. Despite Boland's stated interest in aging women, she does not mention any characters from the myth other than Ceres and Persephone; for her, this relationship is central.

In the ancient world, Demeter's Mysteries were immensely popular, in great part because of the promise of a blessed afterlife for humans who became initiated. Boland is not interested in this aspect of the myth, however. As an Irish Catholic whose religion centers on resurrection and a blessed afterlife, her rejection of the concept of return and renewal is doubled. Boland mourns the loss of her daughter's youth and acknowledges the cycle, not of continual renewal, but of progression and change.

Boland's Ceres poems often take her through the process of initiation from "ignorance" to understanding. Literary gerontologists and feminist theorists such as Valerie Saiving and Carol Christ have argued that humans must embrace death as a part of the life process, and that the process in its entirety is of "the greatest value" (Christ, *SWC*, 207).[14] This acknowledgement is crucial to the Demeter mysteries; it is what initiates were challenged to understand. Ultimately, if she is to become "initiated," Boland's speaker will have to realize this.

In "The Pomegranate," Boland's speaker announces that the Ceres and Persephone myth is "[t]he only legend I have ever loved" (*ITV* 26). She frames her own feelings of stepping outside to retrieve her daughter within Ceres's story:

> I was Ceres then and I knew
> Winter was in store for every leaf
> On every tree on that road.
> Was inescapable for each one we passed.
> And for me.
> It is winter (26)

As "What Language Did" begins with the speaker lamenting growing older, and ends with the chilling chorus of voices begging for "words [they] can grow old and die in," so "The Pomegranate" begins with the speaker's grief at aging, and ends with her realization that, even in the modern world so seemingly removed from the Greco-Roman world of Ceres and Persephone, she can learn an appreciation of the complete lifecycle that includes her daughter growing up and becoming a woman herself. Once Boland's speaker comes to this realization through her identification with the myth, she can articulate her newfound understanding:

> [. . .] what else
> Can a mother give her daughter but such
> Beautiful rifts in time?
> If I defer the grief I will diminish the gift.
> The legend must be hers as well as mine. (27)

Boland's speaker announces early in "The Pomegranate" that as a girl she identified with Persephone and now, as a woman, she identifies with Ceres. Boland's speaker wants to place herself in time. In fact, her identification with the two goddesses seems to place her more fully in the mortal world. Boland's use of the term "legend" as opposed to "myth" suggests, too, that she sees a kernel of historical truth in the mother/daughter relationship, even though the goddesses belong to a fantastical myth. Boland is interested in reality as opposed to fantasy, and identifies with Ceres's grief, while remaining aware of the limitations of the identification. The daughter in the poem must also go through the various seasons of life, and neither mother nor daughter is fixed in the mother/daughter role perpetually. Karen Bennett has argued that in "The Pomegranate,"

> ...we have... the sense that the passage through Hades is a necessary stage on the quest of life and that all the mother can do is watch and *wait for her daughter to emerge* . . . [H]aving already lived it herself, *the mother trusts completely that her daughter will return* . . . Boland's poem reveals an overwhelmingly *cyclical* interpretation of the myth and a quiet acceptance of 'death' as a stage in the constant renewal of life. (22, emphasis added)

In fact, the poem's power is in the speaker's realization that there will be *no* return.

Boland's later Ceres poems confirm that while nature may indeed renew itself, her Ceres's life is not cyclical, but linear and finite. In "The Blossom," the speaker imagines her daughter as an apple blossom who asks:

> *imagine if I stayed here,*
> *even for the sake of your love,*
> *what would happen to the summer?*
> *To the fruit?*
> Then holds out a dawn-soaked hand to me,
> whose fingers I counted at birth
> years ago,
>
> And touches mine for the last time.
> And falls to earth. (*LL* 45, original italics)

Here, the speaker is "so lost in grief" precisely because she cannot retrieve the blossom, as Ceres can (45). The poem's jagged line mirrors the speaker's emotional state and embodies the mother's raw grief.[15] While initiation into Demeter's Mysteries would bring the hope of transformation and rejuvenation to the goddess's worshipers, that hope is missing in Boland's poems.

In Boland's Ceres poems, the aging process is the essential element. In "Ceres Looks at the Morning" she writes, "I wake slowly. Already / my body is a twilight: Solid. Cold. / At the edge of a larger darkness" (*LL* 45). According to Thomas Foster, one dilemma for Irish poets is "how to insist on actual mothers in the face of the all-mother" (3). Against Ceres's timeless experience, Boland focuses on the elements of the mother's body that place her in the ephemeral, human world. In her "Daughter" series the speaker grieves,

> If I wanted a child now
> I could not have one.
>
> Except through memory.
> Which is the ghost of the body.
> Or myth.
> Which is the ghost of meaning. (*LL* 46)

Here, woman is no fertile earth. She is a middle-aged, menopausal mother dealing with a topic not talked about in Irish poetry—the mother who can no longer give birth; the mother who is neither hag nor maiden, but in the strange liminal realm of middle-age. What is her place? What is her purpose? Her body grows "cold"; she is "at the edge of a larger darkness" contemplating the body's "ghosts." Boland's poems are filled with a beautiful sadness depicting the approach of a woman's decline. They allow for a language that faces death head on, and refuses to back away from the complete life cycle that inevitably includes woman's fall and winter.

In these poems, the mother can preserve her motherhood and her daughter's youth only through memory. Thus Boland uses memories to create a revised Ceres myth, and uses that revised myth to preserve memories. Rather than eternally fertile earth mother, the mother in Boland's poems is fully human, aware of her aging body and of the necessity of her daughter's growth away from her. This mother sets her daughter free to live life, not to be the eternal blossom, the perpetual maiden. In "The Bargain" section of "Daughter" the speaker proclaims: "The earth shows its age and makes a promise / only myth can keep. *Summer. Daughter*" (48, original italics). Only myth can promise that eternal return of youth and daughter. In her article "Daughters," Boland calls "the actual, practical experience of a daughter growing up [. . .] one of the true human legends." As a poet, Boland can use her own experiences as she rewrites the mother/daughter myth to include irreversible loss.

Boland's observations on a mother's loss inhabit a mythic time. A revised mythology grows out of the experiences she shares with other mothers. She wonders in *Object Lessons* where myth begins: "Is there something about the repeated action—about lifting a child, clearing a dish, watching the seasons return to a tree and depart from a vista—which reveals a deeper meaning to existence and heals some of the worst abrasions of time?" (*OL* 169). She equates those repetitions to metrical units: "What were all these if not—as language and music in poetry were—a sequence and repetition which allowed the deeper meanings to emerge: a sense of belonging, of sustenance, of a life revealed, and not restrained, by ritual and patterning?" (*OL* 170). On several levels, Boland finds a correlation between myth and poetry, and she uses a currently existing mythology as a means of transforming her personal experience into something shared. She does not subvert Myth as an idea, therefore, but rejects the representations of women in available mythologies. Her Ceres poems offer a model for how women can take this story about a mother and daughter from the patriarchal literary tradition and claim it as their own. She reworks the Ceres myth, demanding that her readers acknowledge the effects of human frailty and the necessity for loss. In so doing she inscribes her aging body into the literary canon.

"Take something and break it": No More Mythologies

If Boland's poetic persona accepts the need to set her daughter free to complete the life cycle, she must accept that freedom for herself, as well. Boland's Ceres poems from *In a Time of Violence* and *The Lost Land* move the speaker toward initiation as she affirms that she was once daughter, then fertile mother, then menopausal mother. The life cycle does not end there, however, as the modern-day conception of Hekate attests.[16] Perhaps due to Boland's mother's death in 2002, *Domestic Violence* (2007), which Boland dedicated to her mother, overflows with meditations on mortality. Rather than continue to identify with the Ceres myth, in which Hekate would represent a new phase in her life to explore, Boland faces the mythic images of daughter and mother in which she has been steeped—and destroys them.

In her poem "Instructions," in which she addresses fellow poets, Boland dismantles the tropes of the apple tree and blossom that were symbols for her daughter in the *Lost Land* poems. Now, Boland's persona conjures the tree, which can be recognized for what it is only when the false images that had been projected onto it are broken away. Much like Adrienne Rich's diver, who finds "the wreck and not the story of the wreck / the thing itself and not the myth," Boland urges the "you" of the poem to break away the mythic and artistic imagery imposed onto the tree until what remains is the tree itself and not the myth. And the tree is dead.

In a single poem, Boland calls into question the worth of her previous mytho-logical poetry. She addresses fellow poets who wish to write about age. "To write about age you need to take something and / break it," the speaker declares emphat-ically (*DV* 77). Boland's long line snaps off into the short, two-word command, as the poet enacts the very thing that she insists must be done. She reveals what she has broken: "A branch, perhaps, girlish with blossom." Persephone is repeatedly called a blossoming maiden in the *Homeric Hymn,* and the daughter figure of the *Lost Land* poems is equated to an apple blossom. Pay no attention to the blossom; keep breaking up the image, she encourages: "Then cut through a promised sum-mer. Continue." In the *Lost Land* poems, we learned that "Summer is a promise that only myth can keep." As her daughter will not return, neither will youth, fertility, and bounty return to the aging speaker. Boland next invokes her persona from the second phase of her life: Ceres, the mother with whom she identified so strongly. In "Instructions," however, the speaker warns, "The spring afternoon will come to your door, angry / as any mother. Ignore her." Rather than empathize with the goddess in their connection to their lost daughters, Boland's persona declares in her brief, instructive dismissal that the goddess is no longer relevant. Finally, she orders her fellow poets to break syntax, the very foundation of written expression.

Boland has effectively chopped to pieces the images she had previously used, and along with them, the myth with which she had identified in her writing for the last thirteen years. "What is left," she says, is: "for you / and you only." While Boland's "you" is addressed to poets, it extends to her entire readership, which means that although each individual must face what Boland is about to reveal, it will be a shared experience. As the hierophant holds up the sacra in the epiphanic moment of the initiation into Demeter's mysteries, here, Boland reveals to us the sacra: "A dead tree. The future. What does not bear fruit. Or / thinking of" (77). Rather than the Greek shaft of wheat, signifying rebirth and regeneration, Boland gives her initiates instructions on how to kill a tree. To what end? Boland implies that each poet has her equivalent of Boland's tree – recycled images and forms that the poet has tried to make accommodate her message. They do not work, argues Boland. When the poet can strip away the artifice, face the truth about aging and dying, and inscribe that personal truth, cultural transformation will occur. That must be the future. Like Adrienne Rich's speaker in "Cartographies of Silence," whose poetry is the modern day equivalent to the Eleusinian sacra, Boland's poem equates to a revelation: the future holds poetry that is divorced from mythology.

Mythology and the poetic tradition have failed to offer Boland aging female characters with whom she can identify. She tells her readers that what poets have attempted for millennia to conceal, that women grow old and die, is a fact that contemporary poets, the "you" of the poem, must begin to write about in mean-ingful ways. She ends her poem with an invitation rather than an answer. She does not push beyond the recognition of tradition's failure to offer a new set of images. She ends the poem without elaborating on what growing old looks or feels like. While Boland exposes a problem with traditional poems and myths, and while she wants to find a language with which to document her own aging body, she stops short of enacting it. Instead, she issues a call to action to present and future revisionist mythmakers and poets to change the nature of poetry. Like Adrienne Rich writing thirty years earlier, Boland calls for "a whole new poetry" that discards used-up images and forms. How and whether this new poetry will engage mythology remains to be seen.

Conclusion

Feminist Mythmaking at the Crossroads

Tired of the elite male monopoly on Classical mythology, many women poets writing between the 1950s and the present transformed previously silent, marginal, passive, or treacherous mythic women into heroines, turning object to subject. As a public forum for redressing personal and historical injustices, women's mythic revision is a discourse of exposures and reversals. All of the poets in this study have challenged culturally weighted stories and have participated in the tradition of revision inherent in mythmaking.

H.D., Sylvia Plath, Adrienne Rich, Margaret Atwood, and Eavan Boland wrestled with what was traditionally expected of them as women and with their sense of themselves as artists, a conflict embodied in their sometimes-frustrated attempts to revise male-constructed mythological literature. Part of their frustration grew from the clash of admiration and anger that they felt toward the classical tradition and canonical literature. These writers grew up reading Western culture's literary canon, which posits that masculine experience equates to universal human experience, and that voices attesting to feminine experience must be marginalized and sometimes actively silenced. The project of revising both classical mythology and the high modernist revision of the classics has constituted a feminist act that represents a commitment to asserting a woman's right to inscribe herself and her experiences into literature and to altering previously male-defined criteria for poetry. At times, those past stories represented so much oppression that even revising them did not provide the kind of satisfaction or inclusion that the poets sought. Like Adrienne Rich, some poets have turned away from mythological revision as a form of protest. Others, like H.D. and Atwood, have envisioned a world where myths can exist in changed, newly-relevant forms. Because Atwood and Boland are still producing poetry, we cannot yet claim to know the definitive legacy of their mythmaking. In all cases, the women manifest the tremendous effort that it takes to engage with a literature that has had a profound and pervasive influence on Western culture and that continues to influence human interactions, even thousands of years after it was produced.

In some ways, revisionist mythmaking at the turn of the millennium still battles the sexism, violence, and objectification of women that permeates contemporary Western culture. In other ways, it is a different project from earlier revisionist mythmaking. Younger generations of poets have grown up reading H.D. and the other poets in this study and often take for granted many of the advances for which second-wave feminists fought. In general, they are no longer revising for poetic legitimacy or out of the anger, frustration, and grief that fueled the first wave of feminist revisionist mythmakers who inscribed their voices into a mythic and poetic canon virtually void of female writers.

As exemplified in the work of H.D. and Adrienne Rich, some earlier feminist poets attempted to identify a female "essence" as separate from male "essence," as they often wanted to create a culture based on "feminine" rather than "masculine" values. By the 1980s, however, the feminist movement had become increasingly concerned with countering the impulse to essentialize gender, looking instead at differences between women and between men rather than positing their sameness. Revisionist mythmaking has mirrored these theoretical concerns.

Following from H.D.'s and Atwood's work decades earlier, and in line with the developing discourses of Masculinity Studies and Gender Studies, revision of male mythic figures allows contemporary women poets to challenge cultural conceptions of masculinity and to redefine expectations for men. Anne Carson's book-length poetic revision of part of the Herakles legend, *Autobiography of Red* (1998), for example, centers on Geryon, a gay, socially awkward boy/teen who falls in love with the leather jacket-wearing, sexually advanced Herakles. The contemporary character, whose Greek mythic counterpart is a red-winged monster whom Herakles kills, struggles with issues of identity. Much like H.D.'s Helen, Geryon learns that identity is not pre-determined, but rather that he can shape his conception of self by choosing elements from various mythologies (both Greek and Quechuan) with which to relate and by rejecting parts that do not work for him. Carson's tender portrayal of Geryon embodies a feminist goal to avoid a counter-scapegoating of men, a goal that lies at the heart of the contemporary revisionist interest in reworking male mythic characters.

As the feminist movement became aware of gaps in the predominantly white, middle-class discourse of the 1960s and 1970s, women began to advocate against ageism, classism, and racism within the movement and society at large. As chapter five attests, literary gerontology developed to study and counter traditional representations of age in literature. Studies of class struggle find their way into Margaret Atwood's recent poetry in her modern-day Helen of Troy, an "exploited" but unapologetic stripper (*Morning in the Burned House* 33). In Atwood's book-length revision of *The Odyssey*, *The Penelopiad* (2005), the epic's hanged maids form a chorus of wry but chipper voices, singing of their lives filled with abuse and denigration. Atwood intersperses their poems throughout the novel, narrated predominantly by Penelope, to establish a counter-narrative that exposes the wretchedness of the lives of the servant girls. A new wave of scholarship, *Classica Africana*, studies the relationship between Black literature and the Classical Tradition in works like Rita Dove's book-length poetic revision of the Demeter and Persephone myth in *Mother Love* (1995).[1]

"That Stranger Was Myself!": Identification With the Other

To conclude this study, I would like to briefly examine examples of poetic sequences from Rita Dove's *Mother Love* and Anne Carson's *Glass, Irony, and God* (1992) that embody a dominant trend in revisionist mythmaking at the turn of the millennium. Rita Dove deliberately places her book-length interpretation of the Demeter and Persephone myth, *Mother Love*, into the tradition of revisionist mythmaking. More specifically, it is a response to Adrienne Rich's *Dream of a Common Language*. In the final sonnet sequence, "Her Island," the African-American poetic speaker, her white, German husband, and their daughter travel to Sicily, known in ancient times as Persephone's island. They hire a native Sicilian to give them a tour, and the speaker notices that "he hasn't seen an American Black before" (69). He "trembles" a bit as he touches her, apparently nervous and unsure of how to communicate until, the narrator tells the reader, "we find a common language" (70). While the literal language that they share is German, the connection that the two develop centers on their interest in seeing the remains of Persephone's grotto and on their common reactions to the remains of an ancient culture that has been destroyed. The family and the guide attempt to find "the center of the physical world," where Persephone was pulled down to Hades, but the sacred spot has been tarred over and turned into a racetrack, and there is "no way to get near" (74, 75). Although they are barred from entering by a giant fence, they circle the spot, using binoculars and unwilling to give up their search.

The excursion signifies contemporary humans' desire to see beyond what is currently visible and to tap into "the ineffable," profound meaning of things (Dove, quoted in Bellin 127). The family and their guide "find a common language" in their desire to bear witness to the spiritual center of human existence. The common language that unites them, therefore, is the transcendent power of myth and the realization that "no story's ever finished" (77). Throughout *Mother Love*, myth is the shared language that allows individuals to get at the ineffable. In the phrase, "we find a common language," and in the volume as a whole, myth unites all of the different voices, rhythms, syntaxes, dialects, races, and cultures, and it unites the speaker's contemporary culture to the past. Dove explains in an interview from a year after *Mother Love*'s release,

> I don't think a universalism that lacks a sense of the specific can be very powerful; at the same time, any culturally drenched perception isn't going to be powerful if it doesn't have some kind of universal reverberation. I guess what I am saying is that "the universal" is a bogus concept. We've come to believe that being "universal" is to transcend difference—again, the incredible trauma of difference in modern society has made us yearn for conformity. Why can't we find the universal in those differences? (quoted in Steffen 176–177).

Her final question gets at the heart of her poetic endeavor and is emblematic of contemporary revisionist mythmaking in general. The poems in *Mother Love* are dialogic, literally, in that they are filled with dialogue; they also speak to one another, as lines from one poem are repeated in another. Sometimes the voices are embodied; sometimes the reader does not know who is speaking. The multiplicity of voices and stories has mythic resonance, and in each case, the particular and distinguishable present becomes a part of the mythic landscape that Dove believes is shared by all humans.

There is also a larger literary dialogue at work, as Dove speaks to other women writers in her epigraphs. Section III's sequence, "Persephone in Hell," begins with an epigraph from H.D.'s *Hermetic Definition*. Another section's epigraph is from Muriel Rukeyser's famous myth poem "The Poem as Mask." Dove's final sonnet sequence, "Her Island," begins with another H.D. quote from "Notes on Thought and Vision." She deliberately places herself in dialogue with other revisionist mythmakers. Most significantly, she endorses Adrienne Rich's statement that "the true nature of poetry [is] the drive / to connect. The dream of a common language" (*DCL* 7). Dove's poetry aims to break down barriers between sexes, classes, races, and nationalities, to "find a common language," to connect, even while acknowledging rather than masking difference (*ML* 70). She and Rich both use the Demeter myth to help them to articulate that common language, and both dream of a poetry that finds the transcendent, shared experience, in particular manifestations and situations. Unlike Adrienne Rich, however, who sought to break with Tradition, Dove, like most of her contemporaries, does not demonstrate an authorial anxiety that plagued many earlier revisionist poets, and there is no overt political agenda. She embraces myth as a common language that lends weight to an individual's particular stories.

Anne Carson, one of the most prolific revisionist mythmakers writing today, also "find[s] a common language" in myth. In her sequence "The Fall of Rome: A Traveller's Guide" from *Glass, Irony, and God*, Anne Carson's speaker goes to Rome to visit his host, Anna Xenia. He warns us that he is no hero: there is "nothing terrific" about him except, he says, that "I can take you to Anna Xenia" (74). Carson's readers may wonder why they would want to know her—a woman whose first name, Anna, is the Italian form of the poet's own name, Anne, and whose last name loosely translates from the Greek to mean "guest / host relationship." Her name, however, is both a clue to the meaning of the poem and a metaphor for how to understand mythic revision at the turn of the millennium.

In ancient Greece, *xenia* was a reciprocal relationship between a guest and a host, each of whom was a *xenos* (guest; host; stranger; foreigner; friend). A traveler arrived at a stranger's home as a stranger himself and as a foreigner; the host would allow him into his home, whereupon the stranger would become a friend. The connection between *xenoi* was hereditary and sacred, divinely sanctioned by Zeus. In Carson's poem, the speaker refers to himself as "a stranger" and "a traveler." The poem is about the difficulties of fitting in, of knowing oneself, and of making meaningful connections to others.

Carson uses the premise of cultural and linguistic barriers to emphasize the difficulty of connecting that is inherent in being human. She provides scenarios that help her reader to relate to this difficulty: "A stranger is someone who stands in the doorway, / drenched in confusion, / and permits the dog to escape," or "A stranger is someone / who sits / very still at the table, / looks down at his knuckles, / thinks some day we will laugh about this, / doesn't believe it" (87, 89). In the midst of a painful series of interactions in which the stranger/foreigner/speaker tries desperately and awkwardly to connect to his host, Anna suggests a trip to Orvieto to show her guest two attractions: a well, the pozzo di San Patrizio, and the Signorelli Chapel in the Orvieto Cathedral.

Each attraction connects to Carson's use of *xenia* and becomes a metaphor for contemporary revisionist mythmaking. In his description of the well, the speaker tells us:

There are 248 comfortable steps
from the top to the bottom of the well: 248 spiral back up.
They are not the same steps.

. . .

Designed concentrically
the two staircases fit

one within the other

like a jackknife blade
within a jackknife,
so that two people

one coming up,
the other going down,
can never meet. (98)

In the next scene, the host and guest visit the Orvieto cathedral chapel, "deco-
rated in 1499 with monumental frescoes/ [. . .]/ illustrating scenes from Dante's
Commedia" (99). Anna Xenia tells the speaker,

Signorelli is painting late in his studio
when they carry in his son,

killed in a riot.
He sits up all night with the body,
making sketch after sketch

and throwing them into a pile.
From that time
all his angels
have the one
same
face. (101)

The well and the chapel are physical metaphors for the interconnectedness of
strangers. The well's two staircases are separate entities that create a whole; they
maintain a barrier, never merging, never allowing the two people to meet, and
yet always intertwined, together making up the entirety of the well. Similarly,
Signorelli's angels each represent different figures, but they are all united by the
same face. These images connect to Carson's conception of *xenia*. The same Greek
word contains a series of opposite meanings that are seemingly distinct from the
other meanings of the word. Yet, a foreigner becomes familiar; a stranger becomes
a friend; and, in the spirit of the reciprocal nature of *xenia*, a host will one day

become guest, and vice versa. The concepts intertwine to create the whole meaning behind the word. The opposites balance each other, help to define each other, and without one, the other loses its full meaning.

Carson uses the ancient concept of *xenia* to highlight contemporary human interactions. Despite the difficulty of making connections, the poetic speaker realizes that Anna Xenia has helped him to understand that the people and situations from which he feels removed and disconnected are somehow a part of him, too, and he exclaims, "That stranger was myself!" (104). The sequence embodies why contemporary women poets consistently return to Greek mythology as subject matter: there is a connection between their own lives and the foreign stories that on the one hand seem ever more remote and subject to question. Like Dove searching for Persephone's sacred site that is buried beneath a racetrack, contemporary female poets search under the surface of their everyday lives, and they weed through the dissonances between their own culture and ancient myth that have been addressed so eloquently by earlier revisionist poets. They do so to uncover the essence of the myths, which will provide entry into hidden or untapped parts of themselves.

None of the poets in this study, no matter how angry with the Greek tradition, chose to rework a character or story with whom/which she felt no personal connection. The women changed the myths to reflect their own experiences and values, but in the process, the poets, too, were changed through their engagement with the powerful and sometimes problematic stories. Revisionist mythmakers like H.D., Plath, and Rich, who challenged the misogyny they found in the men they were taught to emulate, offer to female writers of subsequent generations revised heroines to admire and revised cultural scripts to follow. The earlier women writers now serve as models to inspire younger generations of poets. Whereas H.D.'s Helen struggled to articulate her story, a radical concept in the mid-twentieth century, women today can assert their authority and independence with increased security and surety. This empowerment translates into a new strand of mythmaking, which adopts Greek myth without the anxiety felt by the foremothers of the movement. With increasing frequency, female poets are using mythic revision, not as a political tool for reconstructing notions of gender, but as a transformative personal tool.

Initially, mythic revision marked true rebellion against the tyranny of patriarchal influence. It marked a struggle for survival, and the end goal was a changed world. It has been appropriated for so many purposes in the last twenty years and has become so popular, that readers have come to expect strong female characters when they read poetic revisions of myths. It is not yet clear whether mythic revision remains a subversive genre in which to push against the foundations of culture. Contemporary female poets face a question of whether and how they will keep mythmaking alive and vital in the new millennium.

Anne Carson offers one possible answer. To return to why we, as Carson's readers, should want to know Anna Xenia—the riddle of her name provides the key to the answer. She represents our confrontation with the uncomfortable and foreign elements within myth, but ultimately through that confrontation with what is seemingly most distant, we find ourselves.

Notes

Introduction

1. See Ostriker, Alicia Suskin. *Stealing the Language*. Boston: Beacon Press, 1986.
2. Many scholars have labored to demonstrate the multiplicity of literary modernism. For a study of the conversation between the high and low modernisms, see *High and Low Moderns: Literature and Culture, 1889–1939*. Edited by Maria DiBattista and Lucy McDiarmid. New York: Oxford U.P., 1996. Another excellent study is Peter Nicholls's *Modernisms: A Literary Guide*. Berkeley: University of California Press, 1995. I do not mean to suggest that high modernism was monolithic. When I refer to high or classic modernists, unless otherwise noted, I specifically refer to Eliot and Pound's circle of poets, and exclude James Joyce from the group.
3. Hulme expands on his idea in his essay "Romanticism and Classicism" (1912), in which he "evokes the bare, empirical, and disillusioned landscape of the new classicism. The classical world is dry and hard; the romantic is damp and soft. 'In the classic,' moreover, 'it is always the light of ordinary day,' as opposed to the drugged, hallucinatory romantic light 'that never was on land or sea'" (Gregory 16, Hulme 127). For a discussion of Romantic Hellenism, see David Ferris. *Silent Urns: Romanticism, Hellenism, and Modernity*. Stanford: Stanford U.P., 2000.
4. Much scholarship and theoretical work has been devoted to high modernism and myth. For the purposes of my study I am only interested in the effects of the modernist classical return on later women poets. For that reason I will not attempt to summarize the vast body of work on modernist classicism. For a traditional discussion of twentieth-century myth criticism, see Ted R. Spivey. *Beyond Modernism: Toward a New Myth Criticism*. Lanham, MD: University Press of America, 1988. He discusses theorists such as Campbell, Jung, and Eliade in approaching

literature. For a discussion of a structuralist approach to myth in literature, see Eric Gould. *Mythical Intentions in Modern Literature*. Princeton: Princeton U.P., 1981. For a discussion of Pound and Zukofsky's work with Latin poetry see Hooley, Daniel M. *The Classics in Paraphrase: Ezra Pound and Modern Translators of Latin Poetry*. Cranbury, NJ: Associated U.P., 1988. For a discussion on mythic theory, general mythic patterns and archetypes in stories, and an application of those theories and patterns in the twentieth-century novel, see Meletinsky, Eleazar M. *The Poetics of Myth*. Guy Lanoue and Alexandre Sadetsky, trans. New York: Garland Publishing, 1998.

5. For discussion on Classic Modernism and its claim to "masculine" verse, see Gregory, Eileen. *H.D. and Hellenism*. Cambridge: Cambridge U.P., 1997; Perl, Jeffrey. *The Tradition of Return: The Implicit History of Modern Literature*. Princeton: Princeton U.P., 1984; Laity, Cassandra. *H.D. and the Victorian Fin de Siecle*. Cambridge: Cambridge U.P., 1996; Meisel, Perry. *The Myth of the Modern: A Study in British Literature and Criticism after 1850*. New Haven, CT: Yale U.P., 1987; Ross, Andrew. *The Failure of Modernism: Symptoms of American Poetry*. New York: Columbia U.P., 1986.

6. While Eliot and Pound criticized male as well as female poets for "feminine" style, here Eliot explicitly aligns the adjective with women.

7. Early H.D. is an exception, as I will discuss in Chapter One.

8. See Elizabeth Jane Harrison and Shirley Peterson, Ed. *Unmanning Modernism*. Knoxville: U of Tennessee, 1997. See Gilbert, Sandra and Susan Gubar. *No Man's Land: Sexchanges*. New Haven: Yale U.P., 1989.

9. From *Selected Letters of Ezra Pound and Louis Zukofsky*. Ed. Barry Ahern. New York: New Dirctions, 1987. Pound was in his late-forties when he wrote the letter. His reasoning behind the "under 30" specification is not apparent.

10. In June 1922, Pound wrote in *The Dial*, "The correspondences with Homer are part of Joyce's medievalism and are chiefly his own affair, a scaffold, a means of construction, justified by the result and justifiable by it only" (*Literary Essays* 406). In 1933 he more closely echoed Eliot: "The parallels with the *Odyssey* are mere mechanics . . . Joyce had to have a shape on which to order his chaos" (quoted in *Pound/Joyce* 250).

11. See Hoberman, Ruth. *Gendering Classicism*. New York: SUNY Press, 1997. Hoberman explains the magnitude of this revelation:

    The notion of a previously unimagined pre-history in which goddess-worship and women prevailed over gods and men thus became a crucial factor in the development of modernism. That there could be power, even domination, associated with specifically female body parts working in alliance with nature was an appealing notion to many women, who then found in their identity as women a source of strength, symbolized by their relation to a Magna Mater. (19)

12. See Benstock, Shari. *Women of the Left Bank: Paris 1900–1940*. Austin: University of Texas Press, 1986; see also Lillian Faderman's discussion of Barney's salon on the rue Jacob in Paris (370–372).

13. See Taylor p.200

14. Bonnie Kime Scott, Rachael Blau DuPlessis, Susan Stanford Friedman, Sandra Gilbert, Susan Gubar, and Shari Benstock were some of the first scholars in the 1970s and 1980s to do extensive work to recover lost communities of women writers and to include them as valu-

able members of the predominantly-male canon of modernist writers. More recent studies such as Cassandra Laity's *H.D. and the Victorian Fin de Siecle,* Georgina Taylor's *H.D. and the Public Sphere of Modernist Women Writers, 1913–1946,* Eileen Gregory's *H.D. and Hellenism,* Ruth Hoberman's *Gendering Classicism,* and Gregory Staley's *American Women and Classical Myths* have continued the important work on female modernist writers and communities.

15. While Ostriker's chapter "Thieves of Language: Women Poets and Revisionist Mythology" addresses folk and fairy tales and biblical stories, in addition to Greek mythology, I focus only on the Greek stories. Therefore, when I use the phrases revisionist mythmaking or mythic revision, I am referring only to the poetic tradition of revision of Greek myths.

16. The following is a list of poets who have employed mythic revision and the poems in which they do so. I will list only the book title if more than one poem in the collection makes use of Greek myth. Several of these titles are from Alicia Ostriker's list in *Stealing the Language* (1985) pp.286–288. For a discussion of women's mythmaking in the nineteenth century, see Ostriker pgs. 214–215, and for a list of pre-1960 myth poems, see her notes to chapter six pgs.284–285. Because my study includes poets from the mid-1950s to the present, the list follows these dates.

Julie Agoos, *Calendar Year* (Riverdale-on-Hudson, NY: Sheep Meadow Press, 1996).

Alta, "euridice," *I Am Not a Practicing Angel* (Trumansburg, N.Y.: Crossing Press, 1980), p.6.

Margaret Atwood, *Selected Poems; Morning in the Burned House* (Boston: Houghton Mifflin, 1995); *The Penelopiad* (New York: Canongate, 2005).

Mary Jo Bang, *Apology For Want* (Hanover, NH: Middlebury College Press, 1997).

Eavan Boland, *An Origin Like Water* (New York: Norton, 1996); *In a Time of Violence* (New York: Norton, 1994); *The Lost Land* (New York: Norton, 1998); *Against Love Poetry* (New York: Norton, 2001).

Anne Carson, *Glass, Irony, and God* (New York: New Directions, 1992); *Plainwater* (New York: Knopf, 1995); *Autobiography of Red* (New York: Vintage Books, 1998); *Men in the Off Hours* (New York: Vintage Books, 2000); *The Beauty of the Husband* (New York: Vintage Books, 2001).

Lucille Clifton, *The Book of Light* (1993), *The Terrible Stories* (1996) in *Blessing the Boats: New and Selected Poems 1988–2000* (Rochester, NY: BOA Editions, 2000).

Patricia Dienstfrey, "Blood and the Iliad: The Paintings of Frieda Kahlo," *Newspaper Stories and Other Poems* (Berkeley: Berkeley Poets' Workshop & Press, 1979) pp.28–29.

Sharon Doubiago, *Hard Country* (Minneapolis: West End Press, 1982*); South America Mi Hija* (Pittsburgh: Pittsburgh UP, 1992).

Rita Dove, *Museum* (Pittsburgh: Carnegie-Mellon, 1983); *Mother Love* (New York: W.W. Norton, 1995).

Carol Ann Duffy, *The World's Wife* (New York: Faber & Faber, 1999).

Rachael Blau DuPlessis, *Wells* (New York: Montemora Foundation, 1980); *Drafts* (Elmwood, Conn.: Potes and Poets Press, 1991); *Drafts 15-XXX: The Fold* (Elmwood, Conn.: Potes and Poets Press, 1997).

Kate Ellis, "Matrilineal Descent," in Rod Tulloss, David Keller, and Alicia Ostriker, eds., *USI: Contemporary Writing From New Jersey* (Roosevelt, N.J.: USI Poets' Cooperative, 1980), pp.31–34.

Diana Fahey, *Metamorphoses* (Marrickville, N.S.W.: Dangaroo Press, 1988); *Listening to a Far Sea* (Alexandria, N.S.W.: Hale and Iremonges, 1998).

Kathleen Fraser, *When New Time Folds Up* (Minneapolis: Chax Press, 1993).

Sandra Gilbert, *Emily's Bread* (New York: WW Norton, 1984), pp. 43–44, 82–88

Louise Gluck, *House on Marshland* (1975), *The Triumph of Achilles* (1985) in *The First Four Books* (Hopewell, NJ: Ecco Press, 1995); *Meadowlands* (Hopewell, NJ: Ecco, 1996); *Vita Nova* (Hopewell, NJ: Ecco, 1999).

Jorie Graham, "Self-Portrait as Hurry and Delay (Penelope at Her Loom)," *The Dream of the Unified Field: Selected Poems, 1974–1994* (Hopewell, NJ: Ecco, 1995).

Marilyn Hacker, *Presentation Piece* (New York: Viking Press, 1974).

H.D., *Helen in Egypt* (New York: New Directions, 1961).

Erica Jong, "Alcestis on the Poetry Circuit," *Halflives* (New York: Holt, Rinehart, & Wilson, 1973).

Carolyn Kizer, *Yin* (Brockport, N.Y.: Boa Editions, 1984).

Denise Levertov, *With Eyes in the Back of Our Heads* (New York: New Directions, 1959); *The Jacob's Ladder* (New York: New Directions, 1961); *O Taste and See* (New York: New Directions, 1964); *Relearning the Alphabet* (New York: New Directions, 1970).

Phillis Levin, *The Afterimage* (Providence, RI: Copper Beech Press, 1995); "Mercury," *Mercury* (New York: Penguin, 2001).

Cynthia MacDonald, "Why Penelope Was Happy," *Alternate Means of Transport* (New York: Knopf, 1985).

Alicia Ostriker, *A Woman Under the Surface* (Princeton: Princeton U.P., 1982).

Linda Pastan, *The Imperfect Paradise* (New York: Norton, 1988).

Sylvia Plath, *The Collected Poems* (New York: Harper and Row, 1981).

Katha Pollit, "Penelope Writes," *Antarctic Traveler* (New York: Knopf, 1983).

Adrienne Rich, *Collected Early Poems: 1950–1970* (New York: Norton, 1993); *The Fact of a Doorframe* (New York: Norton, 2002).

Muriel Rukeyser, *Collected Poems* (New York: McGraw-Hill, 1978).

May Sarton, *Selected Poems* (New York: WW Norton, 1978) pp.155–166.

Ann Stanford, "Women of Perseus," *In Mediterranean Air* (New York: Viking, 1977).

Mona Van Duyn, *To See, to Take* (New York: Antheneum, 1970).

Eleanor Wilner, "Iphigenia, Setting the Record Straight," *Maya* (Amherst: University of Massachusetts Press, 1979), pp. 20–21.

17. See Friedman, Susan Stanford. "Creating a Women's Mythology: H.D.'s *Helen in Egypt*." *Signets*. Eds. Susan Stanford Friedman and Rachael Blau DuPlessis. Madison: U. of Wisconsin P., 2000.

18. See *H.D. and Poets After*. The book is dedicated to articles by scholars and poets about the impact of H.D.'s writing on the poets' work. For example, in "My H.D.," Ostriker admits that her volume *A Woman Under the Surface*, which draws heavily on Greek mythology, "is most clearly inflected by H.D." (6). She wrote that until she found H.D., she was "rubbing the salts of anger in my own wounds" (4).

Chapter one: H.D.'s Revision of *Kleos* Culture in *Helen In Egypt*

1. See Eileen Gregory *H.D. and Hellenism* for a detailed study of H.D.'s divergence from mainstream classic modernism. For discussion of Euripides' unpopularity among classic modernists, see Gregory 22–28.

   DuPlessis's first chapter in her book *H.D.: The Career of That Struggle* deliniates H.D.'s attempt to differentiate herself as a woman in her classicism from the classicism of male modernists. See also Diana Collecott *H.D. and Sapphic Modernism* for H.D.'s movement away from Pound , 158–161.

2. See Friedman's article "Who Buried H.D.?: A Poet, Her Critics, and Her Place in 'The Literary Tradition.'" *College English* 36 (March 1975): 801–14. For other responses to her writing from H.D.'s contemporaries, see Collecott 104–107.

3. I use the terms "Greece" and "Greeks" for simplicity, but Greece as it is known today did not exist until 1830, and was in ancient times divided into city-states.

4. For a discussion of H.D.'s interest in Schliemann's finds, see Gregory 29. See Witte *H.D., Archaeology, and Modernism* for a study of the influence of new archeological discoveries on H.D.'s writings.

5. For a discussion of the interlocking concepts of *tīmē* and *kleos*, see Elizabeth Vandiver. *The Iliad of Homer*. Lecture Three. The Teaching Company.

6. See Gregory Nagy, *The Best of the Achaeans*, 222.

7. See Norman Austin, *Helen of Troy and Her Shameless Phantom*, 27–29.

8. Classical scholarship that studies praise and blame poetry began in 1951 with the publication of E.R. Dodds' *The Greeks and the Irrational*. While H.D. was not necessarily familiar with scholarship on Helen and a tradition of blame, her serious engagement with classical texts would not preclude her insight to Helen as a figure of blame.

9. Quoted in Austin, 95. H.D. calls the first section of *Helen in Egypt* "Pallinode," misspelling the Greek word.

10. Herodotus, in his version of the myth, claims that Homer knew the alternative (in his view, true) story but chose not to tell it.

11. Eileen Gregory has most fully explored Euripides's influence in *H.D. and Hellenism*, claiming that Euripides's *Helen* "constitutes the principal classical subtext of her poem." She adds, "*Helen in Egypt* constitutes a Euripidean refiguration of Greek mythology in light of Euripidean tragic themes" (218, 221). She writes of H.D.'s poetic "conversation" with Euripides: "no modernist poet shows a greater literary exchange with an ancient writer" (181). While Euripides is certainly vital to H.D., I place more value on other influences than does Gregory, and I hope to show that H.D.'s decision to adapt multiple Helens is crucial to her work in *Helen in Egypt*. Rachael Blau DuPlessis and Karen Burnett also argue for H.D's appreciation of Euripides. Susan Stanford Friedman briefly discusses H.D.'s deviation from Euripides in her characterization of Helen (*Psyche* 255). Dianne Chisholm argues in *H.D.'s Freudian Poetics* that Euripides's play upholds the "phallocentric structures and figures of classical literature" (171). In *H.D. and Sapphic Modernism* Collecott includes Euripides and Homer together as part of the male-authored tradition from which H.D. broke. She argues, "My own close reading of H.D. . . . has persuaded me that her entire oeuvre can be read as

a creative dialogue with Sappho, and that it is most vivid when so read" (3). Clearly, there has been significant critical disagreement as to the importance and angle of influence of the classical writers on H.D. My argument, for the purposes of this chapter, considers the contributions from each that would have influenced H.D.'s writing of *Helen in Egypt* as a text about reputation and identity.

12. I am indebted to Eileen Gregory for bringing this quote to my attention, 225.

13. For a discussion of H.D.'s interest in the newly discovered fragments and of their influence on her writing, see Gregory 148–161. For an examination of Sappho's influence on H.D.'s life's work, see Collecott *H.D. and Sapphic Modernism*.

14. All quotes from Sappho are taken from Anne Carson, *If Not, Winter*. NY: Vintage Books, 2002.

15. Eileen Gregory mentions that "reference to Homer and to the heroic" has been "little considered" in H.D. scholarship (173). For Gregory, Homer is "the poet of the warrior, of death and the underworld" (178). She adds in her chapter on Euripides that Homer "is *the* Western poet of war" (219). I hope to suggest a different angle of Homeric influence. Gregory also suggests that H.D. is not as deliberately anti-epic as she is pro-Euripidean drama: "Throughout her career Greek drama appears more significant and accessible to H.D. than Homeric epic" (219).

16. See Aeschylus's *The Eumenides*.

17. Lillian Doherty extends this argument to include not only fictive, but "real" women, as well: "I would argue that in an important sense, women in ancient Greece and Rome were all destined for 'sacrifice' [in the] subordination of all their actual and potential abilities to their marital and reproductive functions. I do not mean to suggest that these women did nothing in adult life but have intercourse and give birth. Rather, their adult lives were organized around these functions, and any activities that were thought to interfere with them – including, in Athens, moving freely about the city – were taboo" (Doherty 94–95). On the other hand, Zweig reminds us that we must "remain alert to possibilities of women's roles and status that have historically been overlooked in descriptions that see only total subordination . . . Removing expectations of total domination, subordination, and control, and removing expectations of hierarchical social structures derived from contemporary models, we become open to the possibility of positive interpretations of women's roles. The concept of complementary spheres . . . and the recognition of the extensive significance of women's spiritual and ritual roles will enable us to see women as interactive agents in their societies . . . this is not to say that we will not find evidence of women's subordination, but that when we do, we can more accurately identify the context and note in what areas women may be subordinate and in which ones they may have primary or complete authority and control" (Zweig 169).

18. The term is used by Aristotle in the *Poetics* to describe the plot device of recognition of identity (e.g. the seeming beggar turns out to be Odysseus).

19. There is no suggestion of a relationship between Helen and Achilles in Homer. See Pausanius 3.19.11 for brief mention of Achilles and Helen as lovers after death on Leuke. Austin writes, "In the tradition outside of the Homeric texts the major heroes of the Trojan expedition have passed through the mortal state to a quasi-divine state. Many were thought to have reached islands somewhere far at sea . . . where they became the tutelary spirits of their respective islands. These were collectively the Islands of the Blest" (26n).

20. There are various sources for the relationship between Theseus and the young Helen. He kidnapped her (some say when she was only twelve years old) in an attempt to marry her. His plans failed and he spent four years in Hades after trying to help his friend abduct Persephone. In the meantime, the Dioscuri (Castor and Pollux) invaded Athens and rescued Helen. She figures only as a minor character in Theseus's story. See Apollodorus *Epitomei* and Plutarch *Parallel Lives*.
21. These events would be impossible according to traditional stories in which Achilles dies at Paris's hand *before* Troy falls.
22. See Deborah Kelly Kloepfer's chapter "She Herself is the Riddling," in *The Unspeakable Mother*. See Jeffery Twitchell-Wass for a connection between Pound's *Cantos* and his embrace of fascism and H.D.'s representation of the Command, the iron-ring.

Chapter two: Sylvia Plath's Complex Electra

1. Plath never wrote about her brother Warren as Orestes and there is no known written record of communication between the siblings regarding their father's death and Sylvia's anger.
2. Judith Kroll's *Chapters in a Mythology* (1976) is the definitive study of Plath's interest in the moon goddess and dying god motif.
3. For analyses on Freud's influence on Plath and her Electra Complex, see Van Pelt, Tamise. "Symptomatic Perfectionism: Ideal Ego and Ego Ideal in the Journals of Sylvia Plath." *Literature and Psychology*, 1997. 43(1–2): 47–64; Bremer, Jan Maarteen. "Three Approaches to Sylvia Plath's 'Electra on Azalea Path'." *Neophilologus*, 1992 April. 76(2): 305–16; Bremer, J.M. "Exit Electra." *Gymnasium* 1991 July. 98(4): 325–42; Manners, Marylin. "The Doxies of Daughterhood: Plath, Cixous, and the Father." *Comparative Literature* 1996 Spring. 48(2): 150–71.
4. In her application to Smith College, Plath included Aeschylus's *Agamemnon* in her selected bibliography of favorite literary works that she had read recently.
5. In her fairly exhaustive study of modern versions of the Clytemnestra myth, *Reclaiming Klytemnestra* (2003), Kathleen Komar only references Plath in a footnote to say, "Poets such as Anne Sexton and Sylvia Plath were writing revisionist texts in the 1950s and 1960s but were not focusing on the women of the Trojan War" (20n7). In fact, Plath shows sustained engagement with the mother/daughter pair. Jill Scott concludes in her study *Electra After Freud* (2005) that Plath "chooses the *Oresteia* as her intertext and not either of the later *Electra* tragedies of antiquity," and that Plath's transformation into Clytemnestra signifies a shift "toward the fertile, creative, and nurturing mother" (145, 161). Scott argues that Plath's "lyric 'I' heals herself of any pathological complex . . . most definitely through the experience of mothering," concluding that "maternity in Plath's poetry . . . begins to nurture the speaking subject in ways that move her beyond the angry and vengeful daughter that is Electra and toward a new persona. . . .one thing is sure—this is the voice not of depression and death but of fertility, creativity, and birth. Plath invents and reinvents poetic personas . . . with a vibrancy and vitality that gush with life and love" (164). I have come to a different conclusion, highlighting the need for an investigation into the nature of Plath's fascination with the House of Atreus.

6. A better known version of the myth, not mentioned in *The Oresteia*, says that Agamemnon bragged that he was a better archer than Artemis and was punished for his hubris.

7. Plath's mother had not wanted Sylvia and her brother Warren to see their father's burial; she arranged for a babysitter during the funeral.

8. In *Electra After Freud* (2005), Jill Scott gives a fascinating interpretation of "Electra on Azalea Path" and other Plath poems in light of Freud's *Mourning and Melancholia* and his theory of incorporation and consumption.

9. The Colossus was a giant statue of Helios, the sun god, on Rhodes. It was one of the seven wonders of the ancient world. In her poem, Plath conflates the god with Agamemnon.

10. Mycenae has the lion's gate and Agamemnon describes his army as "the beast of Argos . . . crashing through their walls our bloody lion lapped its fill" (133). Erich Neumann points out in *The Great Mother* (New York: Pantheon, 1955) that the lioness and bees are symbols of the Great Mother goddess Cybele, Artemis (Diana), and Demeter, whose priestesses at Eleusis were called "bees." See also the entry on bees in *The Complete Dictionary of Symbols* (San Francisco: Chronical Books, 2005).

11. Edge" appears as the final poem in *The Collected Poems*. Plath dated it and her poem "Balloons" February 5, 1963. Because the poems were written on the same day, as of the writing of this chapter, there is no way to know definitively which poem was indeed Plath's final poem.

Chapter three: The Mysteries of Adrienne Rich's Radical Feminism in *The Dream of a Common Language*

1. Rich dated each of her poems individually as a more precise historical record than a poetic collection's publication date would indicate.

2. For the complete *Hymn*, see Foley, Helene. *The Homeric Hymn To Demeter*. Princeton: Princeton U.P., 1994. The Orphic version of the myth was slightly different. We know only parts of it from fragments and references made to it in Sophocles, Euripides, Aristophanes, and Plato.

3. Because the gods ate ambrosia, Carlson is probably referring to the grain as a gift for the gods due to the sacrifices humans would make because of a bountiful harvest.

4. The earlier studies also influenced poets from Tennyson, who wrote "Demeter and Persephone" (1889) to H.D. in her "Demeter," "At Eleusis," and "The Mysteries" to Ezra Pound in "The Pisan Cantos." For Victorian through contemporary poetic and fictional revisions of the myth, see Helene Foley, 151–169. For a discussion of Pound's use of the myth, see Lillian Feder, 202.

5. See Eller's *Living in the Lap of the Goddess*.

6. For various feminist interpretations of the Demeter myth see Kathie Carlson, *Life's Daughter / Death's Bride*. Boston: Shambhala, 1997; Carol Christ. *She Who Changes*. New York: Palgrave MacMillan, 2003; Lillian E. Doherty. *Gender and the Interpretation of Classical Myth*. London: Duckworth, 2001; Christine Downing. *The Long Journey Home*. Boston: Shambhala, 1994; Helene Foley, *The Homeric Hymn to Demeter*. Princeton: Princeton U.P., 1994.

7. See Tamara Agha-Jaffar. *Demeter and Persephone*. Jefferson, NC: McFarland & Co., 2002, 16. For a classicist's discussion of the spiritual feminist movement's appropriation of the Demeter myth, see Foley, 168–169.

8. Rich wrote the poems in the volume between 1974–1977.

9. Cynthia Eller's recent study of the early stages of the Goddess movement, *Living in the Lap of the Goddess*, describes the women involved as predominantly white, middle-class, middle-aged, educated, and "disproportionately lesbian" (18). See also Jill Johnston *Lesbian Nation* (1973) and Judy Grahn *Another Mother Tongue* (1984).

10. There is no definitive historical evidence of pre-Greek matriarchal cultures that the conquering Greeks supplanted.

11. In *Of Woman Born* Rich calls Alpert's essay " a search for vindication of the belief that patriarchy is in some ways a degeneration, that women exerting power would use it differently from men: non-possessively, nonviolently, nondestructively" (72).

12. For a comparison of Rich and H.D.'s desire to return to a maternal love-based culture see Friedman's essay "I Go where I Love": An Intertextual Study of H.D. and Adrienne Rich" in *Coming to Light*.

13. Rich's interpretations of the *Hymn* are not substantiated by classical scholarship. The Greek myth is specifically about the mother/daughter relationship and is not meant as a metaphor for all female relationships. When Demeter requires that humans build her a temple, *men* enact the request and are included along with women as Demeter's worshippers. In fact, the Eleusinian Mysteries did not particularly empower women; they empowered the individual over the State. Rich does not mention that the Mysteries were, in fact, not only open to, but run by men, who "temporarily adopted names with feminine endings, as though the transformed understanding of human relationships and of death that the mysteries provides required entrance into a female perspective" (Downing 3). While this concept might have appealed more to Rich during her "androgyny" phase, by the time she began to use the Eleusinian Mysteries as subject matter for her poetry, she had clearly moved past any desire to work with men and did not think that it was possible for them to "enter [] into a female perspective" (Downing 3). While the lasting power of myths is their ability to incorporate different meanings for different readers, and Rich can use the myth for her own purposes, it is worth noting her appropriation of this particular myth as a metaphor for male-enforced sexual separation, when she might have chosen, for example, Sappho's poetry about the separation of female friends and lovers or the Thesmophoria, an *all-women's* celebration for Demeter during which time "mothers, daughters, sisters, friends, and cousins would find each other . . . , even if geography and other constraints of married life had made it difficult for them to see each other daily" (O'Higgins 153). If Rich wanted an exclusively female festival during which women could reunite, she might instead have chosen the Thesmophoria. Although she never mentions it in *Of Woman Born*, her source material and bibliography for the book suggest that she was aware of the ritual. Rich chose the Eleusinian Mysteries as her model, however, and wrote of them as an expression of female power and unity within a patriarchal system.

Chapter four: Margaret Atwood's Transformed Circe

1. Sharon Wilson's essay "Mythological Intertexts in Margaret Atwood's Works" studies Atwood's use of folk tales, fairy tales, and legends in her poetry and fiction, and offers a broad sketch of various motifs and themes in Atwood's mythic intertexts, which she says

indicate characters' cultural contexts, signify characters' entrapment in a pre-existing pattern, deconstruct plots with transgressive language, filling in gaps in female narrative, comment self-consiously on the frame story and on themselves, and structure the characters' imaginative release from externally imposed patterns, offering transformation and highlighting national, political, postcolonial, and gender themes (125–126).

2. See Jan Garden Castro, 216.

3. See Frye. *The Bush Garden: Essays on the Canadian Imagination.* Toronto: Anansi, 1971.

4. For a reading of Circe as a representation of the moon goddess in "Circe / Mud Poems" see Jane Lilienfeld's "Circe's Emergence: Transforming Traditional Love in Margaret Atwood's *You Are Happy.*"

5. For a wonderful study of Atwood's vast range of revisions and the connections between her goddess writing and visual art, see Sharon R. Wilson's "Mythological Intertexts in Margaret Atwood's Works."

6. Kerényi reminds us, too, that pigs were sacred animals of goddesses such as Cybele and Demeter. See Karl Kerényi, *Goddesses of Sun and Moon.* Dallas, TX: Spring Publications, 1979. See, too, Judith Yarnall. *Transformations of Circe.* Urbana, IL: University of Illinois Press, 1994.

7. Of course, Homer's *Odyssey* is a transcription of myth. When I discuss Odysseus's myth or that the characters are caught in the myth, I am referring to the cycle of stories that has developed around them since Homer.

8. Other male characters that fit this description are Peter from *The Edible Woman,* David from *Surfacing,* and Orpheus from *Interlunar.*

9. The first published piece on domestic violence is "The Concept of Matrimonial Cruelty" by John Michael Biggs. London: University of London, Athlone Press, 1962. A watershed study in the United States is R.J. Gelles, "The Violent Home." Beverly Hills, CA: Sage Press, 1974. See also Pizzey, Erin and Alison Forbes, "Scream Quietly or the Neighbors Will Hear." Harmondsworth: Penguin, 1974.

Chapter five: Eavan Boland's Aging Earth Mother

1. The first written record of the Demeter and Persephone myth is the *Homeric Hymn to Demeter.* For the complete hymn see Helene Foley, ed. *The Homeric Hymn to Demeter: Translation, Commentary, and Interpretive Essays.* I use Foley's translation of the *Hymn* in my summary of the myth in Chapter 3 of this book. The Mysteries are also mentioned in works like Aristophanes' *The Frogs* (405 BC), Herodotus's *History* (ca.425 BC), and Ovid's *Metamorphoses.* For excerpts from these texts see C. Downing (ed.), *The Long Journey Home* (Boston: Shambhala, 1994). Boland uses Demeter's Roman name, Ceres, while keeping the Greek name Persephone instead of using the Roman Proserpine. This highlights Boland's lack of fidelity to one particular version of the myth.

2. See Downing p.19.

3. See Downing, *The Long Journey Home;* T. Agha-Jaffar. *Demeter and Persephone* (Jefferson, NC: McFarland, 2002); L. E. Doherty. *Gender and the Interpretation of Classical Myth* (London: Duckworth, 2001), pp. 15–45; Carlson, *Life's Daughter / Death's Bride.*

4. A non-exhaustive list of texts includes Joseph T. Freeman's *Aging, Its History and Literature* (1979); S.F. Spicker, K.M. Woodward, and D.D. Van Tassel's *Aging and the Elderly: Humanistic Perspectives in Gerontology* (1978); Laurel Porter's *Aging in Literature* (1984); Prisca von Dorotka Bagnell's *Perceptions of Aging in Literature* (1989); Barbara Frey Waxman's *From the Hearth to the Open Road: A Feminist Study of Aging in Contemporary Literature* (1990); Christina Jansohn's *Old Age and Ageing in British and American Culture and Literature* (2004);

5. A study by Calasanti and Slevin indicates that much of feminist scholarship focuses on difficulties for younger women, such as "discrimination in the paid labor force; the challenges of childbearing and child rearing; and issues associated with dual-earner families. . ." (cited in Allen and Walker 158–159). See Roberta Maierhofer p. 164 and Ingrid Arnet Connidis p. 125

6. See *Object Lessons* for an account of the influences on her, including Alicia Ostriker's *Stealing the Language* (148).

7. Compare with Keats' 'Cold pastoral! When old age shall this generation waste, / thou shalt remain [. . .].' (ll. 45–47) from 'Ode on a Grecian Urn.' See J. Keats, 'Ode on a Grecian Urn', in Duncan Wu (ed.), *Romanticism: An Anthology*, 2nd ed. (Oxford: Blackwell Publishers, 1998), pp. 1060–1061.

8. 'A Formal Feeling' alludes to Emily Dickinson's poem #341. Dickinson worked in traditional meter and form—hymn and ballad stanzas—but radically challenged the conventional purposes of those forms to subvert patriarchal and biblical orthodoxy.

9. One might argue that, with Keats' 'Urn' for instance, men are also fixed in undying images: 'bold lover, never, never canst thou kiss, / Though winning near the goal—yet do not grieve; / She cannot fade, though thou hadst not thy bliss, / For ever wilt thou love, and she be fair!' (ll. 17–20). Boland dismisses the argument that the problem is one of all art, and not one of gender: "The young man in decorative chase on the side of the urn has the sexual perspective which seeks to possess; the maiden has the erotic task of being simply mute and beautiful" (*OL* 216). While art preserves the man, his desire reflects a masculine perspective that could be associated with the artist, whereas the maiden is entirely objectified. Boland does not discuss images of men that *do* depict aging or flux. There are some famous examples of Irish male poets' depictions of themselves as aged. Boland knew well Yeats' "The Tower," for example, in which he asks, "What shall I do with this absurdity / …This caricature, / Decrepit age that has been tied to me / As to a dog's tail," and his "Sailing to Byzantium," in which he declares that "An aged man is but a paltry thing, / A tattered coat upon a stick." There were also attempts by Irish male writers to depict older female characters. Yeats's 'Crazy Jane' poems and Synge's Nora Burke, in his play *In the Shadow of the Glen*, are examples of potential exceptions that Boland does not address. Synge's Nora was intensely controversial—a peasant woman with sexual needs, fears, and hopes that lay beyond her role as mother and wife. Maud Gonne walked out of the premiere. Arthur Griffith's vituperative attack claimed that Nora would never leave with the tramp because 'Irish women are the most virtuous women in the world' (*United Irishman* 24 October 1903). This outrage at a woman who did not live up to the Virgin Mary-like standard that Irish culture imposed on its women indicates the weight against which Boland must work in her attempt to forge a place in Irish literature for older women with emotions, desires, and dreams that do not fit into the prescribed niche.

10. I do not want to suggest that the Demeter/Ceres myth is simply or uniformly "patriarchal." As many scholars have shown, this myth has numerous variants spanning several hundred

years, and even readings of individual versions vary tremendously. See Doherty, *Gender and the Interpretation of Classical Myth*; Downing, *The Long Journey Home*; and Carlson, *Life's Daughter / Death's Bride*. I will, however, follow Boland's example and place the myth within the larger tradition of patriarchal literature.

11. See A.R.C. Finch,'Dickinson and Patriarchal Meter: A Theory of Metrical Codes', *PMLA*, 102 (1987), pp. 166–176, p. 174. Finch's article discusses Emily Dickinson, but we can apply her argument to Boland.

12. In the variant version found in Ovid's *Metamorphoses*, Ceres never undergoes the transformation into an older woman.

13. see P. Young-Eisendrath. 'Demeter's Folly: Experiencing Loss in Middle Life', in Christine Downing (ed.), *The Long Journey Home* (Boston: Shambhala, 1994), pp. 206–218; C. Downing *The Long Journey Home*, pp. 233–242.

14. see Valerie Saiving, 'Androgynous Life: A Feminist Appropriation of Process Thought', in S. Greeve Daveney (ed.), *Feminism and Process Thought* (New York: Edwin W. Mellen Press, 1981). pp. 18–28.

15. Boland must also have in mind Yeats's 'A Prayer for my Daughter' in which he hopes that 'she become a flourishing hidden tree / [. . .] / O may she live like some green laurel / Rooted in one dear perpetual place. / [. . .] / Assault and battery of the wind / Can never tear the linnet from the leaf.' Boland used the Daphne myth in poems in earlier volumes to revise Yeats's patronizing use of Ovid's myth. In her Ceres poems from *The Lost Land*, she allows, in the inevitable process of time and ageing to which she attests, for this perpetually blooming Daphne to be freed from the tree, to bear fruit and fall to earth.

16. In *The Homeric Hymn to Demeter*, Hekate is not a crone. This interpretation seems to be a modern conception, which includes Hekate as the oldest part of the triple goddess (Persephone, Demeter, Hekate).

17. See Tracey L. Walter's *African American Literature and the Classicist Tradition*; see William W. Cook and James Tatum's *African American Writers and Classical Tradition*.

Bibliography

Aeschylus. *The Oresteia*. Trans. Robert Fagles. New York: Penguin, 1977.

Agha-Jaffar, Tamara. *Demeter and Persephone* (Jefferson, NC: McFarland & Company, 2002).

Alexander, Paul. *Rough Magic: A Biography of Sylvia Plath*. Cambridge, MA: Da Capo Press, 1999.

Atwood, Margaret. *True Stories*. NY: Simon & Schuster, 1981.

———. *You Are Happy*. NY: Harper Row Publishers, 1974.

———. *Morning in the Burned House*. Boston: Houghton Mifflin Company, 1995.

———. *The Penelopiad*. New York: Canongate, 2005.

Auden, W.H. Introduction. *Change of World*. By Adrienne Rich. New York: Norton, 1951.

Austin, Norman. *Helen of Troy and Her Shameless Phantom*. Ithaca: Cornell U.P., 1994.

Bachofen, J. J. *Myth, Religion, and Mother Right* (Princeton: Princeton University Press, 1973).

Bang, Mary Jo. *Apology For Want*. Hanover: NH: University Press of New England, 1997.

"Battle on the Trojan Plain." [London] *Times* 30 April 1915, II, col. 4.

Bell, Michael. *Literature, Modernism, and Myth*. Cambridge: Cambridge U.P., 1997

Bellin, Steven. "Tricking the Muse By Taking Out the Trash" (1993). *Conversations With Rita Dove*. Ed. Earl G. Ingersoll. Jackson: MS: University of Mississippi, 2003.

Bennett, Karen. "The Recurrent Quest: Demeter and Persephone in Modern-Day Ireland." *Classical and Modern Literature*, 23,1 (2003), pp. 15–32.

Bennett, Paula. *My Life A Loaded Gun*. Boston: Beacon Press, 1986.

Benstock, Shari. *Women of the Left Bank: Paris 1900–1940*. Austin: University of Texas Press, 1986.

Biggs, John Michael. *The Concept of Matrimonial Cruelty*. London: University of London, Athlone Press, 1962.

Boland, Eavan. *An Origin Like Water: Collected Poems 1967–1987* (New York: W. W. Norton, 1996).

———. 'Daughters.' *Academy of American Poets — Poetry Exhibits*. 2 April 2000. <http://www.poets.org/LIT/exh/ex009.html>

———. *Domestic Violence*. New York: WW.Norton, 2007.

———. *In a Time of Violence* (New York: W. W. Norton, 1994).

———. *The Lost Land* (New York: W. W. Norton, 1998).

———. *Object Lessons*. New York: W.W. Norton and Co., 1995.

———. Poetry Reading. University of Texas at Austin. 3 November 2005.

———. 'The Woman Poet: Her Dilemma', *Midland Review* 3 (1986), p. 41.

Buchbinder, David. "Weaving Her Vision: The Homeric Model and Gender Politics in *Selected Poems*." *Margaret Atwood: Vision and Forms*. Ed, Kathryn Van Spanckeren and Castro, Jan Garden. Carbondale, IL: Southern Illinois U.P., 1988.

Buck, Claire. *H.D. and Freud: Bisexuality and a Feminine Discourse*. New York: St. Martin's, 1991.

Bunch, Charlotte and Nancy Myron. *Class and Feminism: A Collection of Essays from the Furies*. Baltimore: Diana Press, 1974.

Burnett, Gary. *H.D.: Between Image and Epic*. Ann Arbor: UMI Research Press, 1990.

Bush, Douglas. "H.D.'s Greece." *Mythology and the Romantic Tradition in English Poetry*. 1937. Cambridge, MA: Harvard U.P., 1969.

Byars, Jackie. "The Prime of Miss Kim Novak: Struggling Over the Feminine in the Star Image." *The Other Fifties*. Ed. Joel Foreman. Chicago: University of Illinois, 1997.

Calasanti, Toni M. and Kathleen F. Slevin, Eds. *Age Matters*. NY: Routledge, 2006.

Carlson, Kathie. *Life's Daughter / Death's Bride* (Boston: Shambhala, 1997).

Carson, Anne, trans. *If Not, Winter: Fragments of Sappho*. New York: Vintage Books, 2002.

———. *Glass, Irony, and God*. NY: New Directions, 1995.

———. *Autobiography of Red*. NY: Vintage, 1998.

Castro, Jan Garden. "An Interview With Margaret Atwood: 20 April 1983." *Margaret Atwood: Vision and Forms*. Ed, Kathryn Van Spanckeren and Castro, Jan Garden. Carbondale, IL: Southern Illinois U.P., 1988.

Chisholm, Dianne. *H.D.'s Freudian Poetics: Psychoanalysis in Translation*. Ithaca, NY: Cornell U.P., 1992.

Christ, Carol P. *Rebirth of the Goddess: Finding Meaning in Feminist Spirituality*. New York: Addison-Wesley Publishing Company, 1997.

———. *She Who Changes: Re-Imagining the Divine in the World*. New York: Palgrave Macmillan, 2003.

Cixous, Helene. *The Newly Born Woman*. Trans. Betsy Wing. Minneapolis: University of Minnesota Press, 1986.

Clifton, Lucille. *Blessing the Boats: New and Selected Poems 1988–2000*. Rochester: NY: BOA Editions, 2000.

Collecott, Diana. *H.D. and Sapphic Modernism*. Cambridge: Cambridge U.P., 1999.

Cook, William W. and James Tatum. *African American Writers and Classical Tradition*. Chicago: University of Chicago Press, 2010.

Cooke, Nathalie. *Margaret Atwood: A Biography*. Toronto: ECW Press, 1998.

Crown, Kathleen. "'The mother is the muse H.D. said': Re-membering the Reader in H.D.'s *Helen in Egypt* and Sharon Doubiago's Early Long Poems." *H.D. and Poets After*. Hollenburg, Donna Krolik, Ed. Iowa City: U. of Iowa, 2000.

Daly, Mary. *Beyond God the Father: Toward a Philosophy of Women's Liberation*. Boston: Beacon, 1973.

Dante. *The Inferno*. Trans. Robert Pinsky. London: Farrar, Straus, and Giroux, 1994.

Davey, Frank. *Margaret Atwood: A Feminist Poetics*. Vancouver: Talon Books, 1984.

DiBattista, Maria and Lucy McDiarmid, eds. *High and Low Moderns: Literature and Culture, 1889–1939*. New York: Oxford U.P., 1996.

Djwa, Sandra. "Back to the Primal: The Apprenticeship of Margaret Atwood." *Various Atwoods*. Ed., Lorraine M. York. Ontario: House of Anansi, 1995.

Dodd, Elizabeth. *The Veiled Mirror and the Woman Poet*. Columbia: U. of Missouri Press, 1992.

Doherty, Lillian E. *Gender and the Interpretation of Classical Myth*. London: Duckworth, 2001.

Donovan, Josephine. *Feminist Theory: The Intellectual Traditions, Third Edition*. New York: Continuum, 2000.

Dove, Rita. *Mother Love*. NY: Norton, 1995.

Dowling, Linda. *Hellenism and Homosexuality in Victorian Oxford*. Ithaca, NY: Cornell U.P., 1994.

Downing, Christine. *The Long Journey Home* (Boston: Shambhala, 1994).

duBois, Page. "Sappho and Helen." *Reading Sappho: Contemporary Approaches*. Ed., Ellen Greene. Berkeley: University of California Press, 1996.

DuPlessis, Rachel Blau. *H.D. The Career of That Struggle*. Bloomington: Indiana U.P., 1986.

———. *Writing Beyond the Ending*. Bloomington: Indiana U.P., 1985.

———. "Haibun: "Draw your / Draft." *H.D. and Poets After*. Ed. Hollenberg, Donna Krolik. Iowa City: U. of Iowa Press, 2000.

Edmonds, J.M. [The Berlin Fragments]. "Three Fragments of Sappho." *Classical Review* 23(June 1909): 99–104.

Edmunds, Susan. *Out of Line*. Stanford: Stanford U.P., 1994.

Eliot, T.S. *The Letters of T.S. Eliot*, v.1: 1898–1922. New York: Harcourt Brace Jovanovich, 1988.

———. *Selected Prose*. Ed. Frank Kermode. New York: Harcourt Brace Jovanovich; Farrar, Straus & Giroux, 1975.

———. "Ulysses, Order, and Myth." *Dial*. (Nov. 1923).

———. "A Commentary" [by "Crites"]. *Criterion* 2 (April 1924): 231–32.

Eller, Cynthia. *Living in the Lap of the Goddess* (New York: Crossroad, 1993).

Ellmann, Richard, Ed. *The Norton Anthology of Modern Poetry*. New York: W.W. Norton, 1988.

Euripides. *The Medea*. Grene, David and Richard Lattimore, Eds. Chicago: University of Chicago Press, 1955.

———. *Medea*. Trans. Rex Warner. Chicago: U. of Chicago P., 1946.

———. *Helen*. Trans. Richard Lattimore. Chicago: U. of Chicago, 1956.

———. *Electra*. Trans. Paul Roche. NY: Signet, 1998.

———. *Trojan Women*. Trans. Paul Roche. NY: Signet, 1998.

Evans, Sir Arthur. "The Earlier Religion of Greece in the Light of Cretan Discoveries." *The Frazer Lectures 1922–1932 By Divers Hands.* 1932 Ed. Warren R. Dawson. Freeport, NY: Books for Libraries P, 1967. 248–288.

Faderman, Lillian. *Surpassing the Love of Men: Romantic Friendship and Love Between Women.* London: Junction Books, 1981.

Fahey, Diane. "Working With Greek Mythology." *Feminist Poetics of the Sacred.* Eds. Frances Devlin-Glass and McCredden, Lyn. New York: Oxford U.P., 2001.

Ferguson, Margaret, Ed. *The Norton Anthology of Poetry.* New York: W.W. Norton, 1996.

Ferris, David S. *Silent Urns: Romanticism, Hellenism, and Modernity.* Stanford: Stanford U.P., 2000.

Finch, Anne. 'Dickinson and Patriarchal Meter: A Theory of Metrical Codes', *PMLA,* 102 (1987), pp. 166–176.

Firestone, Shulamith. *The Dialectic of Sex: The Case for Feminist Revolution.* New York: Bantam, 1971.

——— and Anne Koedt, eds. *Notes From the Second Year: Radical Feminism.* New York: Bantam, 1970.

Fogarty, A. "'The Influence of Absences": Eavan Boland and the Silenced History of Irish Women's Poetry', *Colby Quarterly,* 35, 4 (1999), pp. 256–274.

Foley, Helene P. *Female Acts in Greek Tragedy.* Princeton: Princeton U.P., 2001.

———. *The Homeric Hymn to Demeter.* Princeton: Princeton U.P., 1994.

Foster, T. C. 'In from the Margin: Eavan Boland's "Outside History" Sequence', in Alexander G. Gonzalez (ed.), *Contemporary Irish Women Poets: Some Male Perspectives* (London: Greenwood Press, 1999), pp. 1–12.

Friedman, Susan Stanford. "Who Buried H.D.?: A Poet, Her Critics, and Her Place in 'The Literary Tradition.'" *College English* 36 (March 1975): 801–14.

———. "'I Go Where I Love': An Intertextual Study of H.D. and Adrienne Rich." *Coming to Light.* Diane Wood Middlebrook and Marylin Yalom, eds. Ann Arbor: U. of Michigan, 1985.

———. *Penelope's Web: Gender, Modernity, H.D.'s Fiction.* Cambridge: Cambridge U.P., 1990.

———. "Creating a Women's Mythology: H.D.'s *Helen in Egypt*" in *Signets.* Eds. Friedman, Susan Stanford and Rachael Blau DuPlessis. Madison: University of Wisconsin: 1990.

Frye, Northrop. The Bush Garden: Essays on the Canadian Imagination. Toronto: Anansi, 1971.

Gelles, R.J. *The Violent Home.* Beverly Hills, CA: Sage Press, 1974.

Gelpi, Alpert. "'Hazard and Death": The Poetry of Eavan Boland', *Colby Quarterly,* 35, 4 (1999), pp. 210–228.

Gilbert, Sandra and Susan Gubar. *No Man's Land Vol.1.* New Haven: Yale U.P., 1988.

———. *No Man's Land Vol. 2.* New Haven:Yale U.P., 1989.

Glück, Louise. *Meadowlands.* Hopewell, NJ: The Ecco Press, 1996.

Gould, Eric. *Mythical Intentions in Modern Literature.* Princeton: Princeton U.P., 1981.

Graves, Robert. *The White Goddess.* NY: Farrar Straus & Cudahy, 1948.

Greene, D. 'Ancient Myth and Poetry: A Panel Discussion', in Joseph Ronsley (ed.), *Myth and Reality in Irish Literature* (Ontario: Wilfrid Laurier University Press, 1977).

Gregory, Eileen. *H.D. and Hellenism.* Cambridge: Cambridge U.P., 1997.

Gubar, Susan. "The Echoing Spell of H.D.'s *Trilogy*" in *Signets: Reading H.D.* Eds. Friedman, Susan Stanford and Rachael Blau DuPlessis. Madison: University of Wisconsin, 1990.

Guest, Barbara. *Herself Defined: The Poet H.D. and Her World.* New York: Doubleday, 1984.

Haberstroh, P. Boyle. *Women Creating Women* (Syracuse: Syracuse University Press, 1996).

Hammer, Dean. *The* Iliad *as Politics.* Norman: U. of Oklahoma, 2002.

Harding, Mary Esther. *Woman's Mysteries: Ancient and Modern.* New York: G.P. Putnam's Sons, 1972.

Harrison, Elizabeth Jane and Shirley Peterson, Ed. *Unmanning Modernism.* Knoxville: U of Tennessee, 1997.

Harrison, Jane Ellen. *Prolegomena to the Study of Greek Religion* (Cambridge: Cambridge University Press, 1903).

Harvey, Brett. *The Fifties.* NY: Harper Collins, 1993.

H.D. *End to Torment.* New York: New Directions, 1979.

———. *Helen in Egypt.* New York: New Directions, 1961.

———. Letters to Norman Holmes Pearson. *Between History and Poetry: The Letters of H.D. and Norman Holmes Pearson.* Donna Krolik Hollenberg, ed. Iowa City: U. of Iowa Press, 1997.

———. Letters to Richard Aldington. TS. H.D. Papers. Yale Collection of American Literature, Beinecke Rare Book and Manuscript Library. Yale University, New Haven, CT.

———. "Notes on Euripides, Pausanius, and Greek Lyric Poets." TS. H.D. Papers. Yale Collection of American Literature. Beinecke Rare Book and Manuscript Library, Yale University, New Haven , CT.

———. *Notes on Euripides.* San Fransisco: City Lights Press, 1982, 1919.

———. *Notes on Thought and Vision.* San Fransisco: City Lights Press, 1982.

———. *Flowering of the Rod.* New York: Oxford U.P., 1946.

Henneberg, Sylvia. "The Self-Catergorization, Self-Canonization, and Self-Periodization of Adrienne Rich" in *Challenging Boundaries.* Joyce W. Warren and Dickie, Margaret, eds. Athens, GA: University of Georgia, 2000.

Hoberman, Ruth. *Gendering Classicism: The Ancient World in Twentieth-Century Women's Historical Fiction.* NY: SUNY Press, 1997.

Hokanson, Robert O'Brien. "'Is It All a Story?': Questioning Revision in H.D.'s *Helen in Egypt.*" *American Literature* 64.2 (1992): 331–346.

Hollenberg, Donna Krolik. *H.D: The Poetics of Childbirth and Creativity.* Boston: Northeastern U.P., 1991.

———, ed. *Between History and Poetry: The Letters of H.D. and Norman_ Holmes Pearson.* Iowa City: U. of Iowa P., 1997.

Hollis, Hilda. "Between the Scylla of Essentialism and the Charybdis of Deconstruction: Margaret Atwood's *True Stories.*" *Various Atwoods.* Ed., Lorraine M. York. Ontario: House of Anansi, 1995.

Holstein, Martha. "On Being an Aging Woman" in *Age Matters.* Eds. Toni M. Calasanti and Kathleen F. Slevin. NY: Routledge, 2006.

Homer. *The Iliad.* Trans. E.V. Rieu. New York: Penguin, 1950.

———. *The Odyssey.* Trans. E.V. Rieu. New York: Penguin, 1946.

Honninghausen, Lothar. "Margaret Atwood's Poetry 1966–1995." *Margaret Atwood Works and Impact*. Ed, Reingard M. Nischik. Rochester, NY: Camden House, 2000.

Hooley, Daniel M. *The Classics in Paraphrase: Ezra Pound and Modern Translators of Latin Poetry*. Cranbury, NJ: Associated U.P., 1988.

Hulme, T.E. *Further Speculations*. Samuel Hynes, ed. Minneapolis, U. of Minnesota P., 1955.

———. "Romanticism and Classicism." *The Collected Writings of T.E. Hulme*. Karen Csengeri, ed. New York: Oxford University Press, 1994.

Jenkyns, Richard. *The Victorians and Ancient Greece*. Cambridge, MA: Harvard U.P., 1980.

Joplin, Patricia Klindienst. "Epilogue: Philomela's Loom" in *Coming to Light*. Diane Wood Middlebrook and Marylin Yalom, eds. Ann Arbor: U. of Michigan, 1985.

Jung, Carl. 'The Psychological Aspects of Kore', in Carl Jung and Carl Kerenyi (eds), *Essays on a Science of Mythology* (Princeton: Princeton University Press, 1969).

Keane, P. J. *Terrible Beauty: Yeats, Joyce, Ireland, and the Myth of the Devouring Female* (Columbia: University of Missouri Press, 1988).

Keats, John. 'Ode on a Grecian Urn', in Duncan Wu, *Romanticism: An Anthology*, 2nd ed. Oxford: Blackwell Publishers, 1998, pp. 1060–1061.

Kenner, Hugh. *The Pound Era*. Berkeley: University of California Press, 1971.

Kerényi, Carl. *Eleusis: Archetypal Image of Mother and Daughter*. New York: Pantheon, 1967.

Kloepfer, Deborah Kelly. *The Unspeakable Mother*. Ithaca: Cornell U.P., 1989.

Knott, E. *Irish Classical Poetry* (Dublin: Sign of the Three Candles, 1957).

Komar, Kathleen. *Reclaiming Klytemnestra*. Urbana, IL: University of Illinois Press, 2003.

Korg, Jacob. *Winter Love: Ezra Pound and H.D.* Madison: U. of Wisconsin P., 2003.

Kroll, Judith. *Chapters in a Mythology*. NY: Harper & Row, 1976.

Laity, Cassandra. *H.D. and the Victorian Fin de Siecle*. Cambridge: Cambridge U.P., 1996.

Laks, Batya Casper. *Electra*. Jefferson, NC: McFarland & Co, 1995.

Leach, Colin. Introduction. *Helen*. By Euripides. New York: Oxford U.P., 1981.

Levin, Phillis. *The Afterimage*. Providence, RI: Copper Beach Press, 1995.

Lilienfeld, Jane. "Circe's Emergence: Transforming Traditional Love in Margaret Atwood's *You Are Happy*." *Critical Essays on Margaret Atwood*. Ed, Judith McCombs. Boston: G.K. Hall & Co., 1988.

Mardona, Karen. "Sylvia and Ruth." 29 November, 2004. http://dir.salon.com/story/books/feature/2004/11/29/plath_therapist/index.html

Markey, Janice. *A New Tradition? The Poetry of Sylvia Plath, Anne Sexton, and Adrienne Rich*. New York: Peter Lang, 1985.

Meagher, Robert Emmet. Introduction. *Helen*. By Euripides. Amherst: University of Massachusetts, 1986.

Medovoi, Leerom. "Democracy, Capitalism, and American Literature: The Cold War Construction of J.D. Salinger's Paperback Hero." *The Other Fifties*. Ed. Joel Foreman. Chicago: University of Illinois Press, 1997.

Meisel, Perry. *The Myth of the Modern: A Study in British Literature and Criticism after 1850*. New Haven, CT: Yale U.P., 1987.

Meletinsky, Eleazar M. *The Poetics of Myth*. Guy Lanoue and Alexandre Sadetsky, trans. New York: Garland Publishing, 1998.

Meyer, Marvin W., Ed. *The Ancient Mysteries: A Sourcebook*. San Francisco: Harper Collins, 987.

Middlebrook, Diane. *Her Husband: Hughes and Plath, A Marriage*. NY: Viking Press, 2003.

Nagy, Gregory. *The Best of the Achaeans*. Baltimore: Johns Hopkins U.P., 1979.

Neumann, Erich. *The Great Mother*. NY: Pantheon, 1955.

Nicholls, Peter. *Modernisms: A Literary Guide*. Berkeley: University of California Press, 1995.

Nietzsche, Friedrich. *The Birth of Tragedy and The Case of Wagner*. Trans. Walter Kaufmann. New York: Vintage-Random House, 1967.

O'Higgins, D.M. "Women's Cultic Joking and Mockery." *Making Silence Speak*. Eds. Andre Lardinois and McClure, Laura. Princeton: Princeton U.P., 2001.

Ostriker, Alicia Suskin. *Stealing the Language*. Boston: Beacon Press, 1986.

———. "A Wish to Make Real to Myself What Is Most Real: My H.D." *H.D. and Poets After*. Ed. Hollenberg, Donna Krolik. Iowa City: U. of Iowa Press, 2000.

Ovid. *Metamorphoses*. Trans. M. M. Innes. (London: Penguin Books, 1955).

Peabody, Richard and Gretchen Johnson. "A Cage of Sound" (1985). *Conversations With Rita Dove*. Ed. Earl G. Ingersoll. Jackson: MS: University of Mississippi, 2003.

Pereira, Malin. "Going Up Is a Place of Great Loneliness" (1998). *Conversations With Rita Dove*. Ed. Earl G. Ingersoll. Jackson: MS: University of Mississippi, 2003.

Perl, Jeffrey. *The Tradition of Return: The Implicit History of Modern Literature*. Princeton: Princeton U.P., 1984.

Pizzey, Erin and Alison Forbes. *Scream Quietly or the Neighbors Will Hear*. Harmondsworth: Penguin, 1974.

Plath, Sylvia. *The Collected Poems*. Ed. Ted Hughes. NY: Harper Collins, 1992.

———. *The Unabridged Journals of Sylvia Plath*. Ed. Karen V. Kukil. NY: Anchor Books, 2000.

———. *Johnny Panic and the Bible of Dreams*. NY: Harper & Row, 1980.

———. *Letters Home*. NY: HarperPerennial, 1992.

Polson, Deanna L. "A Sublime Blending: H.D.'s *Trilogy* as Memoir, Quest, and Alchemical Allegory." Honors Thesis. U of British Columbia, Okanagan, 2006.

Porter, Laurel and Laurence M. Porter, Eds. *Aging in Literature*. Troy, MI: International Book Publishers, 1984.

Pound, Ezra. "Hugh Selwyn Mauberly." *Selected Poems*. New York: New Directions, 1957.

———. *New Age*, 1 August 1918.

———. Postscript. *Natural Philosophy of Love*. By de Gourmont. New York: Ray Long and Richard R. Smith, 1933.

———. *Literary Essays of Ezra Pound*. Ed. T.S. Eliot. New York: New Directions, 1954.

———. *The Letters of Ezra Pound, 1907–1941*. Ed. D.D. Paige. New York: Harcourt, Brace, & World, 1950.

———. *Selected Letters of Ezra Pound and Louis Zukofsky*. Ed. Barry Ahern. New York: New Directions, 1987.

Powell, Barry, ed. *Classical Myth*, fourth ed. Upper Saddle River, NJ: Pearson Education Inc, 2004.

Rich, Adrienne. *On Lies, Secrets, and Silence*. New York: Norton, 1995.

———. *Diving into the Wreck*. New York: W.W. Norton, 1973.

———. *The Dream of a Common Language*. New York: Norton, 1978.

————. *Of Woman Born*. New York: Norton, 1986.

————. *Blood, Bread, and Poetry*. New York: Norton, 1986.

————. *Collected Early Poems: 1950–1970*. New York: Norton, 1993.

————. *The Fact of a Doorframe: Selected Poems 1950–2001*. New York: Norton, 2002.

Riding, Laura, and Robert Graves. *A Survey of Modernist Poetry*. 1927. St. Clair Shores, Mich: Scholarly Press, 1972.

Roche, Paul. "Introduction to *Electra*." *Euripides Ten Plays*. NY: Signet, 1998.

Rosenberg, Jerome H. *Margaret Atwood*. Boston: Twayne Publishers, 1984.

Ross, Andrew. *The Failure of Modernism: Symptoms of American Poetry*. New York: Columbia U.P., 1986.

Saiving, Valerie. 'Androgynous Life: A Feminist Appropriation of Process Thought', in S. Greeve Daveney (ed.), *Feminism and Process Thought* (New York: Edwin W. Mellen Press, 1981), pp. 18–28, p. 28.

Sarbin, Deborah. "'Out of Myth Into History": The Poetry of Eavan Boland and Eiléan Ní Chuilleanáin', *Canadian Journal of Irish Studies*, 19, 1 (1993), pp. 86–96.

Schuchard, Ronald. "T.S. Eliot as an Extension Lecturer, 1916–1919." *Review of English Studies* n.s. 25 (1974): 163–73.

Scott, Bonnie Kime. *Refiguring Modernism: The Women of 1928, v.1*. Bloomington: Indiana U.P., 1995.

————. *Refiguring Modernism: Postmodern Feminist Readings of Woolf, West, and Barnes, v.2*. Bloomington: Indiana U.P., 1995.

Scott, Jill. *Electra After Freud*. Ithaca, NY: Cornell U.P., 2005.

Seidensticker, Bernd. "Women on the Tragic Stage." *History, Tragedy, Theory*. Barbara Goff, ed. Austin: University of Texas, 1995.

Shakespeare, W. *Complete Sonnets* (New York: Dover Publications, 1991).

Sophocles. *Electra. Electra and Other Plays*. Trans. E.F. Watling. NY: Penguin, 1953.

————. *Philoctetes. Electra and Other Plays*. Trans. E.F. Watling. NY: Penguin, 1953.

Spivey, Ted R. *Beyond Modernism: Toward a New Myth Criticism*. Lanham, MD: University Press of America, 1988.

Spretnak, Charlene, ed. *The Politics of Women's Spirituality: Essays on the Rise of Spiritual Power in the Movement*. Garden City: NY: Doubleday, 1981.

Staley, Gregory, ed. *American Women and Classical Myths*. Waco, TX: Baylor U.P., 2009.

Steffen, Therese. "Rooted Displacement in Form: Rita Dove's Sonnet Cycle *Mother Love*." *The Furious Flowering of African American Poetry*. Joanne Gabbin, ed. Charlottesville: VA: University Press of Virginia, 1999.

————. *Crossing Color*. NY: Oxford U.P., 2001.

Sullivan, Rosemary. *The Red Shoes: Margaret Atwood Starting Out*. Toronto: Harper Collins, 1998.

Swartwout, Susan. "Language Is More Clay Than Stone" (1989). *Conversations With Rita Dove*. Ed. Earl G. Ingersoll. Jackson: MS: University of Mississippi, 2003.

Synge, J.M. *In the Shadow of the Glen* (Boston: J.W. Luce and Company, 1911).

Taylor, Georgina. *H.D. and the Public Sphere of Modernist Women Writers, 1913–1946*. Oxford: Clarendon Press, 2001.

Templeton, Alice. *The Dream and the Dialogue: Adrienne Rich's Feminist Poetics.* Knoxville, University of Tennessee, 1994.

Thurston, Michael. "'A Deliberate Collection of Cross Purposes": Eavan Boland's Poetic Sequences', *Colby Quarterly,* 34, 4 (1999), pp. 229–251.

Toohey, Peter. *Reading Epic.* New York: Routledge, 1992.

Turner, Frank M. *The Greek Heritage in Victorian Britain.* New Haven, CT: Yale U.P., 1981.

Twitchell-Wass, Jeffery. "Seaward: H.D.'s *Helen in Egypt* as a Response to Pound's *Cantos.*" *Twentieth Century Literature* 44.4 (1998): 464–484.

Ude, Wayne. "Having the Picture Coalesce in a Kind of Whoosh!" (1992). *Conversations With Rita Dove.* Ed. Earl G. Ingersoll. Jackson: MS: University of Mississippi, 2003.

Vandiver, Elizabeth. *The Iliad of Homer.* Chicago: The Teaching Company, 1999.

Virgil. *The Aeneid.* Trans. W.F. Jackson Knight. New York: Penguin, 1956.

Watson, Steven. *Strange Bedfellows: The First American Avant-Garde.* New York: Abbeville Press, 1991.

Wagner-Martin, Linda. "'Giving Way to Bedrock': Atwood's Later Poems." *Various Atwoods.* Ed., Lorraine M. York. Ontario: House of Anansi, 1995.

Walters, Tracey L. *African American Literature and the Classicist Tradition.* NY: Palgrave Macmillan, 2007.

Waxman, Barbara Frey. *From the Hearth to the Open Road.* NY: Greenwood Press, 1990.

Wilson, Sharon R. "Mythological Intertexts in Margaret Atwood's Works." *Margaret Atwood Works and Impact.* Ed, Reingard M. Nischik. Rochester, NY: Camden House, 2000.

Winkler, Jack. "Gardens of Nymphs: Public and Private in Sappho's Lyrics." *Reading Sappho: Contemporary Approaches.* Ed., Ellen Greene. Berkeley: University of California Press, 1996.

Witte, Sarah Ellen. *H.D., Archaeology, and Modernism.* Ann Arbor, U.M.I., 1993.

Worman, Nancy. "This Voice Which Is Not One: Helen's Verbal Guises in Homeric Epic." *Making Silence Speak.* Ed. Laura McClure.

Wyatt-Brown, Anne M. and Janice Rossen, Eds. *Aging and Gender in Literature.* Charlottesville, VA: University Press of Virginia, 1993.

Yarnall, Judith. *Transformations of Circe: The History of an Enchantress.* Urbana, IL: University of Illinois Press, 1994.

Yeats, W.B. 'A Prayer for my Daughter', in Richard J. Finneran (ed.), *The Collected Poems of W.B. Yeats, 2nd ed.* (New York: Scribner Paperback Poetry, 1996), p. 188.

———. 'Crazy Jane Talks with the Bishop', in Richard J. Finneran (ed.), *The Collected Poems of W.B. Yeats, 2nd ed.* (New York: Scribner Paperback Poetry, 1996), p. 259.

———. 'Sailing to Byzantium,' in Richard J. Finneran (ed.), *The Collected Poems of W.B. Yeats, 2nd ed.* (New York: Scribner Paperback Poetry, 1996), p. 193.

Young-Eisendrath, P. 'Demeter's Folly: Experiencing Loss in Middle Life', in C. Downing (ed.), *The Long Journey Home* (Boston: Shambhala, 1994), pp. 206–218.

Zajdel, Melody McCollum. *The Development of a Poetic Vision: H.D.'s Growth from Imagist to Mythologist.* Ann Arbor: U.M.I., 1979.

Zeitlin, Froma. 'Cultic Models of the Female: Rites of Dionysus and Demeter', *Arethusa,* 15,1(1982), pp. 129–157.

————. "The Argive Festival of Hera and Euripides' *Electra*." *Oxford Readings in Classical Studies: Euripides*. Ed. Judith Mossman. Oxford: Oxford U.P., 2003.

Zelenak, Michael X. *Gender and Politics in Greek Tragedy*. New York: Peter Lang, 1998.

Zweig, Bella. "The Primal Mind: Using Native American Models for the Study of Women in Ancient Greece." *Feminist Theory and the Classics*. Eds. Rabinowitz, Nancy Sorkin and Amy Richlin. New York; Routledge, 1993.

Index

Studies in Modern Poetry

THIS SERIES BRINGS TOGETHER BOOK-LENGTH WORKS ON PARTICULAR MODERN poets and twentieth-century movements as well as comparative and theoretical studies. Works in the series seek to explore the contributions of twentieth-century poets beyond the well-known major figures of Modernism such as Ezra Pound and T. S. Eliot, in the belief that modern poetry is characterized by its variety, richness, and scope. A particular focus of the series are those books that compare poetic projects from different national and linguistic traditions or explore the interconnections between poetic expression and the other arts. Authors whose critical approaches utilize contemporary literary theory and/or multicultural perspectives are especially encouraged to consider this series. Languages of the poetry studied include, but are not limited to, English, French, German, Italian, and Spanish, though the texts should be written in English and addressed to readers beyond strictly national or disciplinary boundaries. Inquiries and manuscripts should be directed to the general editor:

Peter Baker
Department of English
Towson University
Towson, MD 21204-7097

To order other books in this series, please contact our Customer Service Department at:

(800) 770-LANG (within the U.S.)
(212) 647-7706 (outside the U.S.)
(212) 647-7707 FAX

or browse online by series at:

www.peterlang.com